Credit Management
Principles and Practices

National Association of Credit Management

Credit Management
Principles and Practices

Third Edition

By

Dr. Charles L. Gahala, CCE
Professor of Finance
Benedictine University

National Association of Credit Management

First Edition: 1994
Second Edition: 1996
Printed in the United States of America

10 9 8 7 6 5 4 3 2 1

ISBN 1-888505-17-6

Library of Congress Registration Number: TXu 1-081-744

To my wife, Jan Gahala, who was inestimably important for her words of wisdom and encouragement, and to my parents, Peter and Peggy Gahala, who gave me the wisdom that I hope to pass on to my sons, Eric and Carl.

Table of Contents

Part III: Credit, Collection, and Analysis

Part IV: Secured Credit and Bankruptcy

Preface

Credit Management: Principles and Practices bridges the gap between academic theory and credit practice. This book is intended for use both in college-level finance courses in credit management and by practicing credit executives as a training tool and reference.

Although the material in the text is presented sequentially, college instructors may assign almost any chapter as a self-contained unit. The book can easily be used to customize course lengths. As the body of knowledge in credit management has expanded, the ability to cover all material in one text has become virtually impossible. Moreover, the theory and practice of credit management is dynamic. Therefore, instructors are encouraged to supplement this text with readings.

Each chapter has been engineered as a teaching/learning system. The objectives for each chapter are presented early in the chapter. An end-of-chapter recap of important concepts reinforces key material. There are review questions at the end of chapters that can be used by credit practitioners to prepare for the CBA, CBF, and CCE exams in credit management. One of the most important changes in this third edition is the "Credit Management Online" section at the end of each chapter. Finally, the chapters contain a summary of related readings that can be used to delve more in-depth on a particular subject.

A debt of gratitude goes out to the individuals who have assisted with the preparation of this text. In particular, the services of Caroline Zimmerman of the NACM Communications Department was most helpful.

Other individuals who have influenced the author are far too numerous to mention. However, the professionalism exhibited by the following individuals should be recognized:

Garry Abezetian • Walter "Buddy" Baker • Lowell Belk • Rich Bellis • Paul Bernardoni • Bruce Bialy • Wanda Borges • Paul Brunner • Tom Burke • Stacy Cashman • Linda Chernault • Rita Childers • Dr. Ron Chung • Norm Cowie • Bill Dearhammer • Frank DuBrava • Larry Engels • Doug Ernst • Ross Fisher • Annette Flemming • Marge Frens • Dick Gamble • O.D. Glauss • Ron Gordon • Tom Gordon • Gary Grissom • Hank Haegerich • Mark Hanley • Robert Healy • Joe Jackson •

Dr. Dan Jennings • Dave Judeika • Ruby Kerr • George Kokkines • John Korun • Maury Margotta • Ron Mefford • Fred Morris • Bill Mowers • Bruce Nathan • Madeline Parisi • Nino Pellettieri • Dick Powers • Rocci Primavera • Curt Rothlisberger • Marty Scaminaci • Robin Schauseil • Henry Schmerler • Jim Schmidt • Stan Senalik • Don Slaby • Ray Sojka • Dave Spitler • Gordon Stagge • Rick Stevens • Ray Stober • Charles Tatelbaum • Lee Teigen • Bob Thompson • Bob Togtman • Bob Vodraska • Marty Volpe • Jesse Ward • Bill Weilemann • Tom Wuich

Part I:

An Introduction to Business Credit Management

Chapter 1

THE CHANGING NATURE OF CREDIT MANAGEMENT

"In the past, individuals have come into the credit field without previous preparation. Their entrance into this line was frequently not a matter of deliberate choice and planning."[1]

–Dr. Theodore N. Beckman
Ohio State University

The credit profession is both exacting and exciting. About 80 years have elapsed since Dr. Theodore Beckman authored the above quote in one of the earliest credit management textbooks. During this four score period, thousands of individuals have entered the credit field without adequate preparation.

The complexity of tasks that are often performed by credit managers demand a mastery of skills. Yet the skills essential to manage credit are usually acquired on the job. This book will accelerate the mastery of skills essential to manage credit effectively.

Credit management activities are dynamic in nature. The role of the credit manager goes well beyond the routine task of collecting money. The complexity of tasks, combined with the wide range of required skills, make credit management one of the most challenging of all business occupations.

The **Key Learning Objective** in Chapter 1 is to provide you with an overview of credit management. After reading this chapter, you should be able to master specific additional **Learning Objectives** that include:

1. Recognize the status of the credit manager as a professional.

[1]Theodore N. Beckman, *Credits and Collections in Theory and Practice* (New York: McGraw-Hill Book Company Inc., 1924), vii.

2. Provide a job specification for a credit manager.
3. Identify tasks essential for initial employment and job advancement in the credit profession.
4. Consider a few of the key changes that currently shape the credit profession.
5. Examine the role of the National Association of Credit Management in maintaining the high status of the credit profession.

THE CREDIT MANAGEMENT PROFESSION

The professional status of the credit manager has evolved over time. Accountants, attorneys, ministers, and physicians each qualify as professionals. In order to qualify for the status of professional, an occupation should satisfy certain criteria that can be used to evaluate the occupation.

The specific criteria that can be used to evaluate an occupation as a profession have been developed by Estelle Popham.[2] These criteria are effective in measuring the professional status of any occupation and are useful to recognize the status of the credit manager as a professional.

1. *A Strong Professional Association.* Accountants receive recognition through the American Institute of Certified Public Accountants; attorneys are acknowledged as professionals through their membership in the American Bar Association; doctors maintain professional status through membership in the American Medical Association. Credit managers have the commitment of the National Association of Credit Management (NACM) to advance the established goals of credit professionals. NACM provides the support of a strong professional association, which is essential to elevate the status of credit manager to professional.
2. *Code of Ethics.* The NACM "Canons of Business Credit Ethics" are listed in Table 1-1. These principles govern the activities of business credit grantors. Credit is based upon trust. The credit occupation mandates the application of high ethical standards. The attitude and conduct of credit practitioners is what distinguishes individual credit managers as professionals.
3. *Autonomy Within the Profession.* Autonomy is being used in a self-governing context when recognizing the credit manager as a

[2]Estelle Popham, *A Teaching-Learning System for Business Education* (New York: Bossey Press, 1980).

Table 1-1 **Canons of Business Credit Ethics**
National Association of Credit Management

I. Justice, equity and confidence constitute the foundation of credit administration.
II. Agreements and contracts reflect integrity and should never be breached by either party.
III. The interchange of credit information must be based upon confidence, cooperation, reciprocity and confidentiality.
IV. It is deemed unethical to be a party to unwarranted assignments or transfers of an insolvent debtor's assets nor should creditors participate in secret arrangements.
V. Creditors should cooperate for the benefit of all in adjustment or liquidation of insolvent estates or companies.
VI. Creditors must render all possible assistance to honest debtors who become insolvent.
VII. Dishonest debtors must be exposed and referred to the authorities.
VIII. Cooperation, fairness and honesty must dominate in all insolvent debtor proceedings.
IX. Costly administrative procedures in the rehabilitation or liquidation of an insolvent debtor shall be avoided at all times.
X. Members pledge themselves to uphold the integrity, dignity and honor of the credit profession in all of their business dealings.

Source: National Association of Credit Management, Columbia, Md., 2000.

professional. A good example of the autonomous nature of the credit profession can be perceived through industry credit groups. As a member of an industry credit group, a credit executive must have factual credit and financial information available to share with other group members. Moreover, reciprocity is essential to the nature of openly sharing factual payment information with other creditors. Therefore, credit practitioners set standards for conduct within their profession. NACM members elect fellow members as officers at both the national and affiliate levels. This election process contributes to the autonomous nature of the credit profession.

4. *Contribution to the Welfare of Society.* When credit executives are efficient in allocating credit to customers, they benefit their employers and society. Efficient credit decisions make products more readily available to users. Moreover, product pricing can be held down when carrying costs and bad debts are under the control of credit professionals. Credit executives also help to prevent fraud

through credit investigations that deny repeat abusers the privilege of obtaining new credit.

5. *A Controlled Admission Procedure.* The admission of an individual into a credit-related position varies widely among employers. The credit function in a particular company also can vary widely. The admission of an individual into an occupation or the use of the title "credit manager" does not elevate one to the status of credit professional. The demonstration of competency for credit-related tasks is essential in order to elevate the status of credit manager to that of professional.

   NACM has a credentialing program that includes four designations used to evidence competency for credit-related skills. The CBA, CBF, and CCE designations are geared toward most credit personnel. For the international credit manager, the CICE is available through NACM-FCIB. These designations will be explained later in this chapter. The designations can be useful to demonstrate evidence of competency in the credit profession. However, the lack of an NACM credential does not imply that a credit manager is not a professional.

6. *An Existing Body of Knowledge and Career-Long Learning.* Credit management skills unfold gradually. Most credit practitioners would acknowledge the fact that their real education in credit management came through the college of hard knocks. Over time, credit practitioners recognize the application of technical skills to particular situations. Certain situations become somewhat repetitive; these situations constitute the common body of knowledge. For example, when should a credit manager ask for collateral?

   Other situations require the credit manager to adapt to change; these situations require career-long learning. For example, the Federal Reserve published rules to establish uniform standards for the electronic delivery of disclosures under the Equal Credit Opportunity Act in 2000. How does this change impact a particular credit decision? There are continuing education requirements not only for the CCE in the credit profession but also for members of virtually any profession. Career-long learning has increased in importance due to rapid advances in technology, improved communications, and a globalization of world trade.

What makes a credit manager a professional? The six criteria identified by Popham provide a starting point for all credit practitioners to recognize. However, one final criterion is that the conduct of each individual credit manager should embody the highest level of professional conduct possible on an ongoing basis. In essence, a careful self-evaluation of the status of an individual credit manager as a professional should be made on a regular basis.

REMOVING THE CREDIT MANAGEMENT MYSTIQUE

There is often a mystique associated with the activities that relate to credit management. Academics have historically neglected to encourage students to enter the credit field. Most high school and college students are not aware that careers exist in business credit. Human Resource managers may not know the details for qualifications essential when recruiting credit personnel. Even credit practitioners may not be fully aware of the wide range of activities that the credit department is capable of performing.

Dr. Edward K. Strong, while Director of Vocational Interest at Stanford University, designed a test to measure vocational interest. This type of test does not measure specific abilities nor does it measure intelligence. The test is intended to measure the likelihood of enjoying a particular occupation as a career choice.

Strong analyzed 452 credit managers and determined that credit managers tend to have general business interests instead of narrow interests in a particular area of business. His research suggests that in general, credit managers are not as interested in writing the programs to use a computer as they are interested in using the computer to make decisions. Strong determined that the interests of credit managers are most similar to the interests of operations managers, accountants, and human resource managers. The interests of credit managers are least similar to the interests of mathematicians, architects, carpenters, and ministers.[3]

The research performed by Strong led to the creation of job specifications for credit managers. Table 1-2 contains an updated job specification for credit managers based on the original job specification designed by Strong. Education, experience, and special personal

[3]Edward K. Strong, *Credit Management and the Strong Vocational Interest Test* (New York: Credit Research Foundation and NACM, n.d.), p. 14.

Table 1-2 **Job Specifications for Credit Managers Based on Research by Dr. Edward K. Strong**

Education: College graduate or equivalent with courses in credit and collection principles, accounting, financial statement analysis, commercial law, microcomputers, marketing, management, psychology and economics.

Experience: Five years or more in credit and collection work with exposure to multiple aspects of credit activities, including at least two years in a supervisory capacity in the same or similar industry.

1. Sincere interest in credit work as a career.
2. Fact finding, analysis and interpretation of the financial position of customers.
3. Supervision of the extension of credit and collection of receivables.
4. Familiarity with credit procedure and credit department administration.
5. Training of credit personnel.
6. Familiarity with accounting, order entry, sales, transportation and adjustment procedures.
7. Maintenance of satisfactory customer relations.
8. Contact with financial institutions and sources of credit information.
9. Participation in meetings of credit groups.

Special Personal Characteristics

1. Ability to communicate persuasively and effectively, and resourcefulness in eliciting confidential information.
2. Considerateness and fairness in dealing with people.
3. Emotional stability in handling unpleasant situations with tact and diplomacy.
4. Ability to analyze complex problems constructively.
5. Integrity and ethical standards that are exemplary in nature.

characteristics should each become focal points for the development of credit managers.

Job specifications are essential to effectively recruit and train credit personnel. In order to hone in on the detailed tasks performed by business credit grantors, the author of this textbook surveyed 358 business credit practitioners. The focus of the study was to determine tasks performed by credit personnel. Specific tasks that are essential to initial employment in credit positions and to job advancement in business credit positions were identified.

From among 64 potential tasks, the 10 tasks that business credit managers identified as being most important to gain initial employment in a credit management position are listed in Table 1-3. These tasks suggest that someone who wants to gain initial employment in the credit

Table 1-3 Credit Tasks Necessary for Initial Employment Identified by Business Credit Managers

Tasks listed in order of most frequently reported as necessary for initial employment in business credit positions.

1. Contact banks and suppliers to investigate credit references.
2. Analyze requests for credit in order to extend credit.
3. Analyze financial statements on customers.
4. Extend credit to customers in accordance with established company policy.
5. Establish credit lines for individual accounts.
6. Order reports from credit reporting agencies.
7. Write personal letters to prospective or existing customers.
8. Discuss delinquent accounts with sales personnel.
9. Interpret reports generated by a computer.
10. Manage and control the receivables portfolio by direct involvement with accounts.

Source: An Identification and Analysis of Tasks Performed by Trade Credit Personnel, Charles Gahala, Doctoral Dissertation at Northern Illinois University, DeKalb, Ill., 1983. These tasks were validated by the ACES Credit Group in March of 2002.

field should be able to conduct a credit investigation. Moreover, training for employees new to credit could center upon the competencies necessary to complete the tasks contained in Table 1-3.

Credit managers did not select the same tasks as being "necessary for initial employment" as those tasks that were selected as being "necessary for job advancement." This is not surprising. An overwhelming percentage of respondents identified the tasks contained in Table 1-4 as being essential for job advancement in business credit. Out of 64 possible tasks to select from, the 10 tasks that are most frequently identified as being necessary for job advancement are listed in Table 1-4.

The first task listed in Table 1-4, "attend workshops and conferences to update credit skills," reflects the dynamic nature of credit management. Most credit managers recognize the need to keep in touch with changes that affect their jobs. This suggests that credit managers have lifelong learning needs that can be partially fulfilled by attending workshops and conferences.

Each of the tasks identified as essential for job advancement requires higher-level competencies than those tasks that are essential for initial

Table 1-4 Credit Tasks Necessary for Job Advancement As Identified by Business Credit Practitioners

Tasks listed in order of most frequently reported as necessary for job advancement in business credit positions.

1. Attend workshops and conferences to update credit skills.
2. Establish and monitor standards of performance for credit personnel.
3. Prepare reports for corporate management.
4. Review, at least monthly, the status of collections and past-due accounts.
5. Interpret and delegate approved credit policies to subordinates.
6. Manage and control the receivables portfolio by direct involvement with accounts.
7. Formulate and apply controls to ensure that credit operations conform to standards.
8. Plan a program for the systematic follow-up of collecting accounts receivable.
9. Keep corporate management informed of the status of the accounts receivable portfolio.
10. Experiment with alternative business procedures to correct recurring problems.

Source: An Identification and Analysis of Tasks Performed by Trade Credit Personnel, Charles Gahala, Doctoral Dissertation at Northern Illinois University, DeKalb, Ill., 1983. These tasks were validated by the ACES Credit Group in March of 2002.

employment. Continuing education needs for experienced credit managers are centered more in the areas of credit policy, systems and procedures, and human resources. Training for credit personnel should focus upon fulfilling these needs.[4]

The Association of Credit Executives (ACES) is a group of 35 corporate credit managers, each employed in a different industry, who each have several years of experience at Fortune 500 type companies. The ACES members were asked to review and update the listing of tasks performed by credit managers. The specific tasks identified 20 years ago are still being performed today; however, there are some significant changes reported in the way in which the tasks are being performed. The key changes that were identified by the ACES members appear in Table 1-5.

[4]For a more detailed description of the original research related to credit management tasks, see Charles L. Gahala, *Tasks of Business Credit Personnel* (Columbia, Md.: Credit Research Foundation, February 1985).

Table 1-5 Changes in Performing Credit Tasks Identified by the ACES Credit Group Members in March of 2002

(Changes are not listed in any particular order of importance.)

1. The Internet has become a major force that needs to be more fully utilized in credit decision making.
2. Credit personnel should develop competence in all functional areas of a business in order to work with other departments, as members of cross-functional teams. This will enable credit managers to contribute as agents of change to improve operations.
3. There have been significant improvements in both the speed of accessing, and in the quality of content, concerning credit information.
4. Credit managers have a better image than they had 20 years ago.
5. Many routine tasks have been automated; this allows for the credit function to be more streamlined.
6. Fewer clerical credit employees are needed; credit managers spend more time focusing on non-routine aspects of the credit function. According to one credit manager, this reflects a shift toward being a manager of credit away from being a credit manager.
7. Ethics need to be emphasized in lieu of the Enron debacle.
8. Pressures from employers who subscribe to the profit motive place demands to deliver the credit function in a cost-efficient manner.
9. A need to stay current in the credit profession is essential to be considered for promotion because the changes in the profession are coming more quickly than years ago.
10. The financial tools of analysis are more sophisticated, which requires a higher level of technical competence.

Note that the changes identified by ACES members are not changes in the specific tasks being performed. The ACES members validated the tasks. The tasks are simply being performed in different ways.

The changes in the credit profession are clearly pointing toward a more highly educated credit manager. These changes identified by the ACES members have been addressed and integrated into this edition of the textbook. For example, each chapter includes a Credit Management Online section at the end of a chapter. More contemporary financial tools are integrated into chapters. The real challenge to credit personnel will be to keep in touch with the pace of changes that affect the performance of credit tasks.

NATIONAL ASSOCIATION OF CREDIT MANAGEMENT

One of the essential ingredients necessary to categorize an occupation as a profession is a strong professional association. As one of the oldest and largest business organizations in the United States, the National Association of Credit Management (NACM) provides business credit grantors with an essential vehicle to stay in touch with changes affecting credit management. The basic goal of NACM is to increase the profit of member companies through more efficient and effective credit management. Key activities that contribute to achieving this basic goal are:

- Providing additional training through educational programs, annual conferences, seminars, and the national convention
- Supporting sound legislation and regulation
- Investigating and preventing fraud
- Offering government receivables assistance
- Improving international credit practices
- Publishing a national magazine
- Offering a library of publications to meet members' reference needs

NACM has over 25,000 members located throughout the United States. NACM-affiliated associations offer a variety of valuable services at the local level to assist in the effective management of their member companies' accounts receivable portfolios. These credit management resources include, but are not limited to:

- Business collections
- Industry credit groups
- National, regional, and local business credit reporting
- Distressed business services
- A wide variety of educational seminars, workshops, and classes

Professionalism through Education

The education-related needs of credit personnel are met through a wide range of NACM education-related activities. Formal programs, such as the Mid-Career School and the Graduate School of Credit and

Financial Management, are coordinated by the NACM Education Department. There are also self-study courses, workshops, and seminars at the NACM Credit Congress and sessions at the NACM Legislative Conference to meet the needs of credit managers. There are also online courses and teleconferences that focus on various current issues and problems in credit management. Many NACM affiliates offer courses to members that count toward professional designations.

The Credit and Financial Development Division (CFDD) of NACM is a group of 1,600 members with 46 chapters. CFDD is committed to excellence at both the national and local levels. CFDD provides awards and scholarships to further enhance excellence in the credit profession. NACM members gain an additional opportunity to focus upon education and networking through CFDD.

Professional Certification

In order to demonstrate competence in the credit profession, NACM makes available a professional certification program. NACM makes four specific credentials available to business credit personnel: the Credit Business Associate (CBA); the Credit Business Fellow (CBF); and, for most credit managers, the highest-level credential, the Certified Credit Executive (CCE). For credit practitioners, these credentials represent professional competence and personal achievement.

In 1999 the Finance Credit and International Business (FCIB) and NACM launched a fourth designation: the Certified International Credit Executive (CICE). Senior international credit executives can demonstrate a specialized competence in international credit by obtaining the CICE credential. International skills have become particularly important due to the growth in international trade. The CICE reflects the demand for certain credit managers to develop a specialized international competence that is distinct from the other three credentials.

Each of the four credentials represents a combination of education plus experience; all four designations require the successful completion of a distinct examination in order to earn a specific designation. For more information concerning designation requirements, contact the NACM Education Department via the Internet at http://www.nacm.org or simply call the education department for NACM at 410/740-5560.

ORGANIZATION OF THIS BOOK

Part I of this textbook is designed to provide readers with an introduction to credit management. Chapter 1 introduces readers to the credit profession by examining tasks performed by credit managers and the role of NACM. Chapter 2 incorporates management skills into the credit function. Planning, organizing, and evaluating the credit manager are the focal points contained in Chapter 2. Chapter 3 adds an international dimension to the credit function by examining the role of credit in a global marketplace.

Part II contains four chapters that concentrate upon credit policy and the extension of credit. Chapter 4 provides the reader with the rationale for credit policy and specific credit-related policy focal points. Chapter 5 explains the importance of credit-related government legislation and how the legislation influences credit decisions. Chapter 6 identifies sources of credit information and explains how to utilize those sources. An overview of business credit reporting services is presented in Chapter 7.

Part III consists of three chapters containing information essential to collections and credit analysis. Chapter 8 provides a systemic approach to using alternative collection methods. Chapter 9 provides a primer on financial statement analysis; focal points examined include both common size analysis and ratio analysis. Chapter 10 shows how cash flow analysis can be useful—in particular, the importance of cash flow analysis for highly leveraged transactions.

Part IV is the final section of the textbook. Two highly technical chapters develop subjects of particular interest to business credit personnel. Chapter 11 focuses on the development of secured credit arrangements. Chapter 12 discusses the topics of bankruptcy and reorganization.

Readers will note that each of the 12 chapters in this text could easily be expanded into a specialized full course. Readers who have an interest in a specialized component of a chapter are encouraged to refer to the references and web sites listed at the end of each chapter. The chapters provide a sound foundation in each topic. Because chapters are self-contained, rearranging the sequence for studying material should not present the reader with any particular problems.

CHAPTER 1: FOLLOW UP

Recap of Important Concepts

1. There are six criteria that can be used to gauge the professional status of an occupation. Credit managers have earned the status of being categorized as professionals.
2. NACM has developed the "Canons of Business Credit Ethics." Credit managers should be aware of the details contained in the canons and strive to conduct all activities at the highest level of ethical conduct possible.
3. According to Dr. Edward K. Strong, credit managers tend to have general business interests as opposed to a narrow interest in a particular area of business. Strong has identified specific occupations that are similar to, and other occupations that are divergent from, the interests of credit managers. Having an aptitude for credit management is essential to deriving pleasure from a career in credit management.
4. Credit managers have identified certain tasks that are essential to gain initial employment in business credit positions. In addition, credit managers have identified other tasks that are essential to job advancement in business credit positions. These tasks can be useful for recruiting and training purposes. The wide range of tasks performed by credit managers mandates keeping in touch with change. Credit mangers from the Association of Credit Executives (ACES) have identified key changes that are shaping the credit profession.
5. NACM and its affiliates provide numerous services to credit professionals. Credit managers should be aware of the various services available to them. Becoming actively involved in a professional association can be one of the most enriching experiences available to a credit manager.
6. The title "credit manager" is used loosely, much like the title "accountant." In order to evidence competency necessary to complete credit-related tasks, the NACM credentials of CBA, CBF and CCE have been developed. Through FCIB and NACM, the CICE credential is now available. Credit practitioners can achieve recognition as professionals by completing the requirements necessary for professional designations.

Review/Discussion Questions

1. What criteria can be used to gauge whether an occupation qualifies for professional status? Do you believe that all credit practitioners should be categorized as professionals? If yes, explain why; if not, why not?
2. Which occupations tend to have interests that are similar to those of credit managers? Which occupations tend to have dissimilar interests? How can an aptitude for occupational interest be useful to a credit manager?
3. Why are the Canons of Business Credit Ethics important? Are there any specific canons that are not appropriate? If yes, why? Should there be an additional canon added to the list of 10 canons?
4. Choose one of the 10 changes identified by the ACES Credit Group in Chapter 1. How is this change shaping the way in which you perform on the job? Discuss how you can learn more about how other companies are dealing with this change. (Note: instructors may want to assign and then isolate upon one particular change for discussion purposes in a classroom.)

Test Your Knowledge

1. Why are ethical standards important to credit management? Give two examples of principles that can be used to govern business ethics in credit management.
2. How can a credit manager contribute to the general welfare of society? Be specific.
3. Write a job specification for the position of credit manager. What specific education requirements, experience requirements, and other special personal characteristics are appropriate for a credit manager?
4. What types of educational opportunities are available that can contribute to the skills required in credit management? Try to identify specific credit-related opportunities rather than those available through high school or college courses.
5. You are a corporate credit manager who is trying to fill an entry-level position for a credit analyst. Which tasks are typically performed by someone who is seeking initial employment in a credit management position? How can this knowledge be useful to a corporate credit manager?

6. You are a corporate credit manager who is trying to develop a training program for regional credit managers. What types of tasks should become a focal point for credit managers seeking job advancement in credit management positions? How can this information be useful to a corporate credit manager?
7. Identify three changes that are now occurring in the credit profession that were not addressed in Table 1-5. Rank each of the changes in their order of importance. Justify your rank order. Be specific.

Credit Management Online

There are numerous web sites that can be of use to credit personnel. A few of the sites that are related to the content in each chapter will be recommended.

www.beaucoup/1geneng.html—There are a number of search engines that are useful to navigate through various web sites. This particular web site provides a link to various search engines.

www.ben.edu/faculty/cgahala/index.html—My homepage at Benedictine University is available. There is a link to the Benedictine University site at the bottom of the page; at the BU web page go to the drop-down menu and click on the library. Here you should click on tutorials, then social science, then business and then finance where you will find several web sites that I like to use for teaching purposes.

www.crfonline.org—The Credit Research Foundation (CRF) fulfills the role of enhancing research and education for business credit grantors. CRF has a number of publications of interest to credit managers.

www.learnthenet.com/english/index.html—Surfing the net can be a wonderful experience. This web site is useful in terms of learning about the basics of using the internet.

www.nacm.org—This is the site for the National Association of Credit Management. The site provides an overview of NACM membership, publications, activities, and services. There are several links to topics of interest useful for credit managers at any level in an organization chart.

www.wsj.com—This is the site for the *Wall Street Journal*. I like to joke with students and tell them that "the *Wall Street Journal* will be your textbook for the rest of your business career."

References Useful for Further Reading

Beckman, Theodore N. *Credits and Collections in Theory and Practice.* New York: McGraw Hill Book Company Inc., 1924.

"Certified International Credit Executive." Columbia, Md.: FCIB-NACM, n.d. A brochure describing the CICE designation. Specific reference is to pages 1-16.

Gahala, Charles L. "An Identification and Analysis of Tasks Performed by Trade Credit Personnel." Ed.D. diss., Northern Illinois University, 1983.

Gahala, Charles L. "Changing the Face of Credit Management: Credit Management as a Profession." *The National Credit Review* (May 2002).

Gahala, Charles L. *Tasks of Business Credit Personnel.* Columbia, Md.: Credit Research Foundation, February 1985.

Hoch, Wendy L. "How Earning My CBA Designation Impacted My Career," *Business Credit* (September 2001): 8.

Jamieson, Jacky. "CICE Is Off to a Great Start." *Business Credit* (April 2000): 4.

Leibs, Scott. "Internet Explorers: The Finance Function Finally Goes Online," *e-CFO* (April 2000): 36-44.

National Association of Credit Management. *Professional Certification Program.* Columbia, Md.: 2000.

Osterland, Andrew. "Watching and Waiting: The Web Seemed Poised to Change Everything. What Happened?" *CFO* (January 2002): 25-28.

Popham, Estelle. *A Teaching-Learning System for Business Education.* New York: Bossey Press, 1980.

Slaby, Don. "Current Trends in the Practice of Incentive Programs." *Business Credit* (April 2001): 76-78.

Steve, Bob. "Enhancing Credit Operations with the Internet." *Business Credit* (January 1997): 47-51.

Strong, Edward K. *Credit Management and the Strong Vocational Interest Test.* New York: Credit Research Foundation and National Association of Credit Management, n.d.

Truitt, Phillis L. "CFDD: Your Gateway to Empowerment." *Business Credit* (February 2000): 4.

Wood, Dorman L., and Bruce A. Lobtree. "E-Commerce: The Credit Executive's Latest Challenge." *P.D. News* (Spring 2000): 1-3.

Chapter 2

ORGANIZING THE CREDIT FUNCTION

"The restructuring phenomenon during the last 10 years has led to more central coordination and more integrative management that link credit decision making and receivables activities among business units, subsidiaries and customers."[1]

–Terry Callahan, CCE
Vice President
Credit Research Foundation

Organizing the credit function requires establishing goals. Specific goals could to be broken down into focal points. The focal points could be then be examined so that they can be standardized. Finally, the side effects of anticipated action should be interwoven into other departments in the organization structure.

For example, a company may develop the goal of reducing bad debts. One focal point that could lead to a reduction in bad debts would be to require a completed credit application from all new customers. This focal point could be examined by developing an optimal credit application. The sales force would need to cooperate by implementing the requirement of obtaining a completed application from all new customers. The side effects might create conflict with sales personnel or customers, yet the ultimate results could lead to a reduction in bad debts.

Organizing the credit function requires a vision. While credit managers are often immersed in daily duties, the overall profitability of a business should remain the core of specific credit management

[1]Terry Callahan, "Organizational Alignment of the Credit and Accounts Receivable Function," *Business Credit* (June 2000): 72.

objectives. The purpose of Chapter 2 is to identify critical management focal points essential to organizing the credit function.

The **Key Learning Objectives** contained in Chapter 2 are:

1. Understand the role of benchmarking the credit function.
2. Examine alternative organization structures that can be used to administer the credit function.
3. Recognize the importance of keeping individual credit department personnel motivated.
4. Consider tasks that can be performed through the use of Business Process Outsourcing.
5. Identify specific credit-related tasks that can derive benefits through automation.

An astute reader may be asking this question: What do benchmarking, organization structure, motivating credit department personnel, business process outsourcing, and automation have in common? By addressing these focal points separately and in combination, a credit department can be designed to perform at an optimal level.

BENCHMARKING

Quantitative measures that can be used to gauge the effectiveness of credit department performance can be obtained by benchmarking certain credit department focal points. Benchmarking is a management tool. It can be conducted by using either an external approach or an internal approach. The external approach to benchmarking entails emulating the best business practices of other credit departments. A company may compare itself to an industry average or to a strong corporate role model in an attempt to pinpoint areas that can be improved upon. External benchmarking is limited by the availability of comparable cost data and by difficulties that surface when a firm operates in more than one industry.

An internal approach to benchmarking focuses upon comparing current results to historical norms. The internal approach is limited to a focus on performance measurement for one company. Trends can be established by using the internal approach. Moreover, when a change is made in credit department operations, such as a department downsizing, the results of the change can be quantitatively examined.

Benchmarking performance measures should be quantifiable. Examples of specific credit-related measures that can be used for benchmarking purposes include: (1) aging schedules, (2) credit department expenses per employee, (3) percentage bad debt expenses, (4) days sales outstanding, and (5) best possible days sales outstanding.

Aging Schedules

The purpose of an aging schedule is to break down accounts receivable by the age of the accounts. An aging schedule can be prepared to include all receivables by a corporation or it can be prepared by using specific criteria. For example, an aging can be prepared for a division, product line, geographic area, or sales territory. A monthly aging schedule should be compared to the results obtained 12 months earlier when there is any seasonality in sales.

Table 2-1 shows an aging schedule for Clark Products and for a competitor, Riedel Limited. The aging shows that 10% of the Clark Products receivables are 1-30 days past due while only 8% of Riedel Limited receivables are 1-30 days past due. However, a closer look at the aging shows that Clark Products could serve as an excellent benchmark company for Riedel Limited to emulate.

The aging schedule pinpoints problems in the Riedel Limited receivables; management clearly needs to investigate the problems and perhaps tighten up credit policy at Riedel Limited. The problem could be addressed by using a team from accounting, sales, and credit in order to identify and correct problems.

Certain local NACM affiliates coordinate industry credit groups. The NACM affiliate can act as a clearinghouse to develop an aging schedule for an industry. An individual member of the credit group can then compare an aging to the industry as a benchmark for performance. New goals that bring Riedel Limited more in line with Clark Products can be established.

Credit Department Expenses Per Employee

Credit department operations should develop a focus upon cost containment. The allocation of expenses to the credit department can vary from company to company, so intercompany comparisons can be misleading. However, the internal approach to benchmarking using credit department expenses per employee can be revealing. Total expenses include direct and indirect expenses. Examples of typical credit department expenses include payroll, credit reports, technology-related costs, training, travel, and overhead.

Table 2-1 **Accounts Receivable Aging Schedule**

	Clark Products		Riedel Limited	
Status	Amount	Percentage	Amount	Percentage
Current	$17,000,000	85 %	$16,000,000	67 %
1-30 Days	2,000,000	10	2,000,000	8
31-60	800,000	4	2,000,000	8
Over 60 Days	200,000	1	4,000,000	17
Total AR	**$20,000,000**	**100 %**	**$24,000,000**	**100 %**

Credit department expenses per employee can be calculated by dividing the total annual operating expenses by the total number of employees in the credit department. Trends are important to pinpoint. Moreover, individual operating units and even individual credit offices can be examined separately. The results of benchmarking credit department expenses per employee should be interpreted carefully. The allocation of specific expenses will have a pronounced impact on the results.

For example, if one company allocates cash application expenses to the accounting department while another company allocates similar cash application expenses to the credit department, then the validity of making sound decisions concerning cost containment will become complicated and potentially misleading.

Percentage Bad Debt Expenses

The actual bad debts written off during a year divided by the annual sales volume provides the percentage bad debt expense. This information is available for public companies so external benchmarking can be used. In addition, internal benchmarking can be used to identify trends for the company as a whole or for individual operating units within a company.

The calculation used to benchmark bad debts is relatively simple, yet the interpretation of the results can be tricky. For example, bad debts are closely linked to overall corporate goals. A company experiencing a high growth rate in sales may also experience an increase in the bad debt expense. The important focal point becomes whether the increase in sales raises profits enough to offset the increase in bad debts. By benchmarking a change in the trend for bad debt, the management should be drawn into an evaluation of the effectiveness of the credit policy. Credit policy should be examined in light of overall corporate profitability.

Days Sales Outstanding

Equation 2-1 shows a formula used to calculate Days Sales Outstanding (DSO). This formula will be used to calculate DSO in Equation 2-2.

Equation 2-1. Use of Total Receivables

$$\text{DSO} = \frac{\text{Total Accounts Receivable}}{\text{Credit Sales During Period}} \times \text{Number of Days in Period}$$

For a company that has total receivables of \$8,000,000 and annual credit sales of \$50,000,000, the DSO would be calculated as follows:

Equation 2-2. DSO Example

$$\text{DSO} = \frac{\$8{,}000{,}000}{\$50{,}000{,}000} \times 365 = 58 \text{ Days}$$

The results derived in Equation 2-2 show accounts receivable divided by sales per day; the results show a DSO of 58 days. Most companies try to control their investment in receivables; DSO is useful to gauge this investment of funds into accounts receivable. Using the DSO as a benchmark of performance can be misleading. Credit managers do not control sales terms; an increase in sales when terms are changed could give decision makers misleading information. Consequently, the best possible DSO is often considered to be more useful for benchmarking purposes.

Best Possible Days Sales Outstanding

The best possible days sales outstanding (BPDSO) is particularly useful for benchmarking purposes using the internal approach. This measure can be used for monthly, quarterly or annual periods. The essential difference between BPDSO and DSO is that the BPDSO uses *current* (those receivables not yet due) rather than *total* receivables in the calculation. Equation 2-3 shows the formula used to calculate BPDSO.

Equation 2-3. Use of Current Receivables

$$\text{BPDSO} = \frac{\text{Current Accounts Receivables}}{\text{Credit Sales During Period}} \times \text{Number of Days in Period}$$

For example, if current accounts receivables are \$6,000,000 and credit sales during the year are \$50,000,000, the BPDSO would be 44 days. Equation 2-4 shows the example of the BPDSO calculation.

Equation 2-4. BPDSO Example

$$\text{BPDSO} = \frac{\$6{,}000{,}000}{\$50{,}000{,}000} \times 365 = 44 \text{ Days}$$

The results of Equation 2-4 show a BPDSO of 44 days. When comparing the results of Equation 2-4 to the results of Equation 2-2 for the DSO, the Average Days Delinquent (ADD) can be obtained. The DSO of 58 days minus the BPDSO of 44 days provides an ADD of 14 days. By using the BPDSO to obtain the ADD, the impact of any change in terms of sales is taken into consideration.

Table 2-2 summarizes the aforementioned measures used for benchmarking purposes. Management should consider emulating the company that can produce the best results in an industry, or consider using the industry norm, when analyzing the results. This type of comparison helps to pinpoint areas that need attention when organizing the credit function.

The Credit Research Foundation (CRF) conducts an annual benchmarking survey of credit managers. CRF members furnish data for which CRF acts as a confidential clearinghouse to develop industry results. Credit managers can learn more about the CRF benchmarking process by contacting CRF at www.crfonline.org. Customized benchmarking papers are available from CRF and can be used to implement the benchmarking management technique.

Organizing the credit function starts with a careful self-examination. Benchmarking is one tool that is useful to conduct a self-examination. Benchmarking the performance measures for the credit function is potentially revealing and useful when reviewing the organization of the credit function.

Table 2-2 Benchmarking Performance Measures

Measure	Firm Being Analyzed	Industry Average	Best In Industry
1. Aging Schedule			
Current	67 %	70 %	85 %
10-30 Days Past Due	8	12	10
31-60 Days Past Due	8	10	4
Over 60 Days Past Due	17	8	1
2. Credit Department Expenses Per Employee	\$60,000	\$65,000	\$70,000
3. Percentage Bad Debts	4%	3%	1%
4. Days Sales Outstanding (DSO)	58 Days	50 Days	34 Days
5. Best Possible DSO	30 Days	30 Days	30 Days

DEVELOPING JOB SPECIFICATIONS FOR THE CREDIT FUNCTION

Developing job specifications for the credit function requires focusing upon assigning authority and responsibility. The extent to which authority is concentrated or dispersed depends upon individual circumstances. The goal of organizing the credit function is to engineer the most effective results possible.

A small business normally has a relatively simple organizational structure. Credit operations might be concentrated in one location, enabling the credit department to work closely with other departments. However, as the size of the business increases, the organization of the credit department can become more complex.

An organization chart shows the nature over which authority exists and where decision-making should be made. Table 2-3 shows an organization chart that employs a functional assignment of authority and responsibility. The credit manager reports to a treasurer who empowers the credit manager with the authority and responsibility to control credit operations. There could be a number of additional layers in an organization chart for a large business.

The credit manager in Table 2-3 could have management layers that report to the credit manager. For example, regional credit managers could report directly to the credit manager. The regional credit managers

Table 2-3 **Functional Organizational Chart**

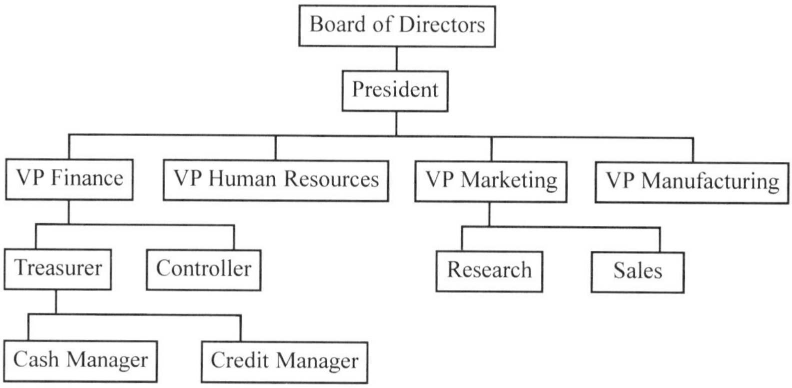

may have area credit managers who report directly to them. Zone managers could report directly to area managers. For many companies, there has been a trend to decrease the number of layers in organization structure.

An organization chart also can be structured by product so that divisions or subsidiary units operate more autonomously. Table 2-4 presents an organization chart that is structured by product line. When product expertise is essential, an organization chart structured by product can be effective.

Table 2-4 **Product Line Organization Chart**

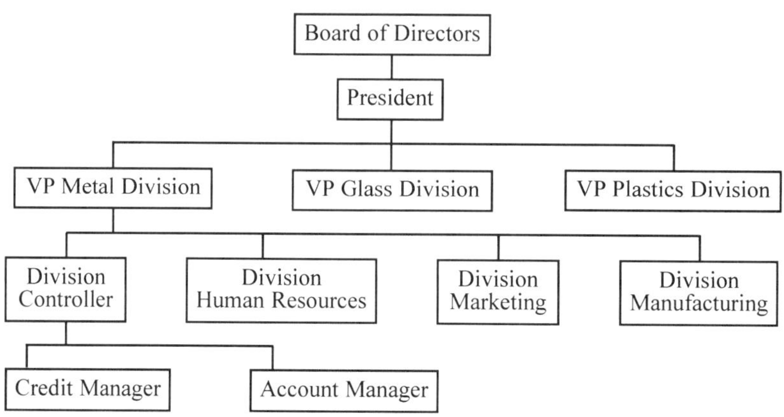

In the organization chart in Table 2-4, each division could have a division credit manager. The division credit manager could develop a specialization in industry-specific product knowledge. The credit manager could then be located at division headquarters to develop a close working relationship with other managers in that division.

Should a company use an organization chart that is structured by function or an organization chart established by product line? Often the crux of the decision is centered upon using a centralized or decentralized approach to management. There are several factors that influence the decision to centralize or decentralize operations.

Advantages of Centralized Credit Operations

1. *Maximum Control.* Credit decisions are usually more consistent when a credit department is centralized. There is less likelihood that a marketing or manufacturing manager will exert pressure on the credit manager to extend credit when the credit manager is located in the corporate headquarters.
2. *Reduced Training.* The ability to develop the skills essential to manage credit can be fostered with consistency. Specific tools used for training credit analysts can be utilized more easily in a centralized credit department. Credit personnel are better able to clearly understand specific credit-related tasks because there is an opportunity to work closely with other credit managers who can guide credit personnel through complex applications.
3. *Economies of Scale.* A centralized credit operation may require fewer credit personnel. Moreover, when divisions have common accounts, the likelihood of duplicating credit analysis is reduced.
4. *More Uniform Policy Implementation.* Credit policy is more likely to be interpreted consistently when a credit department is centralized. The proximity of a corporate credit manager to clarify policy and support decisions provides an improved opportunity for uniform credit decisions. However, there are advantages to dispersing credit operations to various locations.

Advantages of Decentralized Credit Operations

1. *Improved Customer Rapport.* Customers may perceive credit decision making more favorably. Credit personnel may be more aware of the local business conditions.

2. *Closer Interdepartmental Relationships.* When a credit manager is at the same location as sales managers and operating managers, communications often are improved. Managers may become more responsive in certain situations. Interdepartmental conflict can be reduced.
3. *Reduced Response Time.* In general, the larger an organization, the greater the number of decisions that need to be made. In a decentralized credit environment, credit managers may be in a more self-sufficient position, which allows credit decisions to be made in a more timely manner.

A company may use a combination of centralized and decentralized operations. In most cases the company-specific situation dictates the degree to which credit can be decentralized. For example, if a product requires substantial product knowledge and profit margins are high, a company may lean toward decentralization. Corporate politics also play a key role in the decision to decentralize. When division managers are rewarded based on profitability, the division vice president may insist on a decentralized credit operation to maintain more control over credit decisions.

MOTIVATING CREDIT PERSONNEL

During an era of corporate downsizing, fear is a dysfunctional yet powerful motivator. Corporate reorganizations often result in increased demands placed upon credit managers. Maintaining a highly motivated credit department is critically important to the credit function.

Credit managers who perceive their situations as unfavorable are in a position to compromise on ethical standards. Serious morale problems can result in behavior that jeopardizes the integrity of the credit function. Table 2-5 contains examples of dysfunctional behavior that clearly compromises the ethics of the credit profession.

Credit managers are involved in a number of diverse situations in which ethics can be compromised. There is plenty of gray in each of the situations contained in Table 2-5. Ethical behavior can easily be traced to motivation.

Motivation is often complex. For example, although faced with a heavy workload, some credit managers would prefer to play golf than put in more time. Other more complicated situations may require more

Table 2-5 Compromising on Credit Ethics Dysfunctional Behavior

1. Cut deals with customers for extended terms arrangements.
2. Program a computer so that certain customers are not billed late payment service charges.
3. Pad an expense account.
4. Accept a gift from a collection agency in return for forwarding accounts for collection.
5. Absorb an unearned cash discount, showing favoritism to certain customers.
6. Mislead management with a past due report that omits certain past-due accounts.
7. Forge personal credentials on a job application.
8. Order a credit report for a friend who does not have a subscription with the credit reporting agency.
9. Wing it when someone calls to request credit information on an existing customer.
10. Treat subordinates unfairly in a job review, showing favoritism to friends.

personal time off due to family responsibilities. Employees who have more flexibility in their work schedules may experience higher levels of motivation and an increase in job satisfaction.

Credit managers can be motivated in a number of ways. Abraham Maslow created a motivation-related hierarchy of needs in 1954.[2] The basic human needs identified by Maslow, in an ascending order of importance, have stood the test of time. These needs can be used as a starting point when considering motivation.

1. *Physiological Needs.* Basic needs used to sustain human life—such as food, water, clothing, shelter, sleep, and sexual satisfaction—comprise physiological needs. Other incentives will not motivate a person until physiological needs have been satisfied. For example, if a member of the credit department is in dire need of sleep, the individual's work will suffer. A salary increase will not serve to motivate the employee.
2. *Security or Safety Needs.* The threat of physical danger or loss of job is the second level in the hierarchy of needs. Rumors of a corporate downsizing can create serious motivational problems. The need to use a computer could even be perceived as a threat.
3. *Affiliation or Acceptance Needs.* The need to feel accepted is the next level in Maslow's hierarchy of needs. A credit manager who is

[2] Abraham Maslow, *Motivation and Personality* (New York: Harper and Brothers, 1954).

ostracized by other credit department members will have trouble contributing to the overall objectives of the credit department.

4. *Esteem Needs.* After the first three levels of the hierarchy are satisfied, the need to develop self-confidence, status, and prestige should be fulfilled. Sometimes a corner office, a laptop computer, or a job title can contribute to fulfilling this need.
5. *Self-Actualization Needs.* This particular need is a focus on becoming all of what one is capable of becoming. Obtaining the CCE designation could be a temporary goal for certain credit managers; after the CCE is obtained, an individual would then identify a new goal to stay motivated.

There is clearly a need to keep credit personnel motivated. Yet practical suggestions are often as effective as theoretically based motivational techniques. Situations often dictate appropriate motivational strategies.

When credit department turnover is high or employee absenteeism is on the rise, then employee morale is often at a low ebb. There is a need to investigate the cause of the morale problem and to confront the situation using numerous strategies.

Table 2-6 provides a few options that may be used to motivate credit department employees. The motivators identified in this table are general in nature. Readers are encouraged to creatively identify examples for each motivator.

Salaries in credit management have been increasing steadily. Table 2-7 contains a sampling of salaries from the 2000 *Credit and Accounts Receivable Compensation Study* published by CRF. The published study

Table 2-6 **Credit Department Motivation**

1. Promote an atmosphere of contribution by giving managers more power.
2. Encourage education-related activities by providing time away from the job and financial support.
3. Develop a salary system that is based on performance, not just seniority.
4. Ask a credit person to perform a new task and provide essential support to complete the task.
5. Provide an opportunity to make lateral moves.
6. Allow for some flex time in the work week.
7. Encourage innovation in the completion of credit tasks.
8. Promote balance among job-related interests and outside interests.

Table 2-7 **Annual Compensation of Credit Executives**

Title	Average Salary	Median Salary
Chief Corporate Credit Executive	$120,800	$117,500
Export Credit Manager	$ 67,900	$ 73,300
Credit and Collections Manager	$ 74,400	$ 70,500
Division Credit Manager	$ 69,700	$ 65,200
Regional Credit Manager	$ 65,200	$ 62,000
Assistant Credit Manager	$ 54,500	$ 51,000
Credit Analyst	$ 39,300	$ 39,000
Credit Assistant	$ 28,200	$ 27,000

Excerpted from *Credit and Accounts Receivable Compensation Study*, 12th edition, (Columbia, Md.: Credit Research Foundation, 2000).

provides annual salary data on 18 different credit positions, from credit assistant to credit manager to treasurer. It shows, in table format, the average and median salaries for eight different criteria relative to each position: size of receivables portfolio, number of active accounts, number of credit people supervised, region, industry, education, number of years with the company, and number of years in credit.

The sample figures shown in Table 2-7 include salary, bonus, and profit sharing from the CRF survey. The annual salary does not include fringe benefits, stock options, or deferred compensation. There are industry and regional variations that impact the salaries. Further details are available directly from CRF.

The credit function should be engineered to provide credit department employees with a competitive compensation package. There is evidence to suggest that salary does not always motivate employees. Yet, the absence of providing a competitive salary structure can lead to motivational problems.

BUSINESS PROCESS OUTSOURCING

Historically, certain types of credit tasks have been temporarily or permanently performed by outside vendors. This practice is known as outsourcing. For example, a collection agency could be assigned certain problem accounts, a lawyer could be retained to file a lawsuit, or a bank could be used to expedite the receipt of payments via a lockbox system.

These types of tasks have been widely used by credit personnel in order to gain expertise and control costs.

Business Process Outsourcing (BPO) entails the use of long-term contracts usually for the performance of non-core business processes that are to be performed by outside companies. In November of 1999, BP-Amoco entered into contract in excess of one billion dollars to outsource its finance function to PricewaterhouseCoopers. BPO decisions such as this one are often driven by four major goals: (1) the potential to gain access to new technology simultaneously freeing up funds needed for the technology, (2) the emphasis on cutting costs to enhance profits, (3) the potential to gain management expertise in areas where the expertise is in short supply, and (4) the potential to provide managers with an increase in time to use for other more complex core business tasks.

Certain credit-related processes lend themselves nicely to BPO. Processes such as routine collection activity, lien searches, cash application, deduction follow up, credit investigation, and documentation for letters of credit can benefit from the use of BPO. Each process should be examined individually.

Ultimately, the entire credit function could be outsourced. Too often the decision to outsource comes from the top-down approach initiated by top-level management. Credit managers should contribute to the decision-making process. In order for credit managers to contribute to the decision-making process, the costs of servicing credit-related processes and the value added by the credit department or outsourcing firm should be scrutinized.

The quantitative analysis of BPO decisions is similar to a make-or-buy decision that is often included as part of the second course in principles of accounting. This type of analysis identifies incremental cost differences based upon the alternatives of outsourcing or not outsourcing. For example, if a company performs the credit task of performing lien searches, it will need to incur costs such as a portion of credit department salaries, the allocation of fixed costs and overhead for office space and resources, and variable costs associated with each lien search. These costs could be compared to the costs of outsourcing the task of performing lien searches. The alternative with the lower costs pinpoints the potential cost reduction.

The qualitative aspects of a BPO decision are much more difficult to analyze. Several questions that entail the use of sound judgment need to be posed. Will the outsourced process be handled in a more reliable manner? Will there be any differences in the quality and results of the processes being outsourced? For example, if there is an opportunity to outsource credit investigations, a business with many similar small-balance customers could provide BPO with an edge due to economies of scale. However, for a business with large-balance accounts there is often considerable product and industry expertise that may require close personal contact essential to properly complete the credit investigation; this situation might favor handling credit investigations internally.

BPO can conjure up negative feelings from existing employees. The threat of a downsizing if the BPO decision is implemented poses a dilemma. In certain situations, BPO can actually contribute to an increase in costs. Moreover, if credit managers have more time to focus on non-mundane tasks, then the BPO decision could be welcomed by existing personnel.

There has been a shift toward focusing upon value added rather than cost reduction when considering a BPO decision. Since the management of the credit function varies widely from company to company, the decision to use BPO is one more tool that credit managers should become adept at analyzing. In the final analysis, BPO is being driven by the automation of business activities.

AUTOMATING CREDIT ACTIVITIES

Organizing the credit function includes harnessing technological change to facilitate the credit function. Many credit departments have taken a process focus to integrate technology into the credit function. When an existing process is enhanced, a total quality management (TQM) approach is being used. When new processes become the focal point, a reengineering approach is being used.

Harnessing technology with cost-efficient results will be an ongoing challenge. Automated systems have the potential to cause information overload. While automated systems certainly have the potential to process more information, they do not have the ability to synthesize knowledge. Therefore, credit managers will have to roll up their sleeves and get their hands dirty digging for new ways to harness technology.

The expertise essential to tap into the wealth of information available through new technology is in short supply. Many credit managers will have to gain access to new ideas by going outside of their own firms.

Potential sources of ideas include industry credit groups, local NACM affiliates, local colleges, trade journals, consultants, and companies that provide various products.

The array of new products and processes is simply too long to list. Some of the more important credit-related applications that can assist the credit manager are worth noting. Individual providers for specific products often use catchy labels on products that can cause some confusion. Table 2-8 provides process-related technological focal points for credit managers.

Table 2-8 Process-Related Technological Focal Points for Credit Managers

Process	Intended Focus
1. Automated Invoicing	Prompt, accurate invoices with complete access available to credit managers at their workstation.
2. Automated Collection Systems	Collection parameters automatically identify timing and mode of collection while tracking results.
3. Credit Reporting	Online access to credit reports for customers.
4. Credit Scoring/Order Approval	Risk analysis to provide an evaluation of customer creditworthiness.
5. Electronic Credit File	Online maintenance of customer credit information.
6. Electronic Documentation Search	Retrieval of lien information and corporate registration.
7. Financial Analysis	A wide range of analysis tasks such as ratio analysis, common size analysis, and pro forma construction; industry comparisons are readily available.
8. Management Reports	Specific reports generated based upon parameters furnished.
9. Portfolio Analysis	Sort receivables for risk analysis purposes by product, operating unit, or geographical area.
10. Short Payment Analysis/Deductions	Sort customer deductions by size, product, territory, or cause and then channel an immediate follow up.

The process-related focal points contained in Table 2-8 provide topics where technology can be used to produce process reengineering. By relating the topic to actual performance through a benchmarking measure, credit managers can identify certain areas that need improvement. The real challenge is to harness technology in a cost-efficient way. Side effects can necessitate a change in the organization structure that often has an impact on employee morale.

The key focal points in organizing the credit function include: benchmarking, organization structure, motivation of credit department personnel, business process outsourcing, and automation. The focal points need to be designed both individually and in combination. Change is inevitable. The ability to function at an optimal level of efficiency is the ongoing goal of the credit function. Sometimes the process of striving to reach the goal can become as important as achieving the goal.

Several credit departments have moved toward developing a team approach to organization of work. For example, a team approach could combine sales, credit, accounting, and customer service responsibilities. A team member who takes an order makes sure that the order is filled properly. When the customer sends in a payment, another team member also ensures that the cash is applied properly and any discrepancies are quickly recovered. Credit personnel keep sales personnel informed of problems if they arise.

Another organizational focal point for credit managers is total quality management (TQM). The goal of striving for zero defects by doing a job properly is an attitude that TQM fosters. Internal resources are directed toward producing zero defects through preventive maintenance. TQM can be useful by benchmarking a credit department's core expenses: screening costs, collection costs, and bad debts.

Cost-effective innovative performance is at the heart of organizing the credit function. Credit personnel could consider using the checklist at the end of Chapter 4 to map activities to initiate a study to determine if there is need to reengineer the organization of credit function.

CHAPTER 2: FOLLOW UP

Recap of Important Concepts

1. Organizing the credit function is a focus on developing processes that allow the credit function to operate at an optimal level.
2. Benchmarking is an effective management tool for examining the credit function. The approach used can be external or internal. External benchmarking compares the results of a company to those of a superior competitor or to an industry. Internal benchmarking examines the performance of a company over time to identify trends.
3. Specific criteria used to benchmark the credit function include: aging schedules, credit department expenses per employee, percentage bad debt expenses, days sales outstanding (DSO), and best possible days sales outstanding (BPDSO).
4. Organizing the credit function is a focus upon assigning authority and responsibility. An organization chart is often developed by using business functions or by product line.
5. The credit function is often centralized. Advantages of a centralized organization structure include: maximum control, reduced training, economics of scale, and uniform credit policy implementation. For certain reasons, many companies often use a mix of centralized and decentralized credit operations.
6. When credit department morale is at a low ebb, there is a danger that credit personnel behavior will become dysfunctional. Credit personnel may find themselves in positions where professional ethics can be compromised.
7. Business Process Outsourcing (BPO) entails the use of outside companies to perform certain processes. Certain credit activities can be outsourced in an attempt to benefit from technological expertise or in cost-reduction efforts. BPO can also be useful when the credit department workload becomes overwhelming.
8. Abraham Maslow's hierarchy of needs is one of many motivational theories. Maslow's theory is based upon fulfilling low-level needs prior to considering higher level needs. Motivational theory can be a useful starting point when considering morale problems. There are also a number of practical approaches that can be used to motivate employees.

9. Salaries in credit management positions have been on the rise. A study performed by CRF shows that credit department salaries are influenced by several factors including: size of receivables portfolio, number of active accounts, number of credit people supervised, region, industry, education, number of years with the company, and number of years in credit.
10. The ability of credit departments to harness technological change will remain a major concern throughout the decade. Certain activities in the credit department lend themselves to changes in the way in which they are performed.

Review/Discussion Questions

1. What does it mean to benchmark the credit function? Discuss the usefulness of specific measures that can be used to benchmark the credit function.
2. Identify a danger signal where the credit department appears to be lacking in morale.
3. What has been the trend in salaries for personnel in credit management positions? Why do you think the trend is moving in this direction?
4. The following questions pertain to the MGC Company:
   (a) Calculate the Days Sales Outstanding during the year if total receivables at the end of the year are \$20 million and annual sales are \$100 million.
   (b) Calculate the Best Possible Days Sales Outstanding if current receivables are \$15 million and sales during the year are \$100 million.
   (c) What is the Average Days Delinquent when comparing your results in (a) to (b) above?
5. Draw an organization chart for the credit function at your place of employment or for any selected business.
6. What forces are contributing to the surge in Business Process Outsourcing?
7. What credit processes lend themselves to the use of BPO?
8. What caveats should credit managers be aware of when considering BPO?

Test Your Knowledge

1. Provide two examples of unethical behavior by a credit manager.
2. How is the percentage bad debts expense calculated for a company?
3. What is a decentralized credit function?
4. What is the purpose of an organization chart?
5. Explain the Maslow hierarchy of needs theory. How can this theory be useful to a corporate credit manager?
6. What processes in the credit function tend to be excellent focal points for using technological innovation? Try to identify an example where a credit department should be able to reengineer a specific process.
7. Compare and contrast internal benchmarking and external benchmarking. Support your response with examples.
8. What are some of the advantages of using a centralized credit function as opposed to a decentralized credit function?
9. You are hired as a corporate credit manager by a medium-sized company. You notice that morale in the credit department is low. What specific tactics could be useful to provide the credit department with a motivational lift?
10. Business Process Outsourcing (BPO) needs to be examined both quantitatively and qualitatively. Deduction management is a credit-related process that could benefit from BPO. What quantitative and qualitative factors will shape the decision to use BPO for deduction management?

Credit Management Online

www.crfonline.org/surveys/benchmarking—The Credit Research Foundation benchmarking study of the credit and accounts receivable functions is available for purchase at this web site. There are free sample statistics that demonstrate the potential use of benchmarking at this site.

www.fcibglobal.com—The CICE credential available through FCIB-NACM is detailed at this site. The criteria concerning eligibility and nature of the exam are outlined. An application form can be downloaded.

www.nacm.org/education/certification—This web site provides the details for the three credentials available from NACM to credit personnel: CBA, CBF, and CCE. Qualifications, study guides, and exam dates are available here.

www.nacmchicago.org—One of the local NACM affiliates has a web site that can be useful to demonstrate the potential activities for credit personnel to get involved with a local affiliate. This is the web site for the Chicago-area NACM affiliate NACM-Chicago. Membership, services, educational activities, local board membership, and local committees are highlights of this site.

References Useful for Further Reading

Ankenbruck, Eve. "The Credit Department's Technological Future." *The Credit Report* (February 1998): 1, 12.

Callahan, Terry. "Organizational Alignment of the Credit and Accounts Receivable Function." *Business Credit* (June 2000): 72-75.

Credit Professional's Handbook: The Technical Reference Manual for Credit and Customer Financial Management. Columbia, Md.: Credit Research Foundation, Inc., 1999.

Gahala, Charles. "Financial Tools of Analysis: Business Process Outsourcing." *The National Credit Review* (March 2001).

Gundavelli, Veena. "Security in Web-Based Finance." *Business Credit* (November/December 2001): 51-54.

Hansen, Fay. "Global BPO." *Business Credit* (April 2000): 18-20.

Ladwig, Kit. "The Joys of Benchmarking." *Collections and Credit Risk* (March 1997): 97-104.

Old, Forrest. "Outsourcing as a Business Strategy." *Business Credit* (September 1998): 24-26.

Schmidt, David. "Credit and Collections Finds a Home Online." *Business Credit* (October 2001): 47-51.

Walsh, Christopher. "CCEs Speak Out About Today's Business Environment: Smaller Staffs, Bigger Risks, Less Trust." *P.D. News* (Spring 2002): 1-2.

Zava, Mike. "How to Build a Credit Organization." *P.D. News* (Spring 2001): 1-2.

Chapter 3

CREDIT MANAGEMENT IN A GLOBAL MARKETPLACE

"International trade is on the rise, representing 30% of Gross Domestic Product of the United States compared to less than 10% thirty years ago."[1]

–*Gerald Rama*
Vice President, PNC Bank

The growth in international trade from 10% of Gross Domestic Product (GDP) in 1970 to 30% of GDP in 2000 makes it essential to take a global approach to credit management. The devastation created by the World Trade Center and Pentagon catastrophes on September 11, 2001, elevates risk to the forefront of sound credit analysis. Risk control will continue to be the major focus for global credit management for years to come.

The ability to compete in a global marketplace has become a necessity. International trade is expected to continue to grow due to the adoption of the Euro as the common currency in 12 European countries. Furthermore, huge markets in countries such as China and Russia are opening up to foreign trade. Agreements such as the North American Free Trade Agreement (NAFTA) and the Uruguay round of the General Agreement on Tariffs and Trade (GATT) have also contributed significantly to the growth in trade.

At a time when many U.S. companies have witnessed a decline in domestic markets, their international markets have been thriving. Academics refer to this as the negative correlation benefits between marketplaces that can contribute to a stability of earnings. The higher the

[1]Gerald Rama, "Leveraging Export Credit Insurance to Mitigate Foreign Risk and Expand International Sales," *Business Credit* (November/December 2001): 43-46.

negative correlation between markets, the greater the reduction in risk. In this context, global trade can actually create a degree of risk reduction through diversification benefits.

The purpose of Chapter 3 is to provide a foundation for credit management in a global marketplace. The **Key Learning Objectives** in Chapter 3 are:

1. Recognize risks that are unique to operating in a global marketplace.
2. Identify credit analysis focal points that are useful when analyzing sovereign governments and foreign companies.
3. Examine the opportunity to control credit risk through the use of export credit insurance.
4. Utilize strategies that can be helpful to manage foreign exchange risk.

Those firms with comparative advantages in identifiable markets will have the best opportunities to excel in a global marketplace. Credit managers also play a vital role by contributing to the management of risk. This role is emerging as the most important ingredient essential to success in a global marketplace.

The subject of credit management in a global marketplace is deliberately introduced early in this textbook. In addition, specific international topics are integrated into later chapters in the book. The intention is to develop a global way of thinking concerning credit-related subject matter. The topic is so important that the association of professionals in Finance, Credit and International Business (FCIB) and NACM have developed the Certified International Credit Executive (CICE) designation in response to the demand for the unique skills essential to manage credit in a global marketplace.

RISK IN A GLOBAL MARKETPLACE

For most of the topics in this book, the material is applicable to both domestic and global operations. However, there are several types of risk that are unique to managing credit in a global marketplace. These risks need to be examined carefully by credit managers who are involved with evaluating diverse business practices in foreign countries.

The framework in which international credit operates is based upon conventions, laws, culture, mores, and regulations. This framework provides the mechanism to consider risk while establishing credit arrangements. Credit managers face the challenge of understanding how specific factors contribute to risk within an international framework.

For example, the practice of countertrade is somewhat similar to bartering; this can be a cashless process that provides a mechanism to avoid foreign exchange currency risk. Countertrade arrangements vary widely. However, countertrade can create new types of risk depending upon the buyback or compensation agreement. The foreign government willingness to release products or the licensing agreements can impose additional risks that need to be managed carefully.

The practice of forfaiting is another example of a credit tool that can be used to reduce risk while at the same time imposing new risks that need to be managed carefully. Forfait has a French derivation; it implies the purchase of a negotiable instrument (such as a promissory note or a letter of credit) from an exporter on a non-recourse arrangement. The practice of forfaiting is somewhat popular in Europe. If a letter of credit is used as the payment mechanism to fund an export, then the exporting company could discount the letter of credit from a financial institution that then has the responsibility to collect the funds. The new risks for the credit manager using forfaiting involve significant documentation complexities.

Determining the level of risk is essential to conducting business in any country. There are four categories of risk that are unique when operating in a global marketplace: (1) political risk, (2) cultural and language risk, (3) legal risk, and (4) foreign exchange risk. Each of these types of risk contributes to the complexity of decisions made by credit managers.

Political Risk

Political and social forces often contribute to the ability and willingness of a debtor to honor obligations. An individual nation can exercise considerable control over business operations. Political risk includes the risk of expropriation of assets without compensation. Other examples of political risk include radical ideological shifts, rioting, terrorism against personnel or property, and military coups.

Political risk can be assessed by examining the history of a particular country. Factors such as government stability and social conditions influence political risk. In addition, external factors such as ideological orientation and participation in international organizations may be examined to assess political risk.

Cultural and Language Risk

Unique cultural heritages and values can influence the ability to operate successfully in a global environment. At times, cultural norms can conflict with managerial values. For example, the attitude toward alcohol in certain Arab countries may restrict consumption. In some cultures, women may not be accepted as business executives in the same way in which they are accepted in the United States; this can influence negotiation strategy. Even the dress code can create a barrier to open negotiation.

American credit practitioners can be at a disadvantage if they are not fluent in foreign languages. In Canada there are divisions between the French and English-speaking populations. Language risk can be potentially catastrophic. Although more and more foreign business practitioners use the English language, the credit manager who can master local languages holds a distinct advantage.

The risk of making a translation error should not be underestimated. Experienced credit managers often will require two translations to reduce translation errors. Some U.S. credit managers use both a bilingual English-speaking native and a bilingual foreign translator from the host country to compare translations. Translators often have trouble with technical terms.

Language can also be muddled by misunderstood gestures or even misunderstood through unspoken words. The conversational distance may be smaller in the Middle East. A Japanese businessperson may be nodding yes but really thinking no; he or she may be trying to be polite by appearing to be agreeable.

For some credit managers, the issue of receiving or providing gifts and payments to obtain cooperation is a major concern. Although it is common practice in international business to exchange gifts, this issue can become murky. When is a credit manager bribing a public official? When is a private party really asking for an extortion payment? Americans are governed by the Foreign Corrupt Practices Act, which pertains to questionable business practices that relate to bribes and illegal payments. Global credit managers should become familiar with this Act. The U.S. Department of Commerce includes a lesson on the Foreign Corrupt Practices Act in the Basic Guide to Exporting, available on the Internet at www.unzco.com/basicguide/toc.html.

Legal Risk

When credit practitioners enter into business agreements, the laws of the host country govern business transactions. This means that litigation for nonpayment and potential judgments are governed by business practices in the foreign country.

Both the European Community and the United Nations have conventions established for contract disputes when parties from two or more countries are involved. It is also possible to have disputes arbitrated in centers such as Geneva, London, Paris, Hong Kong, or New York. The use of conventions or arbitration clauses should be stipulated in agreements before problems arise. Otherwise, the laws of the host country govern disputes.

There are also a number of governmental laws that can become barriers to international trade:

- *Embargoes* are used to prohibit products that originate from certain specified countries.
- *Quotas* are used to limit the dollar value or quantity for specified products.
- *Tariffs* are fees charged to import goods into a country.
- *Customs* can be a way to limit entry by imposing documentation requirements or assessing fees on imports.
- *Anti-Dumping Regulations* are used to prohibit the sale of products at below-cost pricing.
- *Health and Safety Regulations* pertain to product, packaging and labeling requirements.
- *Antitrust Laws* are commonly referred to as restrictive trade practices in other countries.
- *Tax Laws* may vary widely from country to country. Consumption taxes, value added taxes, income taxes, and capital gains taxes each mandate compliance with host country codes.

Legal risk in international trade is being reduced through agreements such as the North American Free Trade Agreement (NAFTA) and the General Agreements on Tariffs and Trade (GATT). Together, the NAFTA and GATT agreements are a movement toward deregulation that has resulted in an increase in world trade.

NAFTA is the agreement that promotes free trade between Canada, Mexico, and the United States. All three countries can potentially benefit from reduced costs, more competitive prices, and an increase in global trading power. The long-range view is that NAFTA is an economic reform that has opened up trading to facilitate trade between Canada, Mexico, and the United States.

The World Trade Organization (WTO) is an international organization consisting of 144 countries. The WTO is headquartered in Geneva, Switzerland. The role of WTO is to establish trade agreements, monitor trade policies, and handle trade disputes among member nations. The WTO was created by GATT in the Uruguay Round of negotiations.

GATT is an international trade agreement that acts as a mechanism for regulating international trade and trade negotiations. The first GATT agreement, entered into by 23 nations, went into effect in 1948. The Uruguay Round of the GATT agreement was signed by more than 120 countries in 1994. The Uruguay Round of GATT was negotiated over a seven-year period; the results have contributed to the growth in world merchandise trade.

The Uruguay Round contributed to the formation of the General Agreement on Trade in Services (GATS), which is being negotiated. GATS focus is to create an agreement for trade pertaining to accounting, advertising, computer, engineering, education, financial, and other services.

One of the factors that has slowed down the expected growth in international trade relates to the agency issue. The agency issue suggests that there may be a conflict of interests among employees, stockholders, managers (agents), and creditors. In the United States, there is a general belief that the actions that maximize the price of stock also benefit society in general. However, in countries where there are severe social problems, the interests of stockholders are not always a primary concern. The results of the conflict—often caused by social problems—can have a fallout in a debtor's willingness to service obligations. Agents other than stockholders can dominate trade issues.

Foreign Exchange Risk

Credit transactions in a global marketplace are denominated in various currencies. Foreign exchange risk is the risk that the exchange rate used to change one currency into another currency will fluctuate. The potential loss due to a fluctuating currency value is of particular importance to credit managers. This subject will be more fully developed in the last section of this chapter.

Political risk, cultural and language risk, legal risk, and foreign exchange risk each pose unique problems to a global credit manager. In addition, there is business risk inherent in international trade. The next section of this chapter will focus upon the identification of focal points that are useful when extending credit to a sovereign government or foreign business.

COUNTRY RISK

Perhaps the single most limiting factor that retards the growth in international trade is the availability of credit. When credit availability is associated with the obligation of a sovereign government, country risk should be examined. Country risk can be defined as the probability that a loss could be incurred due to events that are under the control of the government. Country risk is a function of political, social, and economic circumstances.

Table 3-1 **Country Risk Analysis Focal Points**

I. **Political Risk Assessment**
   A. Political System: Structure and Evolution
   B. Stability of Leadership
   C. Cooperation with International Bodies
   D. Geopolitical Importance to Western Bloc Countries

II. **Social Risk Assessment**
   A. Disparity of Income; Per Capita Income
   B. Unemployment Levels
   C. Environmental/Governmental Regulation
   D. Social Order
   E. Population Growth Rate
   F. Infrastructure/Transportation Problems

III. **Economic Risk Assessment**
   A. Balance of Payments Flexibility
   B. Inflation Rate/Interest Rates
   C. Natural Resources/Degree of Product Diversification
   D. Growth Rate in Output of Goods and Services
   E. Ability to Service Debt Burden
   F. Ability to Attract Investment
   G. Current Taxation Levels; Flexibility in Future Taxation Levels

Country risk can become complicated for credit analysis purposes because the analysis includes a number of variables that are not normally analyzed by most credit managers. Some credit managers set a country credit limit in order to restrict exposure. Table 3-1 contains a list of focal points for credit managers to consider when analyzing country risk.

The focal points contained in Table 3-1 are a good starting point for country risk analysis. Country risk analysis reports also are available from the Export-Import Bank of the United States. Individual country restrictions can be reviewed at www.exim.gov. There are also commercial providers who can provide credit insurance by country. FCIB, Dun & Bradstreet, Standard & Poor's, and certain major money center banks prepare reports that can be useful for credit analysis purposes.

Default on governmental debt is normally restructured. One of the best gauges to use concerning future governmental obligations is to examine performance on past credit obligations. Sometimes credit managers can reduce their exposure by obtaining guarantees from governmental agencies in the host country. In other cases, export insurance can be used to control credit risk in many foreign countries.

FOREIGN COMPANY ANALYSIS

Credit analysis for a foreign business is similar to analyzing a domestic business, but there are a few important differences. First, the country in which the business is located influences the ability to extend credit to the business. Second, there is a potential for currency fluctuation, which creates an added risk. Finally, the details available by using various sources of credit information are similar to, but somewhat different than, using domestic sources.

When analyzing credit information on a foreign business, there are a number of potential sources to utilize. These sources include resources from FCIB as well as financial statement information, bank references, and commercial agency reports. Chapter 7 will include coverage of commercial agency reports. A few comments concerning the use of international sources of information are included in this chapter.

FCIB. This international arm of NACM is a leading producer of payment records for foreign businesses in more than 130 countries. FCIB publishes a Quarterly Credit and Collection Survey that includes extensive payment records. FCIB members are able to obtain actual credit experience by industry and geographic region. Country and political risk reports are also available through FCIB. The 800 corporate members of FCIB read like a Who's Who of international credit; the membership can be reviewed at www.fcib.com, the FCIB web site.

Non-U.S. Financial Statements. Credit managers should be aware that both the format for non-U.S. financial statements and the principles of accounting used to prepare financial statements in other countries are different than those used in the United States. Since diverse accounting conventions are applied to varying business practices, the results can be easily misinterpreted. For example, Japanese firms tend to use more financial leverage than U.S. firms. Moreover, Japanese firms tend to enter long-term supply contracts and invest into the stock of their suppliers. These differences can result in some unusual gains and losses in an income statement due to fluctuating interest rates and stock market volatility.

Bank References. The availability of information through foreign bank references tends to be more limited in foreign countries than in the United States. In many instances, foreign banks will not share information with suppliers. As a result, credit managers often contact their U.S. bank, who can then contact a correspondent foreign bank to obtain a reference for the credit manager. The U.S. bank often charges a fee for obtaining the reference by increasing the compensating balance requirement on the credit manager's business account.

Not only do sources of information on foreign businesses differ from domestic accounts, the terms of sale may also vary. Trust between the buyer and creditor frequently is not sufficient to establish open account terms. Customers often are reluctant to pay cash in advance. Therefore, export sales frequently are arranged using a letter of credit as a payment mechanism.

EXPORT LETTERS OF CREDIT

Letters of credit allow customers to substitute their creditworthiness for the creditworthiness of an issuing bank. Letters of credit are a type of secured transaction. Chapter 11 in this book contains a thorough discussion of both standby and documentary letters of credit. Documentary letters of credit pertain to both import and export letters of credit.

Credit managers should realize that the foreign customer initiates the letter of credit. The customer's bank issues the letter of credit to an advising bank in the United States. If the credit manager is not comfortable with the creditworthiness of the foreign bank, he or she should request a confirmation of the letter of credit by a U.S. bank. The confirmation allows the credit manager to rely on the creditworthiness of the confirming bank.

The exporter should carefully examine each letter of credit, checking to see if the stated terms and conditions are acceptable. If there are any unacceptable terms or conditions, the creditor should request an amendment to the letter of credit. Any documentation discrepancy is grounds for a bank to refuse the responsibility to comply. Letters of credit should stipulate that they are subject to the Uniform Customs and Practices for Documentary Credits (UPC 500), which became effective on January 1, 1994.

The most common problems concerning letters of credit that are encountered by exporters include: (1) an insufficient dollar amount to cover the credit, (2) an expiration date on the letter of credit that has passed, and (3) an inability to meet the shipping date specified in the letter of credit. Table 3-2 contains a list of the most common discrepancies that surface when banks examine a letter of credit.

These discrepancies can be used as a partial checklist for particular concerns on letter of credit transactions. When a letter of credit arrangement does not appear to be a viable alternative, credit managers can seek to arrange other terms. When a letter of credit is not available, a credit manager can consider obtaining export trade and political risk insurance in order to manage risk.

EXPORT CREDIT INSURANCE

A credit manager can use export credit insurance to control risk on export sales. The insurance company covers the credit so that in the event of a default by a foreign customer, the insurance company will fund the loss. Export credit insurance often includes an agreed-upon deductible amount for claims.

Many countries have established governmental agencies or private consortiums of insurance companies that insure debt obligations. In the Unites States, the Foreign Credit Insurance Association (FCIA) is a private association that includes many commercial insurance companies.

The FCIA works closely with the Export-Import Bank (Ex-Im Bank) of the United States. Ex-Im Bank is an agency of the U.S. government.

Exporters may purchase insurance to cover various types of business transactions through the FCIA. Commercial risk due to a customer

Table 3-2 **Common Documentation Discrepancies in Export Letters of Credit**

- Documents inconsistent with each other.
- Documents presented more than 21 days after date of shipment (or other presentation period specified in the letter of credit).
- Full set of bills of lading not presented or other required documents missing.
- Draft drawn incorrectly or for the wrong amount.
- Draft not signed or not endorsed.
- Invoice does not describe merchandise in exact accordance with the letter of credit.
- Invoice does not show the same shipping terms as specified in the letter of credit.
- Invoice includes charges inconsistent with the shipping terms in the letter of credit.
- Invoice not made out in the name of the applicant shown in the letter of credit.
- Insufficient insurance amount or coverage does not include the risks specified by the letter of credit.
- Insurance certificate or policy not endorsed.
- Insurance certificate dated later than the shipment date. (Acceptable if coverage is warehouse-to-warehouse.)
- Bill of lading not clean (defective condition of goods or packaging indicated).
- Bill of lading does not clearly indicate the name and capacity of the signer and who the carrier is. (Must be signed "ABC Co. as carrier" or "XYZ Co., as agent for ABC Co., the carrier.")
- Bill of lading not correctly endorsed (if endorsement is required).
- Multimodal bill of lading presented when letter of credit calls for port-to-port—or simply "ocean"—bill of lading; "on board" notation does not include the name of the vessel and the port of lading.
- Multimodal bill of lading presented when shipping terms are FOB (i.e., port-to-port).
- Bill of lading not marked "freight prepaid" or "freight collect" as required under the credit or in agreement with the invoice and shipping terms.
- Not all documents show license numbers, letter of credit numbers, or other identification required in the credit.
- Documents not signed in accordance with letter of credit terms (any documents called a "certificate" must be signed).

Source: Walter Baker, Vice President, Bank of America, N.T. & S.A., Exchanging Documents for Money, Chicago, Ill., 1994, pp. 28-29. (Used with specific permission of author.)

default can be covered; political risk coverage also is available through the FCIA. The FCIA homepage can be reviewed at www.fcia.com to learn more about the services available.

Ex-Im Bank publishes a country limitation schedule that includes exceptions and limitations for coverage. Policies can be structured to meet the needs of credit managers. Protection against political or commercial nonpayment is available through Ex-Im Bank. The actual insurance can be purchased to cover a large, one-shot deal or may be structured to provide blanket coverage in a particular country. The insurance coverage can be short-term in nature, or it can be arranged over a long period of time. Insurance can be purchased to cover leased goods, goods shipped on consignment, services, or recurring shipments of goods to a single customer. Since the insurance policies can be structured in many ways, the web site at www.exim.gov is a useful starting point.

Commercial and political risk insurance is also available through private insurance companies. For example American International Underwriters (AIU) has provided trade and political risk insurance since 1974. AIU, which is based in New York City, considers a typical client to be an experienced manufacturer with significant interests in undeveloped countries. The insurance provides protection against large, unexpected losses. The AIU web site at www.aiu.com is a useful site to learn more about the availability of insurance to support exports.

Due to the increasing competitiveness caused by operating in a global marketplace, the selling terms available may create opportunities to increase sales. If a customer is unwilling to pay cash or provide a letter of credit, credit insurance may afford an option essential to control risk.

FOREIGN EXCHANGE RISK

One of the most important differences between domestic and international credit management is that international transactions are often conducted in currencies other than U.S. dollars. Through the years, U.S. credit managers have often conducted international business in dollars. Historically, the dollar has been considered a safe haven with almost universal acceptance. However, the ability to conduct international transactions in U.S. dollars is not always in the best interest of the U.S. exporter. Other currencies are gaining in international stature, particularly the euro.

The euro is the currency now used by 12 European member states as their national currency. Adoption of the euro facilitates trade. The European countries that have adopted the euro as their currency include: Austria, Belgium, Finland, France, Germany, Greece, Ireland, Italy, Luxembourg, The Netherlands, Portugal, and Spain. Foreign exchange risk has been removed for the trade between members of these 12 countries.

Foreign exchange risk is risk caused by a fluctuation in the price of a unit of one country's currency in relationship to the price of the currency in another country. At issue is the transfer of purchasing power using different currencies. For a U.S. exporter, when a sale is made, either the U.S. exporter or the business in a foreign country will bear the foreign exchange risk.

For example, consider the case in which a U.S. exporter sells a product to a firm in Japan. If the transaction is arranged in yen, the U.S. exporter must accept payment from the Japanese business in yen and then convert the yen to dollars. If the transaction is arranged in dollars, the Japanese business must convert yen to dollars in order to pay the U.S. exporter. In either case, foreign exchange risk exists for one of the participants in the transaction.

If the U.S. business insisted upon conducting an export in dollars, the Japanese customer would bear the exchange rate risk. A concern is that the Japanese customer could demand a price concession to bear the exchange rate risk; even worse yet, the Japanese business may change suppliers and purchase from an Australian business that is willing to bear the exchange rate risk.

An international credit manager should be adept at managing exchange rate risk. The basic principles that apply to collecting domestic receivables also apply to collecting international receivables. The key difference is that cash flow is maximized in a cost-efficient way by managing foreign exchange risk in a global marketplace.

In order to manage foreign exchange risk, it is essential for credit managers to isolate upon key points. These points include: (1) understand the differences between using spot and forward market rates, (2) recognize that vehicle currencies are more readily convertible than soft currencies, (3) consider market forces that cause currencies to fluctuate, (4) recognize an opportunity to hedge a transaction, and (5) understand some of the services available from banks to assist in the management of foreign exchange risk.

Spot vs. Forward Rates

The spot rate of exchange is the actual exchange rate between two currencies for their immediate trade. Table 3-3 contains exchange rates at the close of business on June 12, 2002. Exchange rates can be found in the *Wall Street Journal* or in the financial section of most metropolitan newspapers. An online source at www.xe.com/ucc can be useful as a currency converter. The rates contained in Table 3-3 are subject to change on a daily basis.

The forward rates of exchange represent the cost today to obtain a commitment to deliver or to accept an agreed amount of a specific currency on a specific date. Standard forward contract are typically established for 30, 60, 90, or 180 days. Forward contracts trade in the over-the-counter marketplace. However, money center banks can help to arrange the details concerning time intervals for forward contracts. Exchange rates are established at the time that a forward contract is entered into.

The Chicago Mercantile Exchange (CME) provides the largest marketplace in the world for futures contracts in various currencies. The typical contract is for six months. Futures contracts are issued on a quarterly basis. Futures contracts are standarized contracts, whereas forward contracts can be tailored to individual transactions between parties. Both types of contracts are quite useful as a mode to reduce currency risk. However, futures contracts have an excellent secondary market whereas forward contracts have a very limited secondary market. The web site for the CME is www.cme.com; this site can be useful for quotes and for education-related purposes concerning futures contracts.

Currency Convertibility

Currencies such as the U.S. dollar, the euro, the British pound, and the Japanese yen are considered to be bellwether currencies, or vehicle currencies, because other countries frequently use them to conduct business.

There are certain currencies—known as soft currencies—that are not easily converted into dollars. The Ecuadorian sucre or the Pakistan rupee might be considered soft currencies. When dealing with soft currencies, each of two currencies could be converted into dollars. The dollar is being used as a vehicle currency so that an Ecuadorian business can export to Pakistan through the use of dollars. It is important to become

Table 3-3 **Sample Spot Exchange Rates***

Country	Currency	U.S. Dollars Needed to Buy One Unit	Units of Foreign Currency Per U.S. Dollar
Germany	Euro	.943198	1.06022
Great Britain	Pound	1.47018	.680190
Japan	Yen	.00796161	125.603
Canada	Dollar	.651358	1.53525
Mexico	Peso	.103370	9.67400

**as of close of business on June 12, 2002*

familiar with legal and tax situations when dealing in a country with a soft currency. Certain currencies may have a limited convertibility; other countries may place controls on the flow of capital.

Market Forces

Currencies fluctuate based upon several market-related forces. The central bank in a country may defend a currency when market forces are driving down the purchasing power of a currency. Fiscal policy also will influence exchange rates. Forces such as the rate of inflation, the balance of trade, tariffs, taxation policies, or a war can influence currency exchange rates.

Most credit managers realize that they are unable to control the forces that shape currency exchange rates. Therefore, credit managers should identify ways to control the risk associated with exchange rate fluctuation. A hedge can be used to control risk.

Hedging a Transaction

The safest way to conduct an export credit arrangement is to conduct the transaction in U.S. dollars. When a transaction is conducted in a foreign currency, credit managers should consider the opportunity to enter into a hedge transaction by using a currency futures contract. This entails entering into a futures contract to hedge a position in a foreign currency.

Financial currency futures are traded on the Chicago Mercantile Exchange in their GLOBEX around-the-clock electronic marketplace.

Table 3-4 **Sample Currency Futures Hedge**

1. A U.S. exporter sells 1,000,000 aluminum beverage cans to a Japanese customer for 12,560,300 yen. Today's exchange rate is 125.603 yen per U.S. dollar. However, payment will be made in 90 days.
2. If the sale was made for cash today, the U.S. exporter would obtain 12,560,300 yen ÷ 125.603 yen = $100,000 for the aluminum beverage cans. (This is the spot rate of exchange on June 12, 2002.)
3. If the cans are actually paid for in 90 days, the U.S. exporter would be paid using an updated exchange rate. If the yen fell against the dollar to a point where on September 3, 2002, it takes 140.00 yen to purchase one U.S. dollar, the U.S. exporter would obtain 12,560,300 yen ÷ 140.00 = $89,716.43
4. The exporter could have entered into a currency futures contract to avoid the more than $10,000 currency exchange loss. This loss represents the difference between the original spot price of $100,000 and the actual payment of $89,716.43.
5. Over 99% of all futures contracts are closed out through the use of a reversing trade. The exporter would pay a fee to purchase the futures contract (perhaps $50) and also pay brokerage commissions when buying and reversing the futures contract. In addition, there are margin requirements to be maintained during the period in which the contract is held.

The International Monetary Market (IMM) has experienced exceptional growth since trading first began in 1972. Futures contracts typically have four delivery months each year.

A U.S. exporter could enter into a business transaction that is denominated in Japanese yen. If the contract is entered into in June but payment is not expected until September, the U.S. exporter would bear the risk of a currency fluctuation. In order to control the currency fluctuation risk, the credit manager could purchase a September currency futures contract available through the IMM. This would allow the U.S. exporter to lock in the exchange rate today for the funds to be received in September. In this case, the credit manager is said to be in a hedged position.

Table 3-4 provides a sample currency hedge for a U.S. exporter. This example pinpoints the risk for an export denominated in a foreign currency. The Chicago Mercantile Exchange has seminars and courses available online that can be a useful way to hone the skills essential to trading futures contracts.

Banking Services

Banks often are an excellent source of information concerning the management of international payments. Concentration banking involves the use of lockbox services in countries where there is a large volume of transactions. These situations allow banks to collect in-country using local accounts to speed up the availability of funds. Concentration banking is useful when economies of scale can be used to take advantage of detailed cash management services. The details of specific transactions can be made available quickly through the use of computers. Due to bank transaction costs, the use of concentration banking may not be appropriate for small companies.

Banks also are an excellent source for exchange rate quotations. Moreover, large banks conduct training sessions and provide materials that can be particularly useful for credit managers. Several large U.S. money center banks are at the leading edge of using technology to assist credit managers in a global marketplace.

CONCLUSIONS

Due to the tremendous increase in global trade, credit managers will need to develop a global way of thinking. Since the majority of the U.S. exports are conducted through the use of either a letter of credit or some form of prepayment, there is a need to educate credit personnel concerning the use of letters of credit. While only about 1% of U.S. exports are insured, the FCIA, through Ex-Im Bank, can provide a vehicle to reduce risk in certain situations. Commercial banks can provide considerable assistance to credit personnel in the areas of currency hedging and the use of letters of credit.

CHAPTER 3: FOLLOW UP

Recap of Important Concepts

1. Exports have grown from 10% of GDP in 1970 to 30% of GDP in 2000. The adoption of the euro by 12 European countries, the opening of new markets such as China and Russia, and International free-trade agreements such as NAFTA and the Uruguay Round of GATT suggest that the growth in international trade will continue.
2. Credit managers play a vital role in managing the risk associated with the growth in international trade. Many of the basic responsibilities of credit managers in a global marketplace are similar to those in a domestic marketplace. However, there are several specific responsibilities that can be directly traced to operating in a global marketplace.
3. There are a number of risks that credit managers need to control. Specific risks that are inherent to international trade include: political risk, cultural and language risk, legal risk, and foreign exchange risk.
4. Political risk includes the risk of expropriation of assets. Credit managers should monitor ideological shifts, social unrest, acts of terrorism, stability of government, and general social conditions in order to assess the level of political risk.
5. Cultural and language risk should not be underestimated. Priorities should be placed on the ability to speak the language used in the host country, the accuracy of translation, and the unique cultural influences. Corporate policy concerning gifts should be clear. The Foreign Corrupt Practices Act governs questionable business practices such as the payment of bribes.
6. The laws of the host country generally govern business dealings. However, it is possible to use conventions or arbitration clauses in agreements to cover specific potential future disputes.
7. Host countries can create barriers to international trade. Specific concerns include: embargoes, quotas, tariffs, customs, anti-dumping laws, health and safety requirements, restrictive trade practices, and tax laws. Both NAFTA and the Uruguay Round of GATT represent a movement toward deregulation in global markets.

8. Country risk is the probability that a loss could be incurred by events that are under the control of the government. Social, political, and economic focal points should be analyzed to assess country risk.
9. The analysis of the creditworthiness of a foreign business is similar to analyzing a domestic business. However, financial statements are constructed by using different accounting conventions. FCIB and money-center banks are excellent sources of information. Moreover, credit reporting agencies have improved the availability and quality of reports pertaining to foreign businesses.
10. Letters of credit are a commonly used vehicle to arrange for payments in a global market. There are a number of potential documentation discrepancies that relate to using export letters of credit.
11. Export credit insurance can protect the interests of credit managers through political risk insurance and commercial insurance. Both the Export-Import Bank of the United States (Ex-Im Bank) and the FCIA, and other private companies offer ways to reduce risk through the use of export credit insurance.
12. Foreign exchange risk is the risk that is caused by a fluctuation in the price of a unit of one country's currency in comparison to the price of a currency in another country. Global credit managers should be concerned with controlling foreign exchange risk.
13. Credit managers can hedge their position in a business transaction denominated in a foreign currency by entering into a futures contract. This allows the credit manager to control the exposure in exchange rate risk.
14. Banks provide a wide range of services to help credit managers operate effectively in a global marketplace. The use of technology, the improvement in cash flow, and the actual training of credit managers each represent important services available from large banks.

Review/Discussion Questions

1. What is political risk? Identify examples of political risk. Which countries do you believe have a high level of political risk today?
2. What is cultural and language risk? Are there any foreign countries in which the cultural norms may cause problems for credit managers? Give examples to support your answer.

3. Provide an example of governmental laws that are barriers to international trade. What is the global trend in terms of barriers to international trade? Try to identify major agreements to support your response.
4. What is country risk? Identify several focal points used to evaluate county risk.
5. Identify the nature of problems that credit managers encounter when they analyze credit information concerning a foreign customer.
6. If Mexican pesos sell for $.11260 per peso, how many pesos would it take to buy one U.S. dollar?

Test Your Knowledge

1. Why is it important for credit managers to develop a global perspective to managing credit?
2. What is an export letter of credit?
3. What is a tariff? How would an increase in a tariff influence international trade?
4. What is foreign exchange risk?
5. What does the term "expropriation" mean? How can a credit manager try to assess the potential for expropriation?
6. The use of gifts is common in international business. Why should a credit manager be concerned about accepting or giving gifts?
7. Identify at least six common document discrepancies that occur when using documentary letters of credit.
8. How can export credit insurance protect the interests of credit managers on export sales? Be specific.
9. How can a credit manager control foreign exchange risk? Identify a vehicle that can be used to reduce foreign exchange risk.

Credit Management Online

www.cme.com—The Chicago Mercantile Exchange is the largest futures exchange in the world. This site can be useful for currency quotes and education concerning hedging futures contracts.

www.countertrade.org—This is the web site for the American Countertrade Association. The terminology, legal concerns, and mechanics of countertrade are explained in detail at this site.

www.datastream.com—This commercial site contains stock price quotes on over 32,000 companies that are based throughout the world.

www.exim.gov—The Export-Import Bank of the United States is located at this web site. Guidelines for exporting to particular countries can be examined. Insurance availability, costs, and country limitations can be perused.

www.fcibglobal.com—This is the homepage for the Finance Credit and International Business (FCIB). The 800 FCIB member corporations are listed. There are links to FCIB Europe and FCIB Canada at the site. Products and services geared to meet the needs of exporters can be examined.

www.ft.com—The European equivalent to the *Wall Street Journal* can be found at the *Financial Times* web site. The site contains market information, world news, and contemporary topics of interest.

www.unzco.com—The U.S. Department of Commerce guidelines for international trade are located at this site. There is a basic guide to exporting at the site. The table of contents at the site reads like an international textbook. There is considerable information that could be quite useful for training purposes.

www.wto.org—The World Trade Organization homepage contains considerable economic research and also statistics that can be useful to credit managers. The WTO is based in Geneva, Switzerland; trade agreements and a forum for disputes that arise in the 144 member countries can be examined at this site.

www.xe.com—This is a handy web site for currency conversions. There are drop-down menus to use to convert from one currency into a currency of choice.

References Useful for Further Reading

Hansen, Fay. "Working with International Finance Institutions." *Business Credit* (May 2001): 55-59.

Kanaga, Matthew. "Export Credit Insurance: Avoiding the Pitfalls." *Business Credit* (November/December 1998): 51-52.

Ludwig Schaeffer, Mary. *International Credit and Collections: A Guide to Extending Credit Worldwide.* New York: Ioma Publishing, 2001.

Lustig, Carole. "Forfaiting: A European Customer Finance Technique Comes to the U.S." *Business Credit* (November/December 1998): 26-29.

Nathan, Bruce. "Letters of Credit: Satisfy the Documentary Requirements or Risk Nonpayment." *Business Credit* (February 1998): 8-13.

Pagell, Ruth. "Finding International Credit Information." *Business Credit* (March 1998): 15-19.

Rama, Gerald. "Leveraging Export Credit Insurance to Mitigate Foreign Exchange Risk and Expand International Sales." *Business Credit* (November/December 2001): 43-46.

Schlossnagle, Sherry. "Buddy Baker Going Global." *Business Credit* (March 2001): 26-28.

West, Dan. "Countertrade: Part 1 of 2." *Business Credit* (April 2001): 64-67.

West, Dan. "Countertrade: Part 2 of 2." *Business Credit* (September 2001): 42-46.

Whitworth, Ken. "The Role of the International Credit Manager in the 21st Century." *Business Credit* (May 2000): 47-48.

Part II:

Credit Policy and the Extension of Credit

Chapter 4

MANAGING CREDIT POLICY

"Defining and establishing effective credit and collection policies are considered portfolio-level decisions that involve stepping back to look at the forest, not just daily examination of the individual trees."[1]

–Ruby Kerr, V.P - Credit
R.R. Donnelley Co.

Accounts receivable represent about 25% of the total assets for a typical company. The ability to manage this key asset depends upon the formation and implementation of effective credit policy. Due to its complex nature, credit policy should extend credit managers to look beyond individual customers in a way that reflects an understanding of just how credit fits into the overall corporate goals.

Policies that guide the credit function are developed and monitored within the context of a corporate strategic-planning framework. Specific credit policies are formulated to achieve corporate goals. In conjunction with policy, credit procedures help to clarify operating decisions. The mix of specific policies and procedures used to coordinate the credit function are as complex as those of any functional area of business.

The purpose of this chapter is to give you an overview of credit policy and procedures. A hands-on guide for developing credit policy can be accomplished by performing a thorough credit department policy and procedure audit. The audit can be completed by using a checklist contained at the end of this chapter.

The **Key Learning Objectives** in Chapter 4 are:

1. Recognize the role of the credit function in the strategic planning process.

[1]Ruby Kerr, "Gaining an Understanding of Your Customers Using Portfolio Analysis," *Business Credit* (July/August 1998): 43.

2. Focus upon four key credit department objectives.
3. Define credit policy recognizing that credit policy can have both benefits and limitations.
4. Gain an understanding of receivables portfolio analysis.
5. Appreciate the potential use of Economic Value Added (EVA) as a gauge to evaluate policy management effectiveness.
6. Identify specific focal points for which credit department policy and procedures could be developed.

STRATEGIC PLANNING AND THE ROLE OF THE CREDIT FUNCTION

Listening in on the discussion between two credit managers, one credit manager introduced a discussion of a particular credit policy that had worked very well. Yet at the same meeting, another credit manager actually stated that the same policy was one that would be impossible to consider. Why? The reason is simple: not all corporate markets, products, or goals are the same.

Moreover, not all credit managers perform exactly the same tasks. Some credit managers perfect liens under the Uniform Commercial Code (UCC), others do not. Some credit managers use letters of credit, others do not. Consequently, for very good reasons, the credit function varies in terms of policy and procedures from company to company and industry to industry.

Strategic planning is the key ingredient that underlies credit policy and procedures. Strategic planning entails the coordination of long-range plans with a particular focus upon strategies, controls, and desired results. There are, of course, a number of external and internal factors that contribute to the overall strategic plan.

External factors such as social, political, economic, legal, technological, and competitive pressures impact upon a strategic plan. These external forces are assessed in light of internal factors such as production capacity, technology availability, financial strength, human resources, and marketing. The ultimate goal of strategic management is to evaluate these interrelated factors and assess their impact upon risk and reward, which translates into profit or loss.

Judgment always plays a key role in formulating a strategic plan. The tie-in for credit managers is the need to develop credit policies and procedures that remain flexible enough to adapt to the constant change in the interrelated variables, which is part of the strategic planning process.

For example, one company could decide to liberalize credit terms by lending money to customers to boost sales and profits. At the same time, another company could decide to tighten credit policy by eliminating credit cards. The two companies would be moving in the opposite direction with credit policy, yet both companies could improve profits.

The role of strategic planning underlies the framework from which credit policy is formulated. Clearly defined goals impact upon accounts receivable to shape the resulting credit policy. Consequently, the objective of the credit manager is to achieve a desirable balance between changing and conflicting goals.

FOUR KEY CREDIT DEPARTMENT OBJECTIVES

Why have a credit department? Ask any credit person or college student to respond to this question, and then be prepared for some very unexpected surprises. There are four focal points to consider when responding to this question.

1. Develop an Optimal Level of Sales

There is an old axiom that states "Develop sales-minded credit managers and credit-minded sales managers." This axiom highlights a focus upon balancing corporate goals.

This objective can be considered in light of credit policies and procedures used to sell to marginal accounts. The increased sales will usually broaden the market base and affect corporate profits. Internal controls and a high level of skill in exercising judgment are important in selling marginal accounts. Properly managed, these accounts can frequently contribute substantially to profits.

2. Minimize the Carrying Costs for Accounts Receivable.

Average days receivables, better known as Days Sales Outstanding (DSO), is a key focal point measuring credit department effectiveness. A corporate treasurer monitors DSO closely. An example will be used to illustrate the importance of allowing the DSO to increase. DSO can be calculated in two steps to illustrate the importance of monitoring a change in DSO.

Table 4-1 **DSO Calculation**

DSO Step 1. Calculate Sales Per Day

Annual Sales		$730,000,000
Divide by Days in Year	÷	365
To Obtain Sales Per Day		$2,000,000

DSO Step 2. Calculate DSO

Average Receivables		$80,000,000
Divide by Sales Per Day	÷	2,000,000
To Obtain DSO		40 Days

Using the data in Table 4-1, the DSO is 40 days. If the DSO went up to 50 days, the treasurer would need a $20,000,000 source of funds (10 day increase in DSO times $2,000,000 Sales Per Day). The treasurer would use the firm's weighted average cost of capital to calculate the cost of the DSO increase. If the cost of capital for a firm is 12%, it would cost the firm $2,400,000 per year to carry the receivables an extra 10 days throughout the year ($20,000,000 × .12 = $2,400,000).

Credit controls can be used to tighten or loosen credit policy that will cause the DSO to change. Is it better to have a shorter DSO? Is it better to have a longer DSO? It depends!

A shorter DSO is preferred when all other things stay the same. However, if tighter credit controls result in a reduction in sales revenue, those controls need to be thoroughly evaluated in light of their overall contribution to profits.

The challenge to evaluate a DSO as being the optimal DSO is ongoing. As strategic planning goals interact with changes in both external and internal forces, credit managers may need to modify credit policy. These skills usually require considerable experience in credit management.

3. Minimize Bad Debt Losses

Every time a sale is made and goods are shipped to a customer, the risk of incurring a bad debt occurs. The key factor is the assessment of the level of risk in relation to the potential return. If bad debts are abnormally low, credit policy may be too restrictive. On the other hand, there is another old axiom that states "A sale is not completed until the cash is in the drawer."

Table 4-2 Increase in Sales Needed to Offset Bad Debt

Bad Debt Write Off Amount	Profit Margin Percent	New Sales Needed To Offset Bad Debt
$ 1,000	2%	$ 50,000
10,000	2%	500,000
100,000	2%	5,000,000
1,000	5%	20,000
10,000	5%	200,000
100,000	5%	2,000,000

The data in Table 4-2 indicates that incremental new sales must be originated in order to offset a bad debt. The incremental new sales needed is obtained by dividing the bad debt amount by the profit margin percentage. For example, if a company with a 2% profit margin writes off $10,000 to bad debts, that company must find $500,000 in incremental new sales in order to offset the bad debt.

Credit managers are left with several questions. What is the profit margin of a product being sold? Are new sales readily available? How aggressive should the extension of credit be to marginal accounts? Is an economic or industry change going to cause a change in potential bad debts? The answer to these questions can certainly have an impact upon credit policy and procedures.

4. Monitor the Costs Incurred by the Credit Department

Some of the specific costs born by the credit department include: staffing, equipment, space, debt recovery, credit reporting, and training. Lax credit controls may result in costs that erode the credit department contribution to profits. Consequently, controls need to be established that will ensure that the credit department is functioning at a high level of efficiency.

Across-the-board cost cutting often fails to appreciate where the efficiency levers are located. Learning just where the credit department efficiency levers are located is a major challenge. There is a mandate to tie credit policy and procedures to cost control. Updating procedures mandates experimenting with new techniques that employ the investment in technology. The completion of credit tasks more efficiently is an ultimate goal. A corporate chieftain who evaluates credit department cost efficiency does not always know what to look for. As a matter of fact, most employees outside of credit may not even recognize essential credit-related costs. Therefore, credit managers need to link credit policy and procedures closely to cost controls.

ESTABLISHING CREDIT POLICY

The four key credit department objectives identified above can provide a useful basis for identifying specific policy topics. To reiterate, they are: (1) develop an optimal level of sales, (2) minimize the carrying costs for accounts receivables, (3) minimize bad debt losses, and (4) monitor the costs incurred by the credit department. Because every company has a different strategic plan, judgment becomes the dominant factor when considering policy needs. These objectives can serve as a starting point for developing a credit department mission statement.

Credit managers can determine operational constraints at individual companies in order to establish the procedures used to implement specific policies. For example, there could be a corporate policy that requires credit limits to be assigned for all customers. An individual company sets policy to determine how the credit limits should be used: rigidly or flexibly. An individual company also decides to whom the credit limits are communicated. Should the sales department know credit limits? Is the customer made aware of credit limits? The answers to these questions can vary from company to company.

Credit policy can be defined as a general course of action used to guide frequently encountered situations designed to achieve strategic objectives. Effective policy can help to ensure uniformity within an organization. More importantly, effective credit policy enhances corporate profitability. To illustrate, suppose that a person pulls into a mini market and buys $25 worth of gas. Employees at the mini market need to understand credit policy. Is a personal check acceptable? Can a bank credit card be used? Can a customer pay with a $100 bill? In the absence of policy, these questions could be tough to answer; employees would make inconsistent decisions and customers could become upset.

There are potential criticisms concerning the use of credit policy. Occasionally, credit policy is viewed as a straightjacket that impedes flexibility. Another complaint leveled at credit policy is that it is too time-consuming to develop. One final criticism of credit policy is that the policy can lead to disputes with other department managers or customers.

While each of the criticisms of credit policy may have some merit, the benefits of credit policy far outweigh the drawbacks. For example, consider the policy of charging late payment interest. Customers paying late without interest charges use supplier money. This policy may generate complaints. Yet, the policy can also enhance corporate profitability.

SIGNS THAT INDICATE A NEED TO REVIEW CREDIT POLICY

Both external and internal forces can signal the need to modify credit policy. For example, in September of 2001, the Federal Reserve notified all member banks to loosen up policies while working with customers who were experiencing temporary financial difficulty. Needless to say, banks readily complied with this notification.

For business credit grantors, a number of warning signals may point out a need to review what is going on in the credit department in regard to policy. A few of the warning signals that may necessitate a policy shift include:

- A recession (could be a signal more potential bad debts)
- Employer profit margins tightening
- Change in competitive forces
- Change in social or political forces
- Excessive inventory levels
- An increase in bad debts as a percent of sales
- An increase in the DSO period
- An increase in credit department employee turnover
- Credit department budget problems
- An employer recapitalization

This list could continue on and on. However, the key factor to keep in mind is that good judgment underlies any need to alter credit policy and procedure. The need for a shift in policy should be monitored on an ongoing basis. Existing policies can be reaffirmed or altered as conditions require.

The review of credit policy needs to extend beyond the "if it ain't broke don't fix it" mentality. The pace of change in technology and in business conditions mandates regular review of credit policy. Professionalism in credit management necessitates keeping credit policy current.

RECEIVABLES PORTFOLIO ANALYSIS

Credit management has considerable potential to tap into information technology investments. There may be other departments within a given firm that have been more able to tap into the utilization of technology. In particular, there is an opportunity to manage the entire receivables portfolio as an investment that can contribute to the overall profitability of a firm. Portfolio management can be used to evaluate risk and returns by breaking down the impact of a policy change upon the value added by the credit function.

Internal and external forces shape changes in the receivables portfolio. The portfolio should be monitored for shifts in risk and profitability. For example, credit scoring models can be used to screen customers. As the aging of receivables is lengthening, the scores being used for credit approvals may have to be increased. Overall corporate goals need to be recognized and then balanced.

Another situation might involve a company deciding to expand sales. The accompanying anticipated changes in portfolio carrying costs and bad debts should be anticipated and then monitored. Will the increase in sales offset the increase in carrying costs and bad debts? Policy may have to be altered to optimize the risk-reward tradeoff.

Policy changes need to focus upon balancing the risk-reward tradeoff at individual firms. Analyzing the overall receivables portfolio is an effort to look beyond the individual accounts receivable; an effort is being made to see the forest beyond the trees. Benchmarking goals can be used as guidelines for portfolio analysis. Credit managers should view receivables portfolio analysis as a tool that can enhance the value-added by the credit function.

ECONOMIC VALUE ADDED

One approach that can be used to demonstrate the value added by the credit function is through the use of Economic Value Added (EVA). A number of large companies use EVA to evaluate managers. Conceptually EVA is similar to the Net Present Value capital budgeting technique; the real strength of EVA is that even non-financial managers find EVA to be relatively easy to understand.

EVA has become a buzzword in finance. EVA can be defined as net operating profit after taxes less the after tax cost of capital. When considering an income statement, the operating profit is what is left when cost of goods sold and operating expenses are deducted from sales. The operating profit is used on an after tax basis.

The after tax cost of capital includes charges for both interest expense related to debt capital and a cost for equity capital. The charge for equity capital is calculated by using one of several possible methods. Most college finance books demonstrate the cost of equity through the capital asset pricing model approach, the dividend yield plus growth rate approach, and the bond yield plus risk premium approach.

Table 4-3 illustrates the calculation of EVA for the Cardinal Company. The bond yield plus risk premium approach is used to calculate the cost for equity capital. Since equity capital is riskier than debt capital, a risk premium of about 4% added to a firm's bond interest rate. The bond interest rate is often related to a credit rating from Moody's or Standard and Poor's. The example in the table shows that the Cardinal Company has a bond rating that allows it to borrow at 10%. The cost of debt is 10% and the cost of equity is 10% plus 4% to arrive at 14%.

The example in Table 4-3 assumes that Cardinal Company is capitalized by using $5,000,000 in debt capital and $5,000,000 in equity capital. The interest expense is 10% of $5,000,000 or $500,000; the charge for equity is calculated by using the bond yield plus risk premium approach. The 4% risk premium is added to the cost of debt to obtain 14% for the cost of equity. The 14% cost of equity is assessed upon $5,000,000 of equity employed to obtain $700,000. The table flows just like an income statement except that there is a cost for equity funds that were used by the Cardinal Company during the period.

The EVA calculation in Table 4-3 illustrates that there is a charge of $700,000 for equity capital that accountants overlook in an income statement. The cost of equity is taken into consideration through the EVA calculation.

Corporations can use EVA to evaluate divisions, profit centers, or even individual managers. EVA would not be useful in certain situations such as e-commerce companies. It works best for old economy type companies. Individual credit managers may be able to recognize that by cutting the investment in receivables, EVA is sometimes enhanced.

Table 4-3 Economic Value Added Calculation Illustration

The Cardinal Company

Sales	$10,000,000
Cost of Sales	3,000,000
Gross Profit	7,000,000
Operating Expenses	4,000,000
Operating Profit	3,000000
Interest Expenses	500,000
(Debt Capital 10% of $5,000,000 in debt capital employed during the period)	
Profit before Tax	2,500,000
Income Tax (30% Rate)	750,000
Income after Tax	1,750,000
Charge for Equity	700,000
(Equity Capital 14% of $5,000,000 in equity capital employed during the period)	
Economic Value Added	$1,050,000

However, if the investment in receivables is due to a sales increase, EVA might be enhanced by an increase in the receivables portfolio.

The purpose of EVA is to measure the value created for the owners of the firm. Credit policy should also focus upon creating value for the owners of the firm. When credit managers can demonstrate that they create value for a firm by increasing the EVA, they are often rewarded with performance bonuses. The challenge to credit managers is to develop credit policy in a way that strikes an optimal balance between the four key credit department objectives; this will allow the EVA to be maximized.

THE CREDIT DEPARTMENT POLICY AUDIT

Each credit department is different. The purpose of a credit department policy audit is twofold. First, the audit should examine the specific tasks now being performed within the credit function. Secondly, the audit can be used to consider the effectiveness of current credit department activity in conjunction with what the credit department could potentially contribute to overall corporate profitability.

The audit list can be used as a starting point for topics that are essential to consider when formulating credit policy. This list demonstrates the wide range of tasks performed by credit managers. The skills used to complete credit tasks are as varied and sophisticated as those skills needed in any other business-related occupation.

The complexity of each topic precludes writing one policy statement that could fit all companies. These focal points need to be digested in relationship to strategic planning objectives.

Credit department policies and procedures are allocated to each of the four key credit department objectives presented earlier in this chapter. For college students, this list may help to answer the question "What do credit managers do?" For credit practitioners, this list may be helpful when considering the question "What could credit managers be doing?"

Credit Department Policy Subject Matter Checklist

I. Credit policies and procedures that focus upon development of an optimal level of sales.
   A. New customer policy and procedures
      1. Credit application with each request (sample in credit manual).
      2. Procedures that outline expected turnaround time for making a credit decision on new accounts.
      3. Procedures that outline the specific mode for communicating the request for credit and credit decision.
      4. Responsibility for establishing and keeping current credit department files. (Include the nature of contents to be included in file.)
      5. Policy for authorizing and communicating credit limits.
   B. Policies and procedures that relate to terms of sales
      1. Terms established by industry; clear communication internally and to customer.
      2. A discount chargeback policy; procedures for follow up consistently applied and monitored.
      3. A late payment service charge policy; procedures for follow up consistently applied and monitored.
      4. A policy for requests for extended term arrangements. Necessary approvals clearly specified.
      5. A blanket approval policy. (Small orders below a specified amount are either cash or automatically approved.)

6. A policy and procedure for consignment sales.
7. A policy for export sales and letters of credit.
8. A policy for terms for sales to a debtor-in-possession in Chapter 11 bankruptcies.

C. Policy and procedures that govern credit investigations
1. A sign-off policy for responsibility of the control of account developed by the size of account.
2. Use of credit-reporting agencies clarified by the specific requirements for types of reports to be utilized.
3. Policy and procedures that outline obtaining bank references detailing the type of information needed.
4. Policy and procedures that outline obtaining trade references with details of information needed.
5. Financial statement requests from customers and procedures for the analysis of statements with key focal points.
6. Policies and procedures that govern the use of collateral; include sample documentation, specify authorized signatures, and clarify the safeguarding of documents held in storage.
   a. Perfecting liens under Article 9 of the Code
   b. Guarantees (personal and corporate)
   c. Warehouse receipts
   d. Letters of credit (details by types of LC)
   e. Subordination agreements
   f. Lien searches
   g. Pledge of stocks, bonds, or certificates of deposit
   h. Mechanics' liens

II. Credit policies and procedures that focus upon minimizing the carrying costs of receivables.

A. Follow-up system for past-due accounts.
1. Responsibility and time interval for initial follow-up.
2. A systematic program for additional follow-up.
3. Use of the computer for monthly statements or automated dunning letters.
4. Policy and procedures for holding orders and NSF checks.
5. Policy for deductions and open credits.
6. Policy for personal visits. (Written summary report required.)

7. Policy for the exchange of credit information related to customer payment experience.
8. Policy for unauthorized shipments.
9. Policy and procedures for cash application.
10. Policy and procedures for electronic fund transfers

B. Internal credit department reports. (Assign responsibility, clarify timing, and include a distribution list for each report.)
   1. Aging of receivables. (Do all items age out?)
   2. Over credit limits report.
   3. Reports on open items by category and age (deductions, credits, unearned discounts, service charges).
   4. Highly leveraged transaction report.
   5. Report for accounts with collection agencies or in litigation.
   6. Bad debt write off report and reserve for bad debt report.
   7. Travel and expense reports.

III. Credit policies and procedures that focus upon minimizing bad debt losses.
   A. Policy for conversion of an open account to a note. (Interest bearing? Collateralized?)
   B. Policy and procedures governing customer counseling.
   C. Policy for use of collection agencies.
   D. Policy related to the use of outside attorneys and lawsuits.
   E. Policy and procedures related to customer bankruptcy, bulk sales, and assignments for the benefit of creditors.
   F. Policy for credit manager participation on creditors' committees.
   G. Authorization for accounts written off to bad debts.

IV. Credit policies and procedures that focus upon credit department organization and cost containment.
   A. A formal organization chart that clarifies the positions of each member of the credit department (authority and responsibility should be clear).
   B. Policies and procedures that govern human resources within the credit department.
      1. Recruiting and hiring guidelines.
         a. Educational requirements by position.
         b. Experience requirements by position.

2. Training and development guidelines.
    a. Performance review criteria with procedures for a regular periodic performance review.
    b. Membership in professional organizations.
    c. Workshop and tuition reimbursement guidelines.
    d. Promotion and termination guidelines.
    e. Benchmarking (consider use of CRF research).

C. Credit department budget guidelines.
1. Responsibility for preparation and content.
2. Specific items for which policies and procedures need to be developed.
    a. Salaries/incentives
    b. Space and equipment
    c. Supplies
    d. Training and education
    e. Travel and entertainment
    f. Collection/investigation expenses
    g. Computer hardware and software
    h. Internet usage (appropriate web sites to visit)

CHAPTER 4: FOLLOW UP

Recap of Important Concepts

1. Credit policy is a general course of action used to guide frequently encountered situations designed to achieve strategic objectives.
2. Effective credit policy should balance overall corporate goals. A credit department focus should consider countervailing forces such as sales levels, receivables carrying costs, bad debt write-offs, and credit department costs.
3. Credit policy is dynamic. Both internal and external forces shape the need to monitor credit policy on an ongoing basis. Policy needs to be tightened or loosened through strategic and tactical planning.
4. Any discussion of credit policy should consider the potential drawbacks. Credit policy is sometimes considered a straightjacket, too time-consuming to develop, and difficult to implement. These drawbacks need to be carefully examined when establishing credit policy.
5. Credit managers perform a wide range of tasks that should be governed by policies. Disparate corporate objectives preclude writing one set of policy statements that could be used by all companies.
6. There is an evolving focus being placed upon receivables portfolio management. By looking at the overall portfolio, credit managers are more likely to enhance departmental contributions to profits.
7. Economic Value Added can be a useful tool to measure credit department contributions to ownership wealth.
8. A credit department audit should provide a useful starting point for the development of credit policies. Chapter 4 includes a lengthy checklist of potential credit department policy subject matter. Credit policies should be considered with overall corporate profitability as the underlying objective.

Review/Discussion Questions

1. Describe how the credit function should fit into the strategic planning process.
2. For a company with a 1% profit margin and $5,000 written off to bad debts, how much in incremented new sales must be generated in order to offset the bad debt?

3. What risk does a credit manager take when tightening up on credit policy? What risk is taken when credit policy is loosened?
4. What is receivables portfolio management? How can portfolio management be used as an approach to reach credit department goals?
5. How does EVA differ from traditional profit in an income statement?
6. How can a credit department audit be useful for establishing credit policies?

Test Your Knowledge

1. What is meant by a credit manager's reference to "optimal credit policy"?
2. Try to identify specific changes in credit policy that can be viewed as tightening credit policy. What signs can a credit manager look for that might necessitate a need to tighten credit policy?
3. What criticism is commonly leveled at the development of credit policy? Try to cite specific examples of criticism that could be leveled at credit policy changes. How can a credit manager prepare to handle the anticipated criticism?
4. Define credit policy.
5. How would the policy toward conducting a credit investigation differ for a company with numerous small balance accounts from a company with only a few large balance accounts?
6. What are the pros and cons of using a liberal credit policy?
7. Calculate the EVA for The Orioles Company based upon the following parameters:
   - Annual sales are $50,000,000
   - Cost of sales are $15,000,000
   - Operating expenses are also $15,000,000
   - The company has a 40% tax rate
   - Assets are $20,000,000
   - Liabilities are $15,000,000
   - The company can borrow at a 9% interest rate
   - A 4% risk premium exists for equity capital

Case Study

You have just been hired as a corporate credit manager for Ft. Worth Packaging Corporation. Your employer has annual sales of $200 million. The corporate treasurer hired you to fix a situation where credit policy is non-existent or out of control.

Your new employer is nicely positioned in a growth industry. Profit margins for Ft. Worth Packaging are not as high as those for competitors in the industry. The economy is in a slow growth stage.

Your task as the new corporate credit manager is to establish credit policy. In developing your response, identify specific credit policies that you believe are essential to the credit function. Your response should identify focal points. Try not to get hung up in procedures, but rather focus your response upon "optimal" policies so that the credit function can operate effectively.

Credit Management Online

www.crf.com—The Credit Research Foundation published an occasional paper "Current Trends in the Practice of Credit Review Policies and Limits for Good Accounts" in August of 1999. This paper can be downloaded for free.

www.eva.com—Stern Stewart is credited with developing EVA as a tool for the analysis of companies. This is the web site for Stern Stewart & Co. There is an EVA tutor and a wealth of information available concerning EVA.

www.federalreserve.gov/fomc/beigebook—The Federal Reserve Board web site has a report on the current status of the U.S. economy. Economic information is available by district. The beige book contains a detailed report on the current economic conditions for signs of improvement or declines in economic activity; this information is available eight times per year.

www.valuation.ibbotson.com—Ibbotson Associates hosts a web site that contains cost of capital analysis for over 5,000 companies, 300 industries, and 145 countries. This site is geared toward an advanced financial analysis, which can be quite useful for EVA analysis.

References Useful for Further Reading

Barry, Michael. *Credit Management*. New York: John Wiley & Sons, 1997.

Callahan, Terry. "The Changing Role of the Credit Professional." *Business Credit* (September 1996): 14-15.

Cole, Robert, and Lon Mishler. *Consumer and Business Credit Management*. Boston: Irwin/McGraw-Hill, 1998.

Cundiff, Kelly. "Portfolio Risk Management: An Evolving Approach." *Business Credit* (March 2001): 63-65.

Fryer, Bronwyn. "The ROI Challenge: Can You Produce a Positive Return from ERP?" *CFO* (September 1999): 85-90.

Gahala, Charles. "Financial Tools of Analysis: The Economic Value Added." *National Credit News* (November 2000): 12-13.

Kerr, Ruby. "Gaining an Understanding of Your Customers Using Portfolio Analysis." *Business Credit* (July/August 1998): 43-47.

Piumelli, Frederick A. "Transforming the Future of Credit and Collections." *Business Credit* (March 2000): 23-26.

Scherr, Frederick C. "Credit Department Structure and Policy-Making." *Business Credit* (February 1996): 20-21.

Stephens, Kenneth R., and Ronald R. Bartunek. "What Is Economic Value Added? A Practitioner's View." *Business Credit* (April 1997): 39-42.

Chapter 5

LEGISLATION AND REGULATION PERTINENT TO BUSINESS CREDIT DECISION MAKING

"There are one billion credit reports being issued in this country every year—one billion credit reports. Therefore, the Fair Credit Reporting Act is very important. There are privacy issues that should be recognized."[1]

–Stuart Pratt, Vice President
Associated Credit Bureaus

A major challenge to business credit grantors is posed through the need to cope with external forces. Government legislation and regulation shape credit decisions. Legislation and regulation not only create and protect the rights of creditors but also impose limitations on business activities.

This chapter will examine government legislation that is pertinent to credit decision-making. Social responsibility and professionalism are common threads that weave credit managers toward compliance. Failure to comply with federal and state laws can result in severe reprisal.

There is a clear-cut need to become aware of the specific government legislation and regulation that are pertinent to business credit. Moreover, policies and procedures should be in place to ensure that all credit department personnel are acting within the boundaries of the law. Credit managers should consider governmental legislation from the dual perspective of taking advantage of legal rights and for compliance within legal boundaries.

[1]"NACM's 30th Annual Legislative Conference," *Business Credit* (May 2001), 27.

The **Key Learning Objectives** in Chapter 5 are:

1. Identify antitrust legislation with a particular focus upon the Robinson-Patman Act.
2. Examine consumer credit protection legislation with the application geared toward business credit decision-making.
3. Understand the Law of Usury together with an examination of an annual percentage rate (APR) yardstick applied to simple, discount, and add-on interest rates.
4. Provide an overview of the Prompt Pay Act with a focus placed upon government payments to creditors.

AN OVERVIEW OF ANTITRUST REGULATION

In the late 1800s, the U.S. economy moved from an agricultural base toward a manufacturing base. Although common law had forbidden monopolistic restraint of trade, business practices that had been destructive toward small firms were widespread. Price-cutting collusion among companies was a common mechanism used to drive competitors out of business.

The commerce clause in the constitution gave Congress the power to enact antitrust laws. Antitrust legislation is aimed at prohibiting price fixing, price discrimination, and group boycotting. Congress enacted each of the following antitrust acts: (1) the Sherman Antitrust Act of 1890, (2) the Clayton Act of 1914, (3) the Federal Trade Commission Act of 1914, and (4) the Robinson-Patman Act of 1936.

The Sherman Act

In 1890, the Sherman Act became the first of the antitrust laws. The Sherman Act was aimed at two focal points: (1) the prevention of attempts to monopolize and (2) the prevention of conspiracies in restraint of trade. The basic philosophy arising from the Sherman Act is that an industrial concentration of power is not desirable.

The language "restraint of trade" has always caused confusion. Most importantly, credit managers had queried under what circumstances they could be guilty of a conspiracy. In the case of *Catalano Inc. v. Target Sales Inc.*, the U.S. Supreme Court made it clear that credit terms equal price so far as the antitrust statutes are concerned. Therefore, credit managers who agreed to fix credit terms are in violation of the Act.

The Clayton Act

In 1914, the Clayton Act was passed by Congress. The purpose of the Clayton Act was to strengthen the Sherman Act by making illegal practices more specific. For example, the Clayton Act prohibits interlocking directorates that are the result of a member of the board of directors also sitting on a competitor's board.

The Clayton Act includes a provision that prohibits price discrimination for commodities. A seller may discriminate in price in order to meet competition or when differences in quality, quantity, or costs of transportation exist. This provision was later amended by the Robinson-Patman Act.

The Federal Trade Commission Act

Congress also enacted the Federal Trade Commission Act in 1914. This Act created the Federal Trade Commission (FTC). In 1938, the Wheeler-Lea Amendment empowered the FTC to oversee unfair and deceptive business practices.

The FTC is particularly focused upon consumer protection. Changes in technology and the growth in the importance of intellectual property have contributed to innovative problems. For example, there have been numerous consumer complaints concerning cyber-fraud, identity theft, pyramid schemes, deceptive business opportunities, and credit repair schemes. The FTC has a mission to protect American consumers against such deceptive practices.

The Robinson-Patman Act

The Robinson-Patman Act of 1936 is every bit as important as the Sherman Act for credit managers. The Robinson-Patman Act forbids price discrimination where the effect of such price discrimination may be to substantially reduce competition or to create a monopoly.

As *Catalano* has held, terms granted by credit managers are construed as equal to price. Upon complying with rigid requirements, credit managers may meet equal terms offered by a competitor. This could include offering a discount or granting extended payment terms. Documentation that verifies competitive terms must be obtained. More importantly, a credit manager may not obtain the information regarding the competitive terms from its competitor. The documentation should come from the customer or some third party source. Arranging terms with competitors would be a clear violation of the antitrust statutes. As an aside, a credit manager should recognize that there is an increase in credit risk when extended terms are used.

Discounts and late payment service charges should also be considered a part of terms. The Robinson-Patman Act does allow for a seller to reflect certain cost savings in price. For example, certain quantity discounts could be a reason for a difference in price if the cost difference is supported by proof. This type of discount should be made available to all customers.

Table 5-1 provides some general antitrust guidelines for credit managers.

Despite all of the admonishments, the U.S. Supreme Court determined in 1926 that the exchange of completed and factual information concerning terms and other credit information is legal. Any agreement to fix terms will be judged harshly under federal antitrust standards. The penalties for violations are severe. These penalties can include a fine, imprisonment, and monetary damages awarded to injured parties.

CONSUMER CREDIT LEGISLATION PERTINENT TO BUSINESS CREDIT

During the past 30 years, Congress has enacted comprehensive consumer credit protection legislation. Laws such as the (1) Equal Credit Opportunity Act, (2) Fair Credit Reporting Act, (3) Fair Debt Collection Act, (4) Truth in Lending Law, and (5) Fair Credit Billing Act each govern consumer credit. However, business credit grantors are affected by certain aspects of consumer credit legislation.

The Equal Credit Opportunity Act and Regulation B

The Equal Credit Opportunity Act (ECOA) went into effect in 1975. The purpose of the ECOA is to prohibit discrimination by creditors. The Federal Reserve Board issued Regulation B that became effective in 1977. Regulation B is the mechanism used to implement the ECOA.

All creditors must be aware of Regulation B. The requirements for adherence to Regulation B are more strict where consumers are concerned. Nevertheless, business credit grantors are also required to adhere to the provisions of Regulation B.

Table 5-1 Antitrust Guidelines for Credit Managers

1. Do contact your corporate attorney when qualms or questions concerning antitrust arise.
2. Do develop internal policy in consultation with legal counsel that clearly adheres to antitrust legislation.
3. Do extend or deny credit to customers based upon uniform standards of creditworthiness. Stay uniform when charging back unearned discounts and when assessing late payment service charges.
4. Do not attempt to influence the credit decisions made by other credit managers outside of your organization.
5. Do not discuss future terms, future actions, or hearsay comments when exchanging credit information with other credit managers. Only exchange factual credit information.
6. Do not collude with any competitor when establishing credit terms and do not discuss any pricing policy with a competitor.

The ECOA makes it unlawful for any creditor to discriminate with respect to the extension of credit against an applicant on the basis of sex, race, color, creed, national origin, age, or marital status. Strict adherence to this prohibition means that:

1. A creditor is prohibited from inquiring about an applicant's childbearing capacity or birth control practices, race, color, national origin, age, or religion.
2. A creditor may only inquire about marital status if an applicant lives in a community property state or if an applicant requests unsecured credit and relies in part upon property that the applicant owns jointly with another person. The purpose of the inquiry would be to satisfy the creditor's standards of creditworthiness, or to assure the creditor of having the ability to move against the property in question if a debt becomes unpaid.

Regulation B has been amended with its changes effective April 15, 2003. The official staff commentary has also been amended. Some of the language in the official staff commentary is most helpful, in particular, to trade credit grantors. Mandatory compliance with amendments is April 15, 2004.

The following material summarizes the provisions that are to be followed by business trade creditors. Adherence to the ECOA and Regulation B is closely scrutinized when an "adverse credit decision" is made. The definition of an "adverse credit decision" is:

- A refusal to grant credit in substantially the amount or on substantially the terms requested in an application unless the creditor makes a counteroffer (to grant credit in a different amount or on other terms) and the application uses or expressly accepts the credit offered.
- A termination of an unfavorable change in the terms of an account that does not affect all or substantially all of a class of the creditor's accounts.
- A refusal to increase the amount of credit available to an applicant who has made an application for an increase.

Business credit grantors must give an applicant a statement as to the adverse action taken, orally or in writing, within a reasonable period of time. Business credit grantors must also provide the ECOA anti-discrimination statement to the applicants that says "The federal Equal Credit Opportunity Act prohibits creditors from discriminating against credit applicants on the basis of race, color, religion, national origin, sex, marital status, age; (provided the applicant has the capacity to enter into a binding contract); because all or part of the applicant's income derives from any public assistance program; or because the applicant has in good faith exercised any right under the Consumer Credit Protection Act. The federal agency that administers compliance with this law concerning this creditor is the Federal Trade Commission, Equal Credit Opportunity, Washington, D.C. 20580."

While trade credit is referenced in Regulation B, only the Official Staff Commentary gives definition to "trade credit" and it is defined generally as "limited to a financing arrangement that involves a buyer and a seller—such as a supplier who finances the sale of equipment, supplies, or inventory; it does not apply to an extension of credit by a bank or other financial institution for the financing of such terms."

With regard to the extension of trade credit or for business credit to businesses that had gross revenues in excess of $1 million in its preceding fiscal year (or for credit incident to a factoring agreement) a creditor shall:

1. Notify the applicant, within a reasonable time, orally or in writing; and
2. If an applicant makes a written request for the reasons behind the credit decsion within 60 days of being notified of the adverse action, then the creditor must provide to the applicant a written statement of

the reasons for the adverse action together with the requisite ECOA notice.

The issue of obtaining a signature or a personal guarantee from a spouse remains a great concern. The amended Regulation B states: "A creditor shall not require the signature of an applicant's spouse or other person, other than a joint applicant, on any credit instrument if the applicant qualifies under the creditors' standards of creditworthiness for the amount and terms of the credit requested. A creditor shall not deem the submission of a joint financial statement or other evidence of jointly held assets as an application for joint credit."

Regulation B is very specific as to when a spouse's signature may be required. It states: "If a married applicant requests unsecured credit and resides in a community property state, or if the property upon which the applicant is relying is located in such a state, a creditor may require the signature of the spouse on any instrument necessary, or reasonably believed by creditor to be necessary, under applicable state law to make the community property available to satisfy the debt in the event of default if:

(i) Applicable state law denies the applicant power to manage or control sufficient community property to qualify for the amount of credit requested under the creditor's standards of creditworthiness; and
(ii) The applicant does not have sufficient separate property to qualify for the amount of credit requested without regard to community property."

The Fair Credit Reporting Act

The Fair Credit Reporting Act (FCRA) has been in effect since 1971. The FCRA applies to the extension of consumer credit and is also potentially important to business credit grantors. The Federal Trade Commission (FTC) enforces the FCRA.

There are consumer credit reports on nearly 90% of American adults. Under the FCRA, a consumer who is denied credit due to information in a credit report has the right to inspect the credit report.

Two issues have given consumer credit reports a dubious reputation. First, the incidence of errors in the reports could be excessive. Second, a consumer's right to privacy may not be protected when credit reporting agencies sell their database to interested marketers and other subscribers.

The FCRA was amended in 1997. Business credit grantors should be concerned with the authorization of a consumer report. A business transaction in which an individual has accepted personal liability for business debt, such as in the case of a sole proprietor, partner, or guarantor, does provide a permissible purpose under Section 604 of the FCRA to obtain and use a consumer credit report. Under the FCRA, a creditor must certify to the consumer credit reporting agency that there is a permissible purpose for drawing the consumer credit report. In the case where a business creditor obtains a personal guarantee, the creditor may order a consumer report without prior written authorization from the guarantor.

In a situation where an employer would like to order a consumer credit report on a current or prospective employee, the written consent of the current or prospective employee should be obtained. Usually the human resources department will handle the necessary authorization documentation.

Business credit grantors who deal with consumers on an occasional basis must be mindful of the FCRA requirements. One may obtain a consumer report only under the following circumstances:

- In response to the order of a court having jurisdiction to issue such an order, or a subpoena issued in connection with proceedings before a federal grand jury.
- In accordance with the written instructions or permission of the consumer to whom it relates.
- In connection with a legitimate business need for the information.

The Fair Debt Collection Practices Act

In 1978, Congress passed the Fair Debt Collection Practices Act (FDCPA). This legislation pertains to personal debt collected by collection agencies and attorneys from consumers. The FDCPA was aimed at preventing abusive collection practices. Under the FDCPA, debt collectors are prohibited from harassing, furnishing false statements, and making abusive or threatening statements.

This legislation is aimed at consumer credit. The web site for the Federal Trade Commission can be useful to gain a more complete understanding of the details of this law. Information is available at www.ftc.gov/bcp/conline/pubs/credit/fdc.htm.

The Truth in Lending Act and Regulation Z

The Truth in Lending Act mandates disclosure of credit terms to consumers. The purpose of the Truth in Lending Act is to allow consumers to make educated credit decisions through the use of comparable credit terms. The Truth in Lending Law does not govern maximum interest rates; federal and state usury laws establish maximum interest rates.

Standard disclosure forms include the total dollar amount of finance charges and also the annual percentage rate (APR). This information is required by the Act. The finance charge must disclose interest, and also any ancillary fees, credit insurance, and points. Moreover, prepayment penalties, default provisions, and specific collateral are included in disclosure requirements. The APR is basically a simple interest rate that is calculated through an actuarial method. The calculation of an APR will be explained later in this chapter.

The Fair Credit Billing Act

In 1975, the Truth in Lending Act was amended to create the Fair Credit Billing Act. The intention of this legislation is to take the hassle out of billing errors for consumers. Creditors are required to correct errors promptly while at the same time preventing the errors from showing up on consumer credit reports.

This law was designed for consumer credit; therefore, the discussion is limited. For more complete information concerning the Fair Credit Billing Act, please refer to the web site for the Federal Reserve Board and its Consumer Handbook to Credit Protection Laws, available online at www.federalreserve.gov/pubs/consumerhdbk/.

The Law of Usury

The Law of Usury is one of the most complex laws that can affect all types of credit grantors. Under the legal doctrine established in England in 1774, the sale of goods and services was not governed by usury law. This doctrine held true in the United States until individual states began to establish usury laws during the 1950s and 1960s. At this time, usury law became applicable to the sale of goods and services.

Today credit managers should be concerned with both federal and state usury laws. Severe penalties exist for charging an interest rate that is higher than the governing usury ceiling. Penalties often vary. For example, in some states a creditor will forfeit interest, in other states a creditor will forfeit all principal, while in other states a creditor will forfeit twice the amount of all interest.

Usury is the interest rate charged that is in excess of the governing legal rate of interest. Various situations create different usury ceilings. For example, the usury ceiling for credit sales that are secured by liens on residential property may not be the same as the usury ceiling that governs service charges linked to interest on a note.

Business creditors sometimes use terms such as finance charge or service charge instead of interest. When these terms are used in conjunction with the extension of credit and slow-paying debtors, the terms then have the same meaning. Usury laws may be applicable; state laws determine potential usury applications for slow-paying debtors.

Another concern for business creditors is compound interest. Compound interest is the charging of interest on interest. The specific state laws vary concerning whether or not compound interest may be assessed.

Credit managers are urged to refer to the *Manual of Credit and Commercial Laws* to ascertain the application of federal and state usury ceilings. This reference is updated annually. Specific court cases and individual state laws are available for detailed application of the law of usury.

Interest Rate Calculations

Most credit managers encounter situations where a complete understanding of the basic mathematics of interest rate calculations is essential. Usury laws mandate an understanding of interest rate calculations. The Truth in Lending Law requires lenders to disclose an APR to consumer borrowers.

An APR is derived through an actuarial method. An actuarial method is one in which the present value of the payments is equal to the loan's cash value. The laws that govern APR do not in all cases define APR as the effective rate of interest.

Three types of interest rates are commonly used by business credit grantors: (1) simple interest, (2) discount interest, and (3) add-on interest. Seemingly minor misunderstandings concerning the type of interest can lead to major differences in the effective rate of interest. The following examples look at three types of commonly used interest rates through the use of an APR yardstick.

Simple Interest in Dollars. The interest that is assessed to a loan based upon the amount borrowed is the simple interest in dollars. By using the formula of Principal × Rate × Time, the simple interest dollar amount is obtained. For example, a $1,000 loan at 10% simple interest for 60 days would accumulate interest of $16.44 as shown in Equation 5-1 below:

Equation 5-1. Simple Interest Example

$$\$1{,}000 \times .10 \times \frac{60}{365} = \$16.44$$

Note that a 365-day year was used. Sometimes a 360-day year, which is known as a banker's year, is used. The impact of using a banker's year would result in slightly higher interest amount.

Simple Interest Expressed in APR. When a credit manager is looking for the APR on a loan for one year, the calculation is relatively easy. Simply divide the interest in dollars by the principal. Equation 5-2 below shows the calculation of a one-year loan for $1,000 at a 10% rate of interest (APR).

Equation 5-2. Simple Interest Expressed in APR

$$\frac{\$100}{\$1000} = 10\% = \text{APR}$$

When the loan period is for a number of days less than one year, the magic of compounding must be taken into consideration. For a 60-day loan, the loan could be repeated six times during a year. Because of the impact of compounding, the APR would increase. For example, the formula and corresponding results for a 60-day loan for $1,000 at a stated rate of 10% are shown in Equation 5-3.

Equation 5-3. Simple Interest APR Less Than One Year

$$(1 + \frac{\text{Stated Rate}}{\text{T}})^{\text{T}} - 1.0 = (1 + \frac{.10}{6})^{6} - 1.0 = 10.46\% = \text{APR}$$

The "T" in Equation 5.3 represents the number of times that the loan can be replicated in one year. The equation shows that the stated rate is 10% but that the APR is 10.46%. Since the lender receives the principal in 60 days and the loan can be replicated six times during the year, the APR is higher.

Discount Interest. When a credit manager converts an open account to a note, and the face of the note includes both principal and interest, the note is set up on a discount basis. Discount refers to the inclusion of interest and principal in the maturity value. Therefore, the maturity value must be "discounted" in order to determine the principal. The difference between the maturity value and the principal is the interest.

Discount interest will have the effect of increasing the APR. Examples will be shown to illustrate the APR for a full year discount loan in Equation 5.4 and then for a discount loan term less than one full year in Equation 5.5. Equation 5.4 shows an APR of 11.1% for a one-year loan with a stated rate of 10% set up on a discount basis.

Equation 5-4. Example of Discount Interest

$$\frac{\text{Stated Rate \%}}{1 - \text{Stated Rate \%}} \quad \text{or} \quad \frac{10}{1 - 10} + 11.1\% = \text{APR}$$

Equation 5-5 shows the APR for a discount-type loan arrangement with a stated rate of 10% for a two-month period. Note that the interest dollar amount is used in this equation rather than the stated rate of interest that was used in Equation 5-4.

Equation 5-5. Example of Discount Interest Less Than One Year

$$(1.0 + \frac{\text{Interest}}{\text{Face} - \text{Interest}})^{T} - 1.0 = (1.0 + \frac{\$16.67}{\$1{,}000 - 16.67})^{6} - 1.0 = 10.61\%\ \text{APR}$$

Equation 5-5 shows that \$16.67 in interest $(1{,}000 \times .10 \times \frac{60}{360})$ is charged on a two-month loan with a stated rate of 10%. The impact of setting up the loan on a discount basis is to increase the APR to 10.61%. The "T" in this equation represents the number of compounding periods per year.

Add-On Interest. Installment loans used in certain industries often charge interest by using an add-on interest rate. The construction equipment industry, the automobile industry, and the appliance industry often use add-on rates. Add-on interest is paid on the original principal of the loan throughout the life of the loan. Other interest rates recognize the amortization of principal during a loan. The effect of using an add-on rate is to nearly double the stated rate of interest.

An illustration of a three-year \$10,000 loan at 10% add-on will be used to demonstrate add-on interest. A three-step calculation will be used.

Step One: $\$10{,}000 \times 10\% \times 3 = \$3{,}000$ = Total Interest
Step Two: $\$10{,}000 + \$3{,}000 = \$13{,}000$ = Principal + Interest
Step Three: $\$13{,}000 \div 36 = \$361.11$ Monthly Payment

The three-step calculation shows that a \$10,000 installment loan for three years at 10% add-on requires 36 monthly payments of \$361.11. In order to get an approximate APR for this loan, use Equation 5-6 below.

Equation 5-6. Approximate APR

$$\frac{\text{Average Annual Interest}}{\text{Principal} \div 2} - \frac{\$3{,}000 \div 3}{\$10{,}000 \div 2} - \frac{\$1{,}000}{\$5{,}000} = 20\%$$

Equation 5-6 gives an approximate APR for the 10% add-on loan as a 20% APR. The approach used in this equation slightly overstates the actual APR.

Interest Rate Related Concerns

Errors in interest calculations can vary from minor to significant. Usury is a potential hazard with severe penalties for violations. Customers sometimes demand to know how interest has been assessed. Therefore, both legal and practical motives exist for the formulation and communication of policies related to interest rate calculations.

Simple interest is often used to assess service charges for an open account that is paid late. When does the account receive an awareness that this policy exists? When does the interest start accruing? Does the account that chronically pays late have interest assessed on unpaid service charge invoices? Are all customers being treated equally? These are policy questions that have potential usury side effects.

Sometimes a large customer that is experiencing cash flow problems asks to have an open account converted to a note. The note should clearly include the type of interest being used. Notes that require monthly interest payments are often set up on a simple interest basis. Notes that are set up with principal and interest payable at maturity are often set up on a discount basis. A policy governing this area should exist. Sample notes and interest rate calculations should be included in a credit policy manual.

A letter of credit that requires a time draft becomes a banker's acceptance when the bank accepts the vendor's documentation. Many corporate treasurers prefer to discount the banker's acceptance to make the funds available immediately upon acceptance. Discount interest is usually assessed when banker's acceptances are discounted. A policy to double-check the numbers should be in place.

Finally, interest rates should not remain static. As the rate of inflation and the cost of money fluctuates, interest rate levels need to be altered. Some credit managers prefer to peg interest rates to an index, such as the prime rate, in order to reduce interest rate risk. In theory, the prime rate is the lowest rate available from a large money-center bank to a very creditworthy short-term business borrower. When interest rates are tied to prime, usury ceilings should be carefully used as a rate cap on any applicable loan.

Credit professionals often use computers to assess interest rates. The type of interest rate used and specific legal concerns should underlie the computer applications. Interest rate concerns need to be updated on an ongoing basis.

The Gramm-Leach-Bliley Act

On November 12, 1999 the Gramm-Leach-Bliley Act (GLB) was signed into law by President Clinton. GLB replaced the antiquated depression-era Glass-Steagall Act. GLB is a comprehensive overhaul of the regulations that guide financial institutions. The long-standing barriers between commercial banking, investment banking, and insurance have been virtually eliminated.

GLB contains guidelines that protect consumers from the disclosure of information released to third parties. Two provisions of GLB provide the operative guidelines concerning the protection of personal information. These two sections are called Section 502 and Section 503.

Section 502 governs the release of nonpublic personal information. Financial institutions must provide consumers with a notice that informs consumers that information may be disclosed to a third party; consumers are then given the opportunity to keep the information from being disclosed by completing a non-disclosure option.

Section 503 requires financial institutions to divulge their policies concerning the disclosure of personal financial information.

This disclosure is made when an account is opened and then at least once annually.

Prompt Payment Legislation

President Reagan signed federal legislation for the Prompt Payment Act into law in 1982. A major amendment to the 1982 Act went into effect in 1989. In addition, most states have enacted laws that are similar to the federal Prompt Payment Act.

The purpose of prompt payment legislation is simple. For most businesses, cash flow is essential for survival. The government is a very unusual customer; credit risk is minimal, but a bureaucracy laden with paperwork requirements and personnel inefficiency can delay payments. The cost of carrying government agencies should not be allowed to shift to the private sector.

Prompt payment laws are aimed at requiring both federal and state government agencies to pay for goods or services in a timely manner. The amended federal act clarifies the responsibilities for both the government and suppliers. The nuts-and-bolts utilization of prompt payment legislation is well worth the effort of mastering the details.

Stipulations included in the federal prompt payment legislation include:

1. A seven-day constructive acceptance period exists for the government to inspect shipments or work performed. The government also has seven days from the receipt of invoices to review invoices.
2. The deadline for earning cash discounts is determined from the date of an invoice.
3. Remittance information should be included with government checks so that creditors can properly identify what is being paid.
4. Interest for late payments is payable for goods or services if payments are made more than 15 days after a 30-day payment period, except for meat or meat-food products, which call for interest if payments are three days beyond a seven-day payment period, or for perishable agricultural products, which call for interest if payments are made five days beyond a 10-day payment period.
5. The interest obligation begins one day after the appropriate due date. Interest rates are set by the Treasury Department and can change every six months on January 1 or July 1. Late payment interest

should be paid automatically by the federal government without a supplier request.

6. In the event that late payment interest is not paid, creditors need to write a letter that includes specific details for both late interest and an additional penalty on top of the late interest. This request should be made by creditors within 40 days of receiving a late payment.

Prompt payment legislation was revised on September 29, 1999. Although still not perfect, this legislation provides credit managers with a highly desirable mechanism that can be used to induce prompt payment. At a minimum, prompt payment legislation provides a potential tool to use to induce payment from the government in a timely manner or to require the payment of interest.

Federal interest rates are adjusted semi-annually. For the period beginning June 30 through December 31, 2003, the rate of interest was 3.215%. There is a spreadsheet at the Prompt Pay web site that will calculate the interest cost to the government. The site address is www.fms.treas.gov/prompt/ppinterest.html.

CHAPTER 5: FOLLOW UP

Recap of Important Concepts

1. Sound business practice requires the adherence to government legislation and regulation. Credit managers are motivated to comply with laws through both social responsibility and the threat of government reprisal.
2. Antitrust laws have been enacted to prevent conspiracies in restraint of trade. Credit managers should become familiar with the potential application of antitrust legislation to credit management-related situations. In particular, an understanding of the Robinson-Patman Act and how it applies to setting and enforcing terms should be clear.
3. Consumer credit legislation can be pertinent to business credit grantors. The Equal Credit Opportunity Act prohibits discriminatory practices when extending any type of credit. The ECOA also imposes certain requirements upon business credit grantors that pertain to the modification of adverse credit decisions and the retention of credit records.
4. Any business credit grantor who occasionally deals with a consumer needs to become familiar with the Fair Credit Reporting Act. Consumers who are denied credit based upon a consumer credit report are to be notified of the source and nature of the information upon which the denial was based.
5. The Truth in Lending Act mandates disclosure of credit terms to consumers. Part of the disclosure requirement includes the interest rate expressed as an APR.
6. Usury is the rate of interest charged that is in excess of the governing legal rate of interest. The utilization of usury laws is governed by state laws that include a wide number of applications and penalties.
7. Most credit managers encounter numerous situations where an understanding of the mathematics of interest rate calculations is essential. Simple interest, discount interest, and add-on interest can each be converted into an APR.
8. The Gramm-Leach-Bliley Act imposes broad disclosure requirements concerning consumer financial privacy for financial institutions.
9. Prompt payment legislation is aimed at requirements that pertain to federal and state governmental agencies. Credit managers should

become familiar with their rights and responsibilities under the prompt payment laws.

Review/Discussion Questions

1. Describe how credit policy and procedures can be useful tools to foster decisions consistent with the compliance of government legislation.
2. How is antitrust legislation important to credit decision making? Try to identify specific situations where credit managers could be susceptible to an antitrust violation.
3. What types of information can a credit manager legally share with a competitor when exchanging credit information?
4. What types of discrimination are prohibited by the Equal Credit Opportunity Act? Does this part of ECOA apply to business credit grantors?
5. What requirements apply to records retention concerning the ECOA? How do non-trade business creditors differ from trade business creditors concerning adverse credit decisions?
6. What is the purpose of the Fair Credit Reporting Act?
7. What is the purpose of the Truth in Lending Act?
8. What is usury? Who governs the usury laws?
9. What problems can a business credit manager encounter that are governed by the law of usury?
10. Perform each of the following interest rate calculations:
    a. Calculate the simple interest on a three-month loan in the amount of $10,000 with a simple interest rate of 7%.
    b. How much is the APR in (a) above?
    c. How much is the APR for a loan made on discount basis that has a 12% stated rate of interest?
    d. Calculate the monthly payment for a five-year loan that has a principal of $20,000 and a 7% add-on interest rate.
    e. What is the approximate APR for the loan made in (d) above?
11. What is the purpose of the Prompt Payment Act?
12. Are the stipulations that govern prompt payment legislation more in favor of the government or the creditor? Support your response with sound reasoning.
13. How could the Gramm-Leach-Bliley Act constrain sharing of consumer credit information available from financial institutions?

Test Your Knowledge

1. Briefly describe each of the following:
    a. Sherman Act
    b. Clayton Act
    c. Robinson-Patman Act
    d. Fair Credit Reporting Act
2. What is usury?
3. Describe the basic intention and guidelines that pertain to the Prompt Payment Act.
4. How does the Equal Credit Opportunity Act apply to business creditors? Be thorough.
5. How can a business credit manager stay within the guidelines of the Robinson-Patman Act when considering a request for an extended term arrangement?
6. Why is antitrust legislation important to credit decision making? Try to identify specific situations where credit managers could be susceptible to an antitrust violation.
7. What is the purpose of the Fair Credit Reporting Act?

Credit Management Online

www.clla.org—The Commercial Law League of America hosts a web site that contains a considerable amount of information concerning legislation that is important to credit management.

www.creditworthy.com—This web site contains links to the application of several federal laws that are important to credit management.

www.federalreserve.gov/pubs/consumerhdbk—The *Consumer Handbook to Credit Protection Laws* is available at this site.

www.federalreserve.gov/regnsup.htm—Federal Reserve Board regulation is contained at this web site. Application and compliance issues can be examined at this site. Both the Truth in Lending Act and Equal Credit Opportunity Act can be examined.

www.fms.treas.gov/prompt/ppfact.html—Information concerning the Prompt Payment Act is housed at this web site. Updated interest rates and a link to interest payable due to federal government late payment are available.

www.fms.treas.gov/prompt/ppinterest.html—The Prompt Pay web site provides a spreadsheet to calculate the interest cost to the government.

www.ftc.gov—This is the web site hosted by the Federal Trade Commission. Antitrust concerns and guidance for business applications can be examined at this site.

www.nacm.org/govtaffairs.html—NACM hosts a site that recaps government affairs that are pertinent to credit management.

www.sia.com/gramm_leach_bliley—The Securities Industry Association provides considerable information concerning the Gramm-Leach-Bliley Act at this web site.

References Useful for Further Reading

Marcus, Jay E. "The Extent of Personal Guaranties." *The Credit Report* (May 1998): 3.

"NACM's 30th Annual Legislative Conference." *Business Credit* (May 2001): 26-31.

National Association of Credit Management. *Manual of Credit and Commercial Laws*, 93rd Edition. Columbia, Md.: 2002.

Parkinson, Kenneth L. "Why Credit Managers Should Be Concerned with Consumer Credit Laws: A Conversation with Charles Tatelbaum, Esq." *Business Credit* (April 1998): 18-19.

Tatelbaum, Charles M. "Flash! The Equal Credit Opportunity Act Applies to Commercial Credit Grantors." *P.D. News* (January 1998): 1-3.

Tatelbaum, Charles M. "Gramm-Leach-Bliley Act Impacts Business Credit." *Business Credit* (June 2001): 6.

Tatelbaum, Charles M. "Impact of Amended Fair Credit Reporting." *The Credit Report* (December 1997): 1-3.

Tatelbaum, Charles M. "The Privacy, Accuracy, and Fairness of Sensitive Personal Information Under the Amended Fair Credit Reporting Statute." *Business Credit* (November/December 1997: 17.

Wise, Jim. "The Annual Legislative Conference: A Historic Conference for Historic Times." *Business Credit* (February 2002): 6.

Wise, Jim. "Fair Credit Reporting Act and Authorization." *The Credit Report* (July 1998): 1.

Chapter 6

Conducting the Credit Investigation

"The good news is that there are more tools available than ever."[1]

–David Schmidt
Credit Consultant and Author

The term "credit" has a Latin derivation, *credere*, that when literally translated means to believe in or to trust. For most credit managers, the decision to believe in a customer comes down to both the ability and the willingness of a customer to pay. Pressures to reduce costs accompanied by an explosion in the availability of improved information resources have shaped major changes in performing a credit investigation.

Conducting a credit investigation is one of the most common tasks performed by credit managers. Yet the factors that shape the extension of credit can vary widely from company to company. The ultimate goal of a credit investigation is to assess customer business risk so that shareholder wealth can be maximized for the credit manager's employer.

Credit decision making is dynamic. As internal concerns and external forces change, a credit manager will ultimately be in a position to tighten or loosen controls that affect the extension of credit. The ability to assess customer risk is the skill that enables credit managers to confront the dynamics of credit decision making.

Successful credit investigations are earmarked by linking internal controls to the evaluation of external information sources. The goal is to establish effective policy and procedures.

---

[1]David Schmidt, "Get Better Mileage for Your Information Dollars," *Business Credit* (March, 2001): 66.

The **Key Learning Objectives** contained in Chapter 6 are:

1. Examine internal concerns pertinent to conducting a credit investigation.
2. Identify numerous potential sources of credit information.
3. Focus on the essential aspects of a bank reference, trade reference, and industry credit group.
4. Analyze the potential use of empirical credit scoring in a business credit environment.
5. Recognize the importance of monitoring existing credit lines.

Later in this book, we will build on the credit investigation. Chapter 7 will focus on the use of external business credit reporting companies. In Chapter 8, our focus will shift toward maintaining customer relationships. In Chapters 9 and 10, we will examine the importance of financial statements for the credit manager.

THE FIVE Cs OF CREDIT

The ultimate decision to grant or to deny credit rests in the hands of the credit manager. The irony of gathering and interpreting objective credit information is that the final decision is always somewhat subjective. Sound judgment becomes the most important skill for credit managers to develop.

Historically, the five Cs of credit have provided a foundation to broaden the credit manager's focus. The ability to analyze each of the five Cs can provide a well-rounded focus. The five Cs include:

1. *Character.* Many credit managers believe that this is the most important of the five Cs. Does a customer honor commitments? Have there been any prior problems with management? The character reflects willingness to pay. The customer, sales person, bank loan officer, and other suppliers are useful to the credit manager when evaluating character.
2. *Capital.* Financial statement analysis provides the basis to evaluate capital. Focal points include liquidity, cash flow, financial leverage and asset management. An analysis of capital can provide an objective appraisal for a customer's ability to pay creditors.

3. *Capacity*. Does the debtor have the legal capacity to bind a corporation? Are each of the functional areas of the business properly managed: financial, marketing, production, and accounting? The capacity is a subjective indicator for a debtor's ability to pay. Credit managers can consider the length of time a customer has been in business and the legal composition of the business as a reflection of capacity.
4. *Conditions*. The term "conditions" refers to a broad-based focus that extends beyond customer analysis. Changes in tax policy, industry analysis, economic conditions, and geographic area can each become focal points for credit decision making.
5. *Collateral*. Debtor support in terms of specific assets used as collateral can enhance a customer's creditworthiness. Resources such as liens on specific assets, letters of credit, pledges of stock or bonds, and personal or corporate guarantees can each afford an opportunity to ultimately extend credit.

The five Cs of credit can be used as a starting point to assist credit decisions. Internal corporate goals need to be balanced with the five Cs. Credit practitioners should have knowledge of the various resources and the ability to extract the most from their investigation.

PROCESSING APPLICATIONS FOR CREDIT

Most business transactions occur on a credit basis. Both screening new accounts and monitoring existing accounts require credit analysis skills that command a great deal of judgment. In order to effectively process numerous applications for credit, the following focal points are essential: (1) establishing internal controls, (2) recognizing the legal form of the debtor entity, (3) limiting the extent of the credit investigation, and (4) identifying essential sources of credit information.

Establishing Internal Controls

The credit-sales relationship is the foundation for credit controls that govern new accounts. When an initial order comes into the credit department, the order should be logged in. The responsibility for the credit decision should be clear. Any non-routine circumstances should be communicated.

In most orders from new customers, a credit application should be required. The credit department uses the application for an efficient processing of the order. The credit application should be completed in its entirety and signed by the applicant.

Credit managers are urged to include any necessary information essential to processing the application on their credit application form. When credit departments have a need for a quick turnaround time in making their credit decision, the information furnished on an application is vital. Sometimes information culled from a credit application provides much of the information that is essential to use in a credit-scoring model.

The needs of a particular credit department can vary widely. Some credit applications include a built-in personal guarantee form. Other applications include a requirement to furnish a financial statement. Perhaps tax exemption information or an opportunity for comments from a customer or a sales person can prove to be helpful. The point is that credit managers need to develop an application form that works.

Recognizing the Legal Form of the Debtor Entity

The name on the credit application needs to be verified. The legal name of the obligor is critical. When uncertainty concerning the legal name exists, the Corporation Division at the Secretary of State's Office should be contacted to verify the name. Once the name on the credit application is verified, the focus should be placed squarely upon the creditworthiness of the specific obligor. Most entities take on one of three legal forms: proprietorship, partnership, or corporation. However, there are distinguishing modes of operation that can become important such as subsidiary, division, limited liability corporation, an "S" corporation, or a joint venture.

The proprietorship form has the most number of entities in existence, but the corporate form generates significantly more revenue. A proprietor has unlimited personal liability. All partnerships are required to have at least one general partner who also has personal liability. However, limited partners do not have personal liability. For a corporation, there is no personal liability from stockholders unless creditors obtain a personal guarantee or there have been certain acts of fraud.

When dealing with a corporation, creditors should be aware of the legal difference between a division and a subsidiary. A division is an arm of the corporation in which the legal entity is the entire corporation. On the other hand, a subsidiary exists separate and apart from the parent company; creditors can consider requesting a corporate guarantee and a board of directors' resolution that authorizes the corporate guarantee in cases when the subsidiary cannot stand on its own creditworthiness.

A limited liability corporation (LLC) allows stockholders to be protected from personal liability while at the same time provides certain tax advantages that are associated with partnerships. There has been a resent surge in the number of businesses operating as an LLC legal entity. The reduction in risk has made the LLC a popular type of entity. Particular industries are characterized by having many LLC entities: accounting practices, medical practices, and legal firms. The LLC entity creates the risk that is similar to that of other corporations; personal guarantees should be considered when dealing with an LLC.

Regular corporations are referred to as "C" corporations An "S" corporation (formerly known as a subchapter "S" corporation) has the status of a partnership for tax purposes. For corporations that qualify by meeting IRS requirements such as 35 or fewer shareholders, the shareholders are taxed on profits at their own marginal rates; there is no double taxation on corporate profits and dividends as there is for the "C" corporation. Creditors should view "S" corporations in a manner similar to "C" corporations for obligations.

With the explosion in international trade, numerous companies have decided to partner with a business to form a joint venture. Joint ventures create an obligation for the joint venture entity. Therefore, credit managers need to be careful about the legal responsibility; only the joint venture itself, not the businesses that have invested into the joint venture, have liability for joint venture obligations. This might create a need to consider a corporate guarantee from the joint venture investor companies.

Both the name and type of entity of the obligor should be clarified. Once this is done, the credit manager should consider the extent to which the credit obligation will be conducted.

Limiting the Extent of the Investigation

A credit manager can expend considerable time and costs while conducting a credit investigation. The credit manager's time can be viewed as an opportunity cost. In addition, the direct costs associated with the credit investigation can add up; credit reports, phone calls, postage expense, and customer visits will each contribute to credit investigation costs.

Credit policies and procedures should be developed that balance the costs and benefits of thorough credit analysis. The extent of the credit investigation is governed by each of the following factors:

1. The profit potential on the product, if high, can justify a more thorough credit investigation.
2. When there is potential for a long-term supplier relationship, a more thorough investigation is cost justifiable. On the other hand, a one-shot deal may not provide the opportunity to recoup credit investigation costs.
3. A large dollar order can justify an in-depth credit investigation. On the other hand, some companies have a blanket policy for small orders so that credit investigation costs are better controlled.
4. The business risk of the customer can often pinpoint the need to go further or stop with a credit investigation. For example, an application from AT&T or Dow Chemical might be quickly approved. An application from an obscure company may require substantial time and the use of numerous sources of credit information.
5. The nature of the sale can influence a credit investigation. An export sale may require the need to set up a letter of credit. A long-term secured credit sale could require extensive analysis of the collateral and a need to perfect a lien.
6. The timeframe in which a credit decision must be made can vary from one hour to several weeks. Time imposes constraints on the extent of a credit investigation.

Controls that govern credit investigations need to be flexible. Situations dictate a cost/benefit focus that considers each of the factors mentioned in this section. Credit managers need to hone the skill of taking a credit investigation as far as it has to go.

Identifying Essential Sources of Credit Information

Credit managers do not use all sources of information for each of their customers. However, most credit managers encounter certain situations where they want to play a trump card. This is when the knowledge of any existing potential source of credit information can prove to be vital to the ultimate decision.

Table 6-1 Potential Sources of Credit Information

- The Customer
- Your Own Sales Representative
- Business Credit Reporting Agencies:
  - Business Credit USA.COM
  - Dun & Bradstreet
  - Experian
  - NACM
  - Veritas Credit Corporation
- Customer Financial Statements
- Trade References
- Bank Reference from Customer
- Industry Credit Groups
- Use of Creditor's Own Bank to Conduct Investigation
- The Securities and Exchange Commission (10 Ks etc.)
- U.S. Department of Commerce (World Trade Data Reports)
- Public Records (liens, lawsuits) (State and County)
- Utility Companies
- Consumer Credit Reporting Agencies:
  - Equifax
  - Experian
  - Trans Union
- Bond Rating Agencies:
  - Moody's
  - Standard & Poor's
  - Fitch's Investors Service
  - Duff & Phelps
- U.S. Bankruptcy Courts
- Better Business Bureau
- FCIB
- Export-Import Bank
- Customer's Accountant
- Customer's Insurance Company
- Trade Journals
- General Business Publications

Table 6-1 provides an extensive list of resources that can prove useful during a credit investigation. The bread-and-butter resources will be thoroughly discussed. Those sources of credit information that are not often used have been identified in order to plant a seed. There are numerous potential resources, any one of which can make or break a decision to extend credit.

ANALYZING BUSINESS CREDIT INFORMATION

In the previous section of this chapter, our focus was placed upon establishing internal controls, limiting the extent of credit investigations, and identifying sources of credit information. In this section of Chapter 6, our focus will turn toward utilizing key sources of business credit information. The specific key sources to be analyzed include: (1) bank references, (2) trade references, and (3) industry credit groups.

Bank References

The commercial loan officer who handles a prospective customer's account is usually the appropriate contact for a bank reference. Invariably the loan officer will have a close relationship with the customer. The banker may be in a position of wanting to strengthen a borrower's loan relationship, so the banker will usually want suppliers to ship to the bank's customers.

In order to obtain the most information from a bank reference, the trade creditor needs to understand the code of ethics used to exchange credit information. Moreover, the trade creditor should also know the questions to pose to the banker in order to obtain the most meaningful information. Banks have experimented with the practice of charging trade creditors for a reference. This practice has not become widespread due to the number of bank customer complaints.

Table 6-2 Statement of Principles for the Exchange of Credit Information

1. Confidentiality is the cardinal principle in the exchange of credit information. The identity of inquirers and sources should not be disclosed without their permission.
2. All parties involved in the exchange of credit information must base inquiries and replies on fact.
3. The purpose of the inquiry and the amount involved should be clearly stated.
4. If the purpose of an inquiry involves actual or contemplated litigation, the inquirer should clearly disclose this fact.
5. The inquirer should make every effort to determine the subject's bank(s) of account before placing an inquiry.
6. Proper identification should be provided in all credit communications.
7. Replies should be prompt and contain sufficient facts commensurate with the purpose and amount of the inquiry. If specific questions cannot be answered, the reasons should be clearly stated.

Table 6-3 **RMA General Figure Ranges**

To ensure accuracy and consistency when exchanging credit information, the RMA General Figure Ranges should be used. It may be necessary, at times, to clarify these terms so that the inquirer and respondent are "speaking the same language."

Low 4 figures	=	\$1,000 to \$1,999
Moderate 4 figures	=	\$2,000 to \$3,999
Medium 4 figures	=	\$4,000 to \$6,999
High 4 figures	=	\$7,000 to \$9,999

The ranges are adjustable to accommodate all amounts in the following manner:

"Normal"	=	Under \$100
"3 figures"	=	From \$100 to \$999
"4 figures"	=	From \$1,000 to \$9,999
"5 figures"	=	From \$10,000 to \$99,999
"6 figures"	=	From \$100,000 to \$999,999 and so on

Risk Management Associates (RMA), formerly called the Robert Morris Associates, is a trade association for commercial bankers. RMA has established a code of ethics for exchanging credit references. Table 6-2 contains the seven principles that are used for the exchange of credit information. Credit managers are urged to abide by these principles both when obtaining and furnishing information. Both the RMA and the NACM have approved the principles outlined in Table 6-2.

Bankers often provide financial information in general ranges. This is due to the normal fluctuation in deposit and loan balances. Table 6-3 contains the "RMA General Figure Ranges," which are used by bankers when exchanging financial data.

The diligence of the credit manager in posing pertinent questions to a bank loan officer should not be underestimated. Most accounts will be categorized as satisfactory. Credit managers need to know more than the fact that a satisfactory relationship exists to evaluate a potential customer.

Some of the information that can be obtained from a banker includes:

1. Date account opened
2. Average checking account balance
3. Any NSF checks?
4. Type of loans (obtain details)
5. Balance and payment record on loans

6. Collateral on loans (obtain the nature)
7. Any personal guarantees? (personal financial statement?)
8. Any inter-company customer related transactions (specify)
9. Has the bank ever issued a standby letter of credit on this customer's behalf?
10. Does the bank have a current financial statement?
11. What is the trend of the customer's operations?
12. Any expression of the overall account or management?

The 12 pieces of information listed are a good starting point. Each of the points can be developed more fully by posing follow-up questions. Bankers may not be in a position to volunteer derogatory information unless a credit manager frames the appropriate question.

Sometimes bankers will be reluctant to furnish information over the phone. A written inquiry can prove to be sufficient. However, there may be times when it is necessary for the creditor to go back to a credit applicant and ask the applicant to nudge his or her own banker into releasing the necessary credit information over the phone.

A bank reference has the potential to be the most fruitful information obtained by a creditor. Bankers may reside in the same town as a customer. Bankers are usually thoroughly aware of a borrower's situation. The key to a successful bank reference is the ability to pose the essential questions.

Trade References

Trade references provide a vital piece of information to creditors: the willingness of a customer to pay. Actual payment experience is an excellent indication of future payment patterns. Reciprocity is a key ingredient when considering the exchange of information.

Many of the pieces of information obtained from a bank reference apply to trade references. In addition to the topics introduced for bank references, a supplier can be questioned concerning various aspects of customer relations. For example, Have orders ever been held? Are discount chargebacks a problem? Have there been any disputes? When was the last sale made to this customer? What is the current status of the account?

In most situations, credit managers can pick up the phone and obtain a trade reference. However, some creditors have a policy of not releasing information over the telephone; they respond only to written inquires.

Other companies may want to ensure that the caller is not fictitious, so they will call back to the creditor with the reference.

Sometimes the practice of reciprocity is not honored. Professionalism is diluted when a creditor refuses to give out information over the phone, then at a later date, turns around and requests a reference over the telephone. Credit practitioners should strive to maintain reciprocity in order to maintain a high level of professional status.

Industry Credit Groups

Industry credit groups provide a forum whereby many years of experience can be shared, thereby enabling one to keep in touch with change. The factors that affect one company tend to have a similar effect upon other companies in the same industry. Direct involvement and interchange with other credit managers in the same industry can often be the most valuable source of information available.

The primary purpose of an industry credit group is to exchange factual historical information among members who share a common customer base. In addition to sharing factual information, industry groups have an educational side wherein they address professional concerns that range from organizational issues to computer systems to participation on creditors' committees. The opportunity to interchange data and keep current with changes underlies most educational activity.

Each industry group generally establishes bylaws whereby the group clarifies its activities. Groups are careful to set forth principles that ensure that no discrimination exists in any activities. Factors for the group to clarify include: member dues, number of meetings per year, type of reports to exchange, election of group officers, and an agenda for any credit education-related topics. Written credit reports, oral account discussion, and education-related activities are ongoing benefits of group membership.

Written Credit Reports

Most industry credit groups will clear or report on accounts on a regular basis. Credit managers typically request information for a slow payment record, a first order, a change of ownership, or any extraordinary concern.

Most written credit reports are custom designed. The reports will show payment patterns that are typical within an industry. The written credit reports are generally discussed at the next industry group meeting.

Some industry groups clear all past-due accounts, while other groups will limit the number of accounts thereby allowing for more in-depth discussion.

Oral Account Discussion

The primary advantage of an oral interchange of payment history is the freshness of the information. Discussion of accounts represents a key focus of the formal industry group meetings. Superior-quality historical factual information is exchanged in confidence. The personal contact among credit managers promotes a cooperative attitude. Perhaps the oral exchange of current factual information fosters more group trust than any other single activity.

In addition to obtaining typical payment history, credit managers can address practical procedural questions. For example, when can a customer be reached? Who is really making the decision to pay when a customer is called for payment? What numbers will the government require before sending a payment? Are any other credit managers experiencing quality claim concerns? Are deductions typical? Experienced credit managers can furnish answers to these questions. One can readily understand why credit managers recognize that the benefits of an industry group are vital.

Education-Related Activities

The opportunity for credit managers to gather with a group of peers is important to recognize. Credit managers need to keep abreast of changes and discuss how their jobs will be affected by socioeconomic developments. In the education portion of meetings, industry groups may ask a member to lead a discussion on a particular topic of interest to the group. At times, outside speakers are used to address common concerns. Varying topics of industry specific concerns are reviewed during these discussions such as:

- *Technological Breakthroughs.* Examples include the use of electronic funds transfers (EFT), the Internet, credit scoring models, electronic data interchange, and computer software utilization.
- *Demographic Shifts.* Changing demographics have an effect on customer performance within specific industries.
- *Corporate Restructuring.* Credit managers are faced with dual concerns because both customers and employers going through a

restructuring process. Either concern could be an important agenda item at an industry meeting.

- *International Trade Concerns.* Banks, freight forwarders, or government agencies can recommend and provide potential guest speakers on timely topics. A focus by continent and/or country would be relevant to certain industries. The use of letters of credit or other export terms represent viable topics in the area of international trade.
- *Macroeconomic Forces.* For example, a change in the gross national product affects the auto industry much more than the food industry. The economic impact of proposed government legislation may prove to be a cause for credit managers to oppose or support specific legislation as a collective body.

The written reports, oral discussion of accounts, and education-related activities tend to be indispensable tangible benefits of industry credit groups. Active participation is a key ingredient of an industry credit group. An individual relatively new to credit management has the opportunity to gain a practical edge in applying credit skills. One can learn from seasoned credit managers who have taken on leadership roles. For both the individual new to credit and the seasoned credit managers, the industry group can provide a mechanism for personal growth.

AN ANALYSIS OF CREDIT SCORING SYSTEMS

The use of credit scoring has exploded into the business credit environment. The reasons are simple. Scaling down the credit department is a common reality that has been experienced by many credit managers. The cost-cutting trend suggests that credit managers simply have less time to manage more accounts. Simultaneously, there have been significant improvements and developmental cost reductions related to business credit scoring systems. Many business credit managers are now employing some type of a credit scoring systems.

The focus upon credit scoring in a business credit management reduces the need for human judgment. Judgmental credit analysis relies upon a credit analyst's ability to gather and interpret customer-related information. Credit scoring systems rely upon scorecards to replace the judgment exercised by a credit analyst. While the need for human judgement to override the scoring system will always be there, the benefits of computer scoring can be significant.

Credit scoring systems attempt to assign points to a number of variables that characterize customers. The points are then totaled in order to generate decisions relating to the extension of credit. In order to provide credit managers with guidelines to consider the use of a credit scoring system, the following areas will be discussed.

1. An overview of the development of credit scoring and the mechanics of three types of credit scoring models.
2. A demonstration of a simplistic credit scoring model.
3. An identification of the benefits achieved through a properly developed credit scoring system.
4. Critical discussion of the major drawbacks related to credit scoring systems as they pertain to business credit grantors.

The Development and Mechanics of Credit Scoring Systems

Credit scoring systems have progressed significantly since they were first used during the 1930s, when mail-order businesses used numerical systems to make an accept/reject decision. The early credit scoring systems were based upon a trial-and-error experimental process. The underlying basis of the credit decision was made by accumulating points rather than a credit manager exercising judgment.

The primary users of credit scoring systems in the 1990s included large banks, insurance companies, utilities, oil companies, and other retail credit grantors. Since the 1990s, many business creditors have implemented credit scoring systems. Improved computer technology has allowed creditors to identify predictor variables from a large sample of customers. The predictor variables are assigned point values. Credit extension decisions are then based upon customer accumulation of points. Using this tool can help the credit manager arrive at more consistent credit decisions.

Credit scoring can be based upon any of three different approaches to developing the scoring model: (1) behavioral models, (2) rules-based models, or (3) neural models. The models are each concerned with developing a prediction of nonpayment or for the prediction of a bankruptcy. The models are used to generate scorecards; some credit managers use several scorecards for various industries.

Behavioral Models. Behavioral-based scoring systems require a substantial pool of customers. Customer records are scrutinized for anywhere from 20 to 200 specific factors on each customer. Certain factors are identified as predictive variables, which are then analyzed by using multiple discriminate analysis or multivariate regression analysis. The analysis is concerned strictly with statistical predictability applicable to a designated number of accounts.[2]

Rules-Based Models. At the heart of a rules-based model is the application of a set of rules. The rules tend to be relatively simplistic in nature. For example, several readily available variables—such as D&B rating, number of years in business, standard industrial classification (SIC) code, and public record information—could be assigned weights. The weights are then used on a scorecard that determines creditworthiness. New accounts might be in need of garnering more points until they can establish themselves as creditworthy.

Neural Models. The basis of a neural-based credit scoring model is the use of a computer to combine mathematics with logic. The model employs the parallel processing of math-based historical experiences and logic-based patterns. The model is engineered through the use of a substantial number of processing elements similar to the neurons that influence the human brain. The processing elements are layered based upon experience. Eventually the neurons signal the credit decision. (See the *Credit and Financial Management Review*, Fourth Quarter 2001, to review an academic study of neural-based credit scoring.)

A Demonstration of a Credit Scoring Model

In order to furnish a simplistic example of a rules-based scoring model, a creditor could analyze each customer by examining 100 various factors. Perhaps only 10 of the 100 factors are statistically significant. The 10 statistically significant factors are then combined with judgmental factors that predict willingness to pay, such as payment history and trade references.

Implementation of a credit scoring system does not necessarily eliminate the need for judgment. In many cases, business credit grantors use a two-tiered system that streamlines the use of judgment. For example, in a 10-factor system with each factor weighted equally

[2]Edward Altman, *Corporate Financial Distress* (New York: Wiley Publishing Co., 1983). Readers are urged to review Altman's Z Scoring Models for a thorough discussion of statistical procedures. Although designed for bankruptcy prediction, the process is conceptually similar in credit scoring models.

(usually factors have different weights) at 10 points, a credit manager could automatically approve all accounts scoring above 80 points, reject all accounts below 50 points, or exercise judgment on all accounts scoring between 50 and 80 points. The weights enable the credit manager to determine the odds that the new account will turn out to be a favorable or unfavorable risk.

A credit manager could easily tighten or loosen credit approval policy by moving the points for the cutoffs. A more restrictive credit policy would simply move the minimum level of points to 60 from 50. Under certain conditions, the credit manager may want to exercise judgment on more accounts. The judgment area could widen to include scores between 45 and 85 points to be used as the revised cutoff levels for review.

Cutoffs are set based upon the probability of payment. The cutoff levels should be monitored and reviewed on a regular basis in order to maintain optimal control. In doing so, the credit manager identifies and accumulates everything known about the population under consideration.

Credit Scoring Examples

Table 6-4 contains a sample of the type of system that is used for credit scoring. The sample is based upon the use of a rules-based analysis for historical bad debt losses. Certain predictor variables are identified and then weighted on a scorecard. The total score is then used to accept or reject new credit applicants.

There are eight variables that have been introduced through the use of eight questions in Table 6-4. Based upon the points scored for each question, applicants can be evaluated for creditworthiness. Variables such as annual income are weighted based upon actual loss experience with previous bad debts.

The scores can be used to predict the probability of a bad debt. For example, Table 6-4 shows that an applicant who scored a 75 would be in the top 30% of all credit applicants and have a 2% probability of becoming a bad debt.

A company could set up its credit policy using a system similar to the example in Table 6-4. Perhaps 4% is an acceptable bad debt threshold. Then scores above 50 would be acceptable as a cutoff. Another approach could call for accepting all scores above 70; any score between 20 and 69 could be reviewed by a credit manager who might order a credit report to base a decision; and all scores below 20 could be rejected. Parameters could be adjusted based upon experience. If credit policy is tightened, simply raise cutoffs.

Table 6-5 shows a hypothetical credit scorecard that can be used if there are many applications from small balance companies. The variables are identified and weighted by using numerous data from historical bad debts. The system is not meant to be a panacea; credit analysts should have the ability to override the system when judgment is used.

For the company with many applications in small dollar amounts, the system used in Table 6-5 can be practical. If bad debt results are not successful, the system should be combined with other sources of credit information. The time and costs associated with credit investigations can be drastically reduced. Moreover, if the system is properly designed, bad debts can be reduced.

Potential Benefits Achieved Through Effective Credit Scoring Systems

Credit scoring systems can provide a number of favorable outcomes:

1. *Reduced Credit Investigation Costs.* The cost of credit reports for each current and potential customer can be prohibitive. A properly designed credit scoring system may substantially reduce the need for credit reports. In particular, credit grantors who handle a high volume of new accounts benefit from the reduced investigation costs.
2. *Reduced Response Time for New Accounts.* For large credit departments, judgmental systems may create situations for credit managers to exercise judgment that is applied inconsistently. A scoring system facilitates consistency with the improved clarity of pertinent factors and the empirical assignment of weights useful when assessing the factors. The response time can be reduced with improved results.
3. *Improved Management Control.* When the economy slips toward a recession, corporate policy may become more conservative. The point system cutoffs can easily be moved to reflect a tighter credit policy. Conversely, controls can be loosened by lowering the number of points necessary to qualify for credit.

Table 6-4 Credit Scoring Scorecard for an Individual

Points Earned

____ 1. How much is your annual income?

0 to $20,000 (-10) $20,001 to $35,000 (5)
$35,001 to $70,000 (10) Over $70,000 (15)

____ 2. How many years have you been employed at your current job?

less than 1 (-15) 1-2 (2) 3-5 (10) Over 5 (16)

____ 3. What is your highest education level?

No H.S. diploma (-10) H.S. diploma (5) College grad (10)

____ 4. What is your current living arrangement?

Own home (15) Rent (2) Other (0)

____ 5. What is your age?

Under 24 (5) 24-33 (10) 34-42 (4) 43-51 (15) Over 51 (20)

____ 6. Do you have a bank credit card?

Yes (10) No (0)

____ 7. How many other credit cards do you own?

0 (5) 1-4 (10) 5-10 (12) Over 10 (4)

____ 8. Do you have a telephone?

Yes (10) No (0)

Using the Scores for Each Applicant

Score	Layer	Probability of Bad Debt %
100-108	Top 5%	.5%
85-99	15%	1%
70-84	30%	2%
50-69	50%	4%
20-49	75%	6%
Less than 20	100%	10%

4. *A Potential for Reduced Discrimination.* The Equal Credit Opportunity Act prohibits discrimination on the basis of race, color, religion, national origin, and immigration status when using a credit scoring system. However, the Act states that age may be used in a credit scoring system when "the system is demonstrably and statistically sound."

Table 6-5 **Credit Scoring Scorecard for Corporate Applicants**

Points Earned

____ 1. How many years has the business been in operation?

0-1 (0)   1-4 (-5)   5-8 (6)   Over 8 (20)

____ 2. How many people are employed by this company?

1 (3)   2 to 10 (4)   11-50 (8)   Over 50 (12)

____ 3. How many customers does the business have?

1 (-5)   2 to 10 (3)   11-100 (10)   Over 100 (16)

____ 4. Is there a bank loan outstanding?

Yes (10)   No (0)

____ 5. Has any of the existing management team ever been affiliated with a previous bankruptcy?

Yes (-20)   No (0)

____ 6. During the past year, in what direction have sales changed?

Increased (6)   No change (0)   Decreased (-4)

____ 7. What is the rating available from a credit reporting agency? (Use composite)

1 (15)   2 (5)   3 (0)   4 (-6)   Not rated (0)

____ 8. During the past year, in what direction have profits changed?

Increased (9)   No change (0)   Decreased (-5)

Using the Scores for Each Applicant

Score	**Layer**	**Probability of Bad Debt %**
75-87	Top 10%	.1%
65-74	Top 25%	1%
40-64	Top 50%	2%
20-39	Top 75%	5%
Less than 20	Top 100%	18%

Furthermore, experts believe that a judgmental system is more difficult to defend against discrimination claims. A scoring system by nature is purely objective.

The potential benefits of credit scoring systems underlie their widespread use. Literally millions of credit decisions made by thousands of credit grantors are based upon credit scoring models each year.

PROBLEMS RELATED TO CREDIT SCORING SYSTEMS

Business credit grantors should recognize the serious practical drawbacks that relate to credit scoring systems. Major drawbacks suggest that credit scoring should not be attempted in certain circumstances. Potential drawbacks include:

1. *An Insufficient Pool of Customers.* When a business has relatively few customers or very large balance customers, a credit scoring system may not be appropriate.
2. *A Heterogeneous Pool of Customers.* Business credit grantors may sell into markets that vary so substantially that judgment is essential. Statistical analysis may not be able to identify variables that can consistently predict repayment, or variable weights may not adequately identify an accept or reject decision. For example, how much weight should be given to a previous bankruptcy?
3. *The Obsolescence of Historical Information.* The nature of credit scoring systems is to develop predictor factors based upon historical performance. What happened in the past may not occur in the future. As dollar exposure per account increases, the risk of relying upon historical information becomes greater.
4. *The Prohibitive Cost of Developing a Scoring System.* Scoring system costs have declined dramatically during the past few years. However, a less expensive generic type of a system may prove to be ineffective as a risk assessment tool. Moreover, the system may need to be modified on a regular basis. A cost benefit analysis may be difficult to interpret. Shortcuts should be avoided if benefits are to be achieved.
5. *Statistical Difficulties.* Statistics relating to credit scoring systems are as complex as any that the credit manager can expect to encounter. Problems relate to obsolete data, insufficient data, selection of predictor variables, and the weighing of predictor variables. For more information on statistical problems, see the article by Robert Eisenbeis.[3]

Any one of the five problems identified could cause a particular credit grantor to dismiss the potential utilization of a credit scoring system.

---

[3]Robert A. Eisenbeis, "Pitfalls in the Application of Discriminant Analysis in Business, Finance, and Economics," *The Journal of Finance* (June 1977): 875-900.

However, only when the problems are carefully weighed against the potential benefits can a proper decision be rendered.

The important question to consider is: What are the benefits inherent in using credit scoring as a risk assessment tool? The response is that each credit manager needs to find the best way to assess risk in a cost-effective manner in order to optimize profits. Business credit grantors have made tremendous inroads in utilizing scoring systems efficiently.

MONITORING EXISTING ACCOUNTS

The information used to analyze a new customer may be more extensive than for long-term customers. According to Dr. Fred Scherr, over 85% of large firms use credit limits to control accounts.[4] At issue is the difficulty of balancing the costs of updating credit information against the benefits of more closely monitoring risk.

Just like Moody's or Standard and Poor's review bonds, credit managers should review accounts on a regular basis. Changes in the overall economy, within an industry, or at a particular company can trigger a need to consider revising a supplier relationship. Computers can be used to alert credit managers to a change in payment patterns. There are also companies that will alert credit managers to changes in publicly available information. Yet many problems do not get detected until it is too late to benefit from placing a hold on orders for a deteriorating account.

Bust-outs present a particularly difficult type of a problem. A bust-out is a scheme to deliberately defraud creditors. The bust-out handles payments by paying in a timely manner early in a relationship, and then later, when large orders are placed, files for bankruptcy. Bust-outs are not easy to detect. When credit information includes a false corporate name or address, or when a customer places a very substantial order after having placed several small orders, credit managers should be skeptical. A thorough credit investigation is in order.

Conducting credit investigations for existing customers on an ongoing basis may entail more skill than is needed with new customers. It can be quite difficult to work out of a deteriorating situation. The personal judgment used during negotiation requires fresh information and significant creativity. Conducting a thorough credit investigation may never be more important.

---

[4]Frederick C. Scherr, "Optimal Credit Limits," *Financial Management* (Spring 1996): 71.

CHAPTER 6: FOLLOW UP

Recap of Important Concepts

1. Historically, the five Cs of credit have been used as a starting point to conduct a credit investigation. The five Cs should be combined with an analysis of internal concerns that are pertinent to making decisions. Internal controls that foster a cohesive credit-sales relationship should be developed. A functional credit application and an effective system of communicating can provide the sound foundation that is necessary to conduct a credit investigation.
2. Alternative sources of credit information should be used to the extent necessary. A cost/benefit approach becomes the driving force in utilizing potential credit information sources. Chapter 6 includes a lengthy list of potential resources. In addition, several practical factors are identified that can be used to limit the extent of the credit investigation.
3. Banks can be one of the most useful sources of credit information. Credit managers should abide by the RMA's Code of Ethics when exchanging information. Creditors should be familiar with the appropriate types of questions to pose to bankers; framing the proper questions can lead to the development of pertinent information.
4. Credit references from trade suppliers reflect a potential customer's payment history. Reciprocity and the RMA's Code of Ethics should be honored when using trade references.
5. For some credit managers, industry credit groups are the single best source of credit information. Both the discussion of open accounts and the ability to clear accounts with other suppliers in written reports provide useful information for credit investigation purposes. Industry groups also provide a unique opportunity to keep abreast with change through education-related activities.
6. Empirical credit scoring systems are growing in popularity with business credit grantors. The growth is fostered by improvements in computer systems. There are benefits and problems related to credit scoring systems that need to be carefully examined when considering the use of a credit scoring system.
7. There is a need to update credit information on existing accounts on a regular basis. The costs and benefits of monitoring risk is a role that credit managers need to address.

Review/Discussion Questions

1. What information should be included on a credit application form? Why?
2. Why is it important to limit the extent to which a credit investigation is conducted? What factors might limit the investigation?
3. Discuss the use of each individual source of potential credit information. (This question is intended for business practitioners.)
4. Why is there a need to establish principles for the exchange of credit information?
5. Why is a bank loan officer an appropriate resource for a credit investigation? What questions should be introduced during a telephone conversation used to obtain a bank reference?
6. Explain the banking phrase "mod 5." Give an example of a mod 5 balance.
7. What is the cardinal principle in the exchange of credit information?
8. Why is it important to verify the exact legal name for a new customer? How can the legal name be verified?
9. What internal controls can be used to facilitate the credit investigation process?
10. What type of business credit grantor is most likely to use a computer credit scoring system?
11. a. Use Table 6-4 to score each of the following credit applications:

	(1) Mike Huffy	(2) Benji Workman	(3) Anita Luk
Annual Income:	$18,000	$47,000	$29,000
Years at Employer:	Less than one	10	4
Education Level:	H.S. Diploma	College Grad	College Grad
Living Arrangement:	Rents	Owns	Rents
Age:	Under 24	45	34
Credit Card Bank:	None	Yes	Yes
Other Credit Cards:	None	5	None
Telephone Status:	None	Yes	Yes
Score:	________	________	________

b. Based upon the following credit policy, would you grant credit to any of the applicants?

Approve scores above 75
Investigate score between 40 and 74
Reject scores below 40

c. What are some of the benefits and pitfalls of using a credit scoring approach to granting credit?
d. If a credit manager wanted to loosen credit policy, what changes could be made when using a credit scoring system? What factors could cause the policy to be loosened?

Test Your Knowledge

1. Explain each of the five Cs of credit.
2. List 10 potential sources of credit information.
3. What are the RMA principles that are used to exchange credit information? Describe the RMA general figure ranges in detail.
4. Describe in detail the information available from a trade supplier when obtaining a credit reference.
5. How can industry credit groups be useful to a credit manager?
6. What are the factors that should be considered when investigating the usefulness of a computer credit scoring system? Be thorough.
7. Provide an overview of the three approaches that can be used to develop credit scoring systems.
8. What is a bust-out? Are there any precautions that a creditor can take to reduce the likelihood of being burned in a bust-out?
9. Is there a difference in the obligation created by a division of a company in comparison to a subsidiary? If so, why is this difference important?
10. Why have LLC corporations grown in importance? Can credit managers do anything to limit risk when dealing with an LLC corporation?

Credit Management Online

www.crfonline.org/publications/abstracts.asp—The Credit Research Foundation publishes *The Credit and Financial Management Review,* which is a quarterly journal. The journal regularly includes articles that delve into various aspects of credit analysis. Abstracts can be reviewed; copies of articles can be ordered online.

www.dnb.com/dbproducts/descriptions.html—D&B has developed a commercial credit scoring model. A sample report can be viewed, and information concerning credit scoring can be examined at this site.

www.myfico.com/myfico/Home.asp—This web site has been developed by Fair, Isaac and Company. The site provides the details for the development of FICO scores, which are the credit scores that are used at the three major consumer credit reporting companies.

www.nacm.org/affiliates/industrygroups/industry-index.html—This is the National Association of Credit Management site that is useful to look up any of the NACM Industry Credit Groups. Simply enter a keyword to find out where the industry group is hosted.

www.rmahq.org/Ed_Opps/publications.html—RMA is a bank trade association. Numerous publications, including the *RMA Journal*, can be referenced from a wide range of potentially useful publications.

www.standardpoors.com/ProductsAndServices/RiskManagementSolutions/index.html—Standard and Poor's can provide an assessment of credit analysis methodologies and a review of an existing credit portfolio. Default probabilities are driven by historical information.

References Useful for Further Reading

Altman, Edward. *Corporate Financial Distress.* New York: Wiley Publishing Co., 1983.

Banasiak, Michael, and Eileen O'Hare. "Behavior Scoring." *Business Credit* (March 2001): 52-55.

Blakeley, Scott E. "Bust-Outs on the Rise: What You Can Do to Protect Your Credit Sales." *Business Credit* (October 1995): 8-9.

Davis, Karron T. "Credit Scoring Software: A Brief Look." *Business Credit* (February 1999): 32-34.

Eisenbeis, Robert A. "Pitfalls in the Application of Discriminant Analysis in Business, Finance, and Economics." *The Journal of Finance* (June 1977): 875-900.

Fensterstock, Albert. "The Application of Neural Networks to Credit Scoring." *Business Credit* (March 2001): 58-59.

Gahala, Charles L. "Changing the Face of Credit Management: Credit Scoring Models at the R. R. Donnelley Company." *National Credit News* (April 2002): 3-4, 23.

Middleton, Martha. "High Speed Commercial Credit." *Collections & Credit Risk* (February 1997): 39-42.

Parkinson, Kenneth L., and Joyce R. Ochs. "Using Credit Screening to Manage Credit Risk." *Business Credit* (March 1998): 23-27.

Richard, Christine. "Sign of Times: Credit Analysis Is Cool." *The Wall Street Journal* (July 1, 2002): R4.

Robida, Chuck, and Grant Gilkerson. "How Many Scorecards Do I Need for My Business Lending Environment?" *Business Credit* (June 2000): 36-38.

Sargent, John. "Rules Based Credit Scoring." *Business Credit* (March 2001): 56-57.

Scherr, Fred C. "Optimal Trade Credit Limits." *Financial Management* (Spring 1996): 71-85.

Schmidt, Bonnie A. "Making Credit Decisions Without Financial Statements." *Business Credit* (February 1997): 52-53.

Schmidt, David. "Get Better Mileage for Your Information Dollars." *Business Credit* (March 2001): 66-69.

Simon, Ruth. "Your Credit Score: Fair Issac Can Help." *The Wall Street Journal* (March 19, 2002): A1 and A10.

Snyder, Jesse. "Opportunity Knocks at Scoring's Door." *Collections & Credit Risk* (April 1997): 53-58.

Wallis, Lyle. "The Future of Decisionmaking in the A/R Process." *Business Credit* (March 2001): 50-51.

Yegorova, Irena, Bruce H. Andrews, John B. Jensen, and Steven Walczak. "A Successful Neural Network-Based Methodology for Predicting Business Loan Default." *The Credit and Financial Management Review,* Vol. 7, No. 4, Fourth Quarter 2001.

Chapter 7

Business Credit Reporting Services

"The first delivery system for credit information was verbal...subscribers sent out their confidential clerks or came themselves, to the Mercantile Agency, to have credit letters read aloud."[1]

–Travis B. Blackman, describing credit reports circa 1850

Football players have changed from the early years of professional football. Today, players are bigger, faster, and stronger than ever before. In a much more pronounced way, business credit reporting services have changed. During the past 160 years, business credit reports have become more pertinent and user friendly.

Business credit reporting companies provide detailed credit information for a fee. During the past decade, substantial enhancements have occurred in the quantity and quality of credit reporting services. Creditors now have the ability to draw online reports via the Internet for most American businesses.

The use of credit information services should entail an evaluation of the benefits provided by the information weighed against the costs of the information. The costs of business credit reports are based upon the fees charged by the credit reporting agency, the type of report ordered, and the quantity of reports ordered. The fees for ordering reports are often posted on the web site by the reporting agency when using the Internet.

Credit reporting services can provide substantial benefits. The turnaround time for a credit investigation is often instantaneous.

[1]Travis B. Blackman, *The Story of Dun & Bradstreet* (Murray Hill, N.J.: D&B Information Services, 1991): 3.

Monitoring key accounts can be more closely controlled. Costs for completing a credit investigation can be reduced. Moreover, the quality of information now available in business credit reports can often exceed the information available if conducting a routine in-house credit investigation.

The **Key Learning Objectives** in Chapter 7 are to:

1. Provide an overview of business credit reporting services.
2. Examine the nature of a D&B Rating, and the sections of a D&B Business Information Report.
3. Analyze the information available in an Experian Business Profile Report.
4. Identify business credit reports that are available from other credit reporting companies.
5. Become familiar with the use of consumer credit reports for business credit reporting purposes.

BUSINESS CREDIT REPORTING SERVICES

An indirect credit investigation can save time while often furnishing superior information, in comparison to a credit investigation performed directly by a credit analyst. A cost benefit analysis should be performed to determine the needs of an individual user. One focal point should include a close look at the information needed to support screening new accounts and monitoring existing accounts.

For example, when considering relatively small balance accounts, a full report may not be necessary. The costs of the full report might be hard to justify. Perhaps just a snapshot of a business could be sufficient. On the other hand, for marginal accounts or key accounts, a full report might be essential.

Another focal point might be placed upon avoiding the duplication of information. Particularly in decentralized credit environments or multi-divisional companies, there is a potential to order more than one report on the same customer. This can drive costs to excessive levels.

There was once a time when D&B seemed to have a virtual monopoly on the business credit reporting industry. Both domestic and international competitors have made significant inroads in the business credit reporting industry. The result is a marketplace that is more responsive to the needs of credit professionals.

Various types of concerns—such as a lack of clarity in the fee structure, a one-report-fits-all-user-needs mentality, and a lack of compatibility in technology needs—each seem to have been addressed. For credit managers, the results can be characterized as outstanding. Yet there is a new problem of product differentiation that now takes on more importance than ever. This new problem will be addressed by examining individual credit reporting companies next in this chapter.

D&B Corp.

D&B Corp. was formerly known as the Dun & Bradstreet Corporation. The company was split into three separate companies when Moody's Investment Services and R. H. Donnelley were spun off. Now D&B can be more focused in its role of providing business credit information services. D&B is generally considered to be the world leader in providing high-quality business credit information, yet some credit managers believe that the leadership edge is shrinking.

The origin of D&B can be traced to Lewis Tappan, who founded the Mercantile Agency in New York in 1841. One of Tappan's employees, R.G. Dun, purchased the Mercantile Agency in 1851 and then changed the business name to R.G. Dun and Co. John M. Bradstreet founded a rival credit agency in Cincinnati in 1849. The two firms merged in 1933 to form what is now called D&B Corp.

Today D&B's information base contains more than 70 million companies worldwide. For most credit managers, there is a need to:

- Understand the nature of a D&B rating.
- Utilize the components of a Business Information Report.
- Recognize the potential utility for other D&B products.

The D&B Rating

D&B ratings contain three digits. The first two digits are based upon a firm's capital, which is often called net worth. The capital is simply the difference between a firm's assets and liabilities. Table 7-1 shows that D&B net worth ratings range from 5A to HH for those companies where D&B has a balance sheet. When an estimated net worth is used by D&B, the first two digits in a D&B Rating are either 1R or 2R.

The third digit in a D&B rating indicates the composite credit appraisal. A composite credit appraisal can range from a 1 for high quality to 4 for limited quality. The composite credit appraisal does not

Table 7-1 **D&B Ratings**

	Balance Sheet Net Worth	Composite Credit Appraisal			
		High	Good	Fair	Limited
5A	$50,000,000 and over	1	2	3	4
4A	$10,000,000 to 49,999,999	1	2	3	4
3A	$1,000,000 to 9,999,999	1	2	3	4
2A	$750,000 to 999,999	1	2	3	4
1A	$500,000 to 749,999	1	2	3	4
BA	$300,000 to 499,999	1	2	3	4
BB	$200,000 to 299,999	1	2	3	4
CB	$125,000 to 199,999	1	2	3	4
CC	$75,000 to 124,999	1	2	3	4
DC	$50,000 to 74,999	1	2	3	4
DD	$35,000 to 49,999	1	2	3	4
EE	$20,000 to 34,999	1	2	3	4
FF	$10,000 to 19,999	1	2	3	4
GG	$5,000 to 9,999	1	2	3	4
HH	up to $4,999	1	2	3	4

	Net Worth Based on Estimated Balance Sheet	Composite Credit Appraisal		
		Good	Fair	Limited
1R	$125,000 and over	2	3	4
2R	up to $124,999	2	3	4

Source: D&B Corp., 2002

apply to a business whose rating is based upon an employee range (ER) for the D&B rating.

When a blank (—) rating is used by D&B, there was insufficient information available to D&B. A blank rating is not necessarily unfavorable. In many cases, private firms do not release financial statements so the net worth is not available.

Certain industries do not readily lend themselves to classification under the traditional D&B rating system. Banks, insurance companies, and other financial service businesses operate in industries where net worth can be misleading. In these situations, D&B uses an employee range (ER) instead of a balance sheet net worth. Table 7-2 provides the D&B ratings that are based upon an employee range.

Using Table 7-2, a bank with 200 employees would have an ER3 rating from D&B. Note that the 3, which is the third digit in the rating,

Table 7-2 **D&B Employee Range Ratings**

Rating	Number of Employees
R1	1,000 or more
ER2	500 to 999
ER3	100 to 499
ER4	50 to 99
ER5	20 to 49
ER6	10 to 19
ER7	5 to 9
ERN	Not Available

Source: D&B Corp., 2002

does not represent a composite credit appraisal. The third digit simply represents a comparable number of employees at the bank.

The D&B Business Information Report

Credit managers can access D&B reports online by using the Internet. Reports can be purchased by using a credit card or through the use of a subscription number that is assigned to each buyer. Any questions concerning a particular report can be directed to D&B at their corporate web site (www.dnb.com) or by calling the D&B customer resource center at 800-234-3867.

For many credit managers, the Business Information Report is one of the most complete sources of credit information available. D&B assigns each entity its own DUNS number. Credit information that pertains to any report ordered is privately shared with a customer, and fees are assessed for each report.

Each report available via the Internet is organized through the use of a tabular format. There are five tabs that can be examined by clicking on a tab at the top of the page or going to the specific information desired in a tab which is listed on the left side of the page. The following tabular headings are used by D&B in a Business Information Report:

1. *Overview.* The overview of a report provides credit managers with a quick read-out on the customer. Information that appears in the overview of the report includes the DUNS number, business name, address, phone number, chief executive officer, standard industrial classification (SIC) code, D&B rating, D&B PAYDEX, year started,

number of employees, summary financial statement data such as annual sales and net worth, history, and financing.

2. *History and Operations.* The intention of this portion of a Business Information Report is to provide an overview of the ownership. Affiliated companies, business registration, a review of the operations, and the industry information are included in this section. For example, a change in ownership or a bankruptcy would be reported here.
3. *Payments.* This section is useful to gain detailed information concerning the payments made to other suppliers. D&B furnishes a D&B PAYDEX for both a three-month period, to provide information about current patterns, and also for a 12-month period, to identify any changes in the payment patterns. PAYDEX uses a unique dollar weighting for the manner in which payments are made and reported by D&B vendors. A high PAYDEX score is preferable. Table 7-3 shows the PAYDEX score key available from D&B.
4. *Banking and Finance.* There are financial statements, if available, for the most recent three-year period. The accountant's opinion is furnished. Certain financial ratios are compared to industry norms. A bank reference is also provided in this section.
5. *Public Filings.* Business Information Reports contain a summary of publicly available records. Public filings include judgments, suits, liens, UCC filings, and government activities.

A Business Information Report from D&B can provide the basis for a credit decision. Yet the ultimate accept/reject decision is always made by the credit manager. When there are errors in reports or incomplete reports, D&B should be contacted directly so that the reports can be improved upon.

Other D&B Products

There are numerous products available from D&B Corp. A menu can be accessed at the D&B web site that includes three pages of products that are now available. The days of one type of report for all credit situations are over. There are products available for purchasing managers and for marketing managers. One of the best ways to appreciate the wide range of products and services now available is to test the products and services on the D&B web site.

For the credit manager, D&B has numerous products that can be used based upon the needs to meet a particular situation. Some of the more

Table 7-3 **Key to D&B PAYDEX**

Paydex	Payment History
100	Anticipate
90	Discount
80	Prompt
70	Slow to 15 Days
60	Slow to 22 Days
50	Slow to 30 Days
40	Slow to 60 Days
30	Slow to 90 Days
20	Slow to 120 Days
UN	Unavailable

Source: D&B Corp., 2002

interesting products include Predictive Scoring Reports, Industry Credit Score Reports, Credit Limit Reports, Financial Stress Scoring Reports, and Strategic Risk Analysis Reports. The reports can provide a wealth of pertinent information that should be balanced with the costs and needs of the situation.

D&B has operations in numerous countries with data gathering capabilities in over 200 countries. The number of Business Information Reports available for international companies is expanding rapidly. Improvements in global communication, acquisitions made by D&B, and expansions in global trade suggest that credit managers will be utilizing more international resources from D&B.

R.G. Dun published the first reference book in 1859. D&B reference books are still available today. Subscribers lease the reference books that contain business lists by county. D&B ratings and SIC codes for each business are the basic information contained in the reference books. D&B updates its online information database every 3.9 seconds. The explosion in available information almost makes the reference books seem obsolete.

Experian

Experian Information Services, Inc. began in 1976. It was formerly called TRW until it was divested by TRW and the name was changed to Experian. Most individuals recognize Experian as one of the big three companies that prepares consumer credit reports. The Experian Business

Information product line has been instrumental in driving the entire industry to higher quality levels.

Experian Business Credit has several products available for credit managers. Most credit managers should become adept at using the Business Credit Profile, which is Experian's general report for credit managers. Experian also has a Business Summary, an Intelliscore, and International Profiles.

The Business Credit Profile Report

The web site for Experian Business Credit Reports is located at www.businessreportsusa.com. The phone number for customer service is 800-315-7678. The seven-part Business Credit Profile can be examined at this web site. Visitors can walk through each part one at a time. Simply click on the highlighted section that is to be examined.

The Experian Business Credit Profile is a comprehensive business credit report that assists credit managers in making informed accept/reject decisions quickly. The unique aspect of the Business Credit Profile is the format. Experian has developed a seven-part report based upon extensive analysis of historical payment performance. The Experian Business Credit Profile has the following components:

1. *The Executive Summary.* The executive summary includes a brief description of the business. In addition, an actual and predicted Days Beyond Terms (DBT) is furnished. The actual DBT is a dollar-weighted average for the actual number of days that a business is using to pay its suppliers. The predicted DBT includes historical payment trends and other pertinent factors such as industry, public records, and years in business. The executive summary also includes a general credit evaluation, historical payment information, and any significant derogatory data.
2. *Trade Payment Information.* Experian uses thousands of actual accounts receivable records contributed by businesses to compile extensive trade payment information. Actual payment records are summarized by industry over a six-month period. Quarterly payment records are summarized over a 15-month period.
3. *Payment Trends.* Payment patterns reflect change during the past six months. Publicly available information such as bankruptcy, tax liens, and judgments are detailed.
4. *UCC Profile.* Any lien filings under the Uniform Commercial Code (UCC) are shown in this section.

5. *Company Background Information.* A brief history of the company, such as the principal officers and year founded, are furnished.
6. *Standard & Poor's Information.* Detailed discussion and analysis of financial information is included for publicly traded companies.
7. *Federal Government Information.* Selected financial and contract data for any transactions with federal government agencies are included in this section.

The Experian Business Credit Profile can be useful for new account investigations, controlling existing accounts, ensuring the stability of suppliers for a purchasing selection, or screening prospects for marketing opportunities.

Business Summary

Experian believes that 90% of all businesses fit into its categorization of small businesses. Experian Business Summary is intended to meet the needs of credit managers with account balances less than $1,000.

Intelliscore

The Intelliscore uses a statistical approach to weight up to 14 variables to derive an Intelliscore. Experian recommends setting in-house decision parameters when using Intelliscore. This report is best suited to high-volume, small-balance credit decision making situations. The Intelliscore can be used to predict payment problems or credit risk.

Other Business Credit Reporting Companies

In addition to D&B Corp. and Experian Business Credit Services, there are other credit reporting companies. Several industry-specific credit reporting services exist. In addition, there are certain countries where credit reports are available through a host country credit reporting source. A brief overview of alternative credit reporting sources follows.

Business Credit USA. Credit reports are available for $5 through Business Credit USA. Reports are brief. There are 14 million businesses in the database. The reports could be useful to verify existence, or to find an address or telephone number. Its web site is located at www.businesscreditusa.com.

FCIB Credit and Country Reports. FCIB can provide credit reports for foreign companies that are customized. There are also country reports available for most foreign countries. Reports can be ordered at the FCIB web site: www.fcibglobal.com.

Graydon America, Inc. Graydon specializes in credit reporting in Europe. Graydon can develop credit reports for companies in every country in the world. Graydon's reports include bank and trade references, public filings, litigation, and industry comparisons. The Graydon web site is located at www.graydonamerica.com.

Veritas Credit Corporation. Veritas specializes in preparing commercial credit reports in North, Central, and South America (including the Caribbean). A Veritas report contains detailed payment history that compares a business to industry data through the use of a graph. In addition, Veritas reports contain bank references, legal, technical, public record, and financial information. Veritas has been in business since 1989 and is growing through the acquisition of other credit reporting businesses. A sample report can be viewed at their web site, which is www.veritas-usa.com.

CONSUMER CREDIT REPORTS

There are over 450 million credit reports drawn on consumers each year. Reports are available on over 90% of American adults. There are circumstances when it is permissible for business credit grantors to draw a consumer report.

The Fair Credit Reporting Act (FCRA) governs consumer credit reporting. Under the FCRA, a consumer credit report may be drawn when the information is used in connection with a business credit transaction. The transaction should entail an extension of credit when an individual's personal creditworthiness supports the business transaction. A permissible purpose is required in order for a business credit grantor to draw a consumer credit report.

Three companies are engaged in the development of consumer credit databanks: (1) Equifax, (2) Experian, and (3) Trans Union. There are certain types of information that are common to each credit reporting company personal credit report. Consumer credit reports include information such as payment history, judgments, liens, and bankruptcies. Extensive use of coding systems can be useful to gain specific details for the records contained in consumer reports.

Equifax, which is slightly larger than its two formidable competitors, is based in Atlanta, Georgia. The company stock trades publicly on the

New York Stock Exchange under the ticker symbol EFX. Equifax has a strong regional presence in the Southeast and in the South. Its corporate web site is located at www.equifax.com.

Experian is based in Nottingham, United Kingdom, with U.S. headquarters located in Mesa, California. It was formerly a part of TRW until it was spun off. It has a strong regional presence on the West Coast. Not only is Experian a strong competitor to D&B Corp. in business credit reporting, it is also positioned as one of the three largest consumer credit reporting companies in the world. The Experian consumer credit reporting web site can be accessed at www. Experian.com.

Chicago-based Trans Union is a subsidiary of The Marmon Group. Although it has a strong regional presence in the Midwest, there are Trans Union operations in all 50 states and in 24 countries. The corporate web site is www.transunion.com.

The three consumer credit reporting companies are each known for being adept in the area of credit scoring. All three companies are growing rapidly. A three-in-one credit report that contains the information available from each of the three consumer credit reporting agencies can be obtained at www.econsumer.equifax.com.

CHAPTER 7: FOLLOW UP

Recap of Important Concepts

1. Credit reporting services have been in existence in the United States for over 160 years. Both the quantity and quality of information now available in credit reports is indispensable to credit decision making.
2. Products now available from credit reporting companies should be examined from a cost/benefit analysis approach.
3. D&B Corp. is generally considered to be the world leader in providing credit information services. Credit managers should become adept in scrutinizing D&B ratings, Business Information Reports, and other D&B products. There are Business Information Reports available through D&B for over 70 million businesses located throughout the world.
4. Since 1976, Experian has grown to become a formidable contender to D&B as the world leader in business credit reporting services. Experian furnishes Business Credit Profile reports, Business Summary reports, and Intelliscore reports that afford unique potential benefits to credit grantors.
5. There are other industry-specific and international credit reporting services. Credit managers should consider experimenting with various business credit reporting services to gain access to the best services for their particular employer.
6. There are three primary providers of consumer credit reports: Equifax, Experian, and Trans Union. Under certain circumstances, business credit grantors may draw a consumer credit report to access information relevant to the extension of credit.

Review/Discussion Questions

1. Describe a D&B rating of BB2. Be specific.
2. What information is contained in the heading of a D&B Business Information Report?
3. How can a credit manager use D&B to assist a purchasing manager?
4. What other products are available to business credit managers from D&B?
5. Describe the components of an Experian Business Credit Profile report.

6. How can an Experian Intelliscore report be useful to a business credit grantor?
7. From whom can a credit manager obtain reports for a business outside of the United States?
8. What companies provide consumer credit reports? What type of information is disclosed in a consumer credit report?

Test Your Knowledge

1. What does a D&B rating represent?
2. The Experian Business Credit Profile report contains an extensive database. What type of information is Experian known for including in this report?
3. What specific type of information is contained in a D&B Business Information Report or an Experian Business Credit Profile? Thoroughly summarize the type of information contained in either report.
4. Under the Fair Credit Reporting Act, when can a business credit grantor draw a report on a consumer?
5. What type of internal controls can be used to monitor the effectiveness of business credit reporting services?
6. Describe the way in which a credit manager could utilize business credit reports to assist a purchasing manager.

Case Study

D&B furnishes a sample report for the Gorman Company at its corporate web site. The report is 12 pages in length. Go to the D&B site at www.dnb.com/product/printer_friendly_ebir.htm and review the report for Gorman Manufacturing Company, Inc. Examine the report to identify the various types of information found in the report. Is any derogatory information contained in the report?

Next, go to the web site for Experian Business Credit. Please go to www.businessreportsusa.com and progress through each of the seven areas found in the report. The sample report for Sample Computer Co. will be developed while you highlight each section of the report. What types of information are contained in the report? Is there any derogatory information?

Compare the types of information found in the sample reports from D&B and from Experian. Do the reports differ in nature? Do you have a preference for either report? Support your response with details.

Credit Management Online

www.businesscreditusa.com—Business credit reports available from Business Credit USA are available at this site. The reports tend to be both brief and inexpensive.

www.businessreportsusa.com—Experian business credit reports can be reviewed at this site. The components of each of the seven parts contained in an Experian report are explained and then demonstrated in a sample report.

www.dnb.com—The home page for D&B Corp. is hosted at this site. The many D&B products can be reviewed. Product pricing is also included. There are samples for products with discussion of the niche that each product is intended to fill.

www.econsumer.equifax.com—The consumer credit reporting Equifax Consumer Services, Inc. hosts this site. A sample Equifax Credit Profile is furnished. Three-in-one reports that include information from Equifax, Experian, and Trans Union are demonstrated at this site.

www.experian.com—This is the home page for Experian. There are links to consumer reports, business reports, and international reporting at this site.

www.graydonamerica.com—This is the home page for Graydon America. Graydon reports can be ordered at this site.

www.myfico.com—Fair, Isaac and Company demonstrates FICO scores at this site. There is also a link to a nifty financial calculator that may be of use for numerous consumer-related financial calculations.

www.nacm.org/services/credit_reports.html—This web page from the National Association of Credit Management describes credit reports.

www.transunion.com—Consumer credit reporting giant Trans Union Corporation hosts this web site. The basic contents of a consumer credit report are described at this site.

www.veritas-usa.com—The Veritas Group makes its credit reports available at this site. The criteria that are used in its formula are described here. Sample reports from numerous countries also can be reviewed at this site.

References Useful for Further Reading

Blackman, Travis. *The Story of Dun & Bradstreet.* Murray Hill, N.J.: Dun & Bradstreet Information Services, 1991.

The Business Information Report. Murray Hill, N.J.: Dun & Bradstreet Information Services, 2002.

Cole, Robert H., and Lon Mishler. *Consumer and Commercial Credit Management.* Burr Ridge, Ill.: Irwin McGraw-Hill Inc., 1998.

Fensterstock, Albert. "The Internet: The Future of Credit." *Business Credit* (October 1999): 29-32.

Hansen, Fay. "The Revolution in Online Credit Resources." *Business Credit* (October 2000): 26-30.

Schmidt, David. "Get Better Mileage for Your Information Dollars." *Business Credit* (March 2001): 66-69.

Snyder, Jesse. "Who's On First?" *Collections and Credit Risk* (September 1996): 63-68.

Whiteside, David E. "Commercial Credit Data Gets Crowded." *Collections and Credit Risk* (December 1996): 39-44.

"Veritas: Decision Support Is Our Business." New Haven, Ct.: The Veritas Group Reporting Corporation, n.d.

Part III:

Credit, Collection, and Analysis

Chapter 8

A Systematic Approach to Effective Collection Activity

"Have patience with me, and I will pay thee all."

–Matthew 18:29

After doing some soul searching, most credit managers would agree that collection activity is central to most types of credit management activity. Garnering the ultimate receipt of the cash for sales that are made on a credit basis has created jobs for credit managers for many years. Technology has revolutionized collection activity. The pivotal focus should now be placed upon efficiently harnessing technology to integrate collection activity with the overall goals of a firm.

Collection activity can be optimized by using a systematic approach that integrates multiple focal points. In a systematic approach, a credit manager recognizes the interrelationships of the many component factors that impact collections. For example, in a systematic approach, order entry, prompt accurate billing, internal controls for screening new accounts and monitoring existing accounts, alternative collection strategies, deduction management, and legal concerns are each considered both individually and simultaneously.

Customer knowledge acquired from conducting a credit investigation (in Chapter 6) and obtaining agency reports (in Chapter 7) is put to use in developing a comprehensive collection system in this chapter. Moreover, financial statement analysis (Chapters 9 and 10) and legal concerns (Chapters 11 and 12) each play important roles in collection activity. Therefore, credit managers are challenged with assessing multiple focal points in order to apply the concepts that are integral to an effective collection system.

A sound analysis of a collection system includes several areas of concentration. While the focus includes components of the collection system in a piecemeal approach, the actual system is interactive.

The **Key Learning Objectives** contained in Chapter 8 are:

1. Examine the technological changes that have altered the approach to collection activity.
2. Recognize the way in which various terms of sale affect the collection system.
3. Identify internal controls that can be useful in maintaining credit availability.
4. Analyze alternative modes of collection available to the credit manager.
5. Focus on customer deductions as a component of collection activity.

INTEGRATING TECHNOLOGY INTO THE COLLECTION SYSTEM

Enterprise resource planning (ERP) embraces the use of an integrated approach to technology. Technology can be designed to perform a wide array of business applications that are compatible for the needs of various departments and users within an organization. Systems such as PeopleSoft, SAP, and Oracle have been among the leaders in ERP installations. There are also several software application packages that are not necessarily integrative that can be quite useful for specific credit applications.

Coupling the needs of credit managers to the available ERP packages has been, and will continue to be, a major challenge. Credit and collection needs are not often among the key applications integrated into ERP systems. Complicating technology needs is the fact that credit department needs can vary widely from company to company. One ERP system will not fit the needs of all users.

The real challenge is to obtain meaningful credit information in a timely, cost-efficient manner. Successful use of technology will free up time for credit managers to focus upon less-mundane types of tasks. Applications include credit scoring, deduction management, collection management, automated prioritized follow-ups, automated customized correspondence, and management reports.

The ability to harness technology underlies the development of the rest of this chapter. Technology is useful when considering setting terms and then developing a collection management system. Managing receivables efficiently requires access to meaningful information that can be used to control risk.

TRADE CREDIT TERMS

One of the most important factors to consider in a collection system is a focus upon establishing and then enforcing the terms of sale. Used in this context, terms of sale represent the period for which the credit is granted. Although most business transactions occur on a credit basis, the terms used in the credit period need to be carefully considered.

Many firms use a lockbox system in order to speed up the inflow of funds available for the Treasurer to use. A lockbox is a system where incoming checks are directed to a post office box. The funds are deposited at a bank that is as close to the customer and a Federal Reserve bank as possible. The checks will clear through the Federal Reserve more quickly; the funds are then available for use. Credit managers are made aware of receipts via an electronic transmission of data so that their rccords coincide with actual payments received.

Selling terms can be readily separated into four categories: (1) cash, (2) open account, (3) special, and (4) electronic payment arrangements. Since there are many variations of terms, each of the four categories will be scrutinized. Whatever terms are put to use with a customer, the terms should be clearly communicated in writing. A paper trail can be useful if an account ever needs to be litigated.

Cash Terms

Credit should be earned. When a customer is not creditworthy, cash terms become an alternative means to make a sale. There are a number of ways for a credit manager to establish cash terms. The following cash terms vary in risk:

Wire Transfer. Rather than obtaining a check, a credit manager can negotiate for a wire transfer. A customer in a hurry for merchandise may arrange to have a bank wire funds to a creditor's bank. The fees are nominal. The credit manager should alert his or her own bank to the incoming transfer and then have the bank call the creditor as soon as the wired funds are received so the order can be released.

Cashier's Check. This type of check is drawn by a bank on the bank's own funds. The creditor looks to the bank for the risk of payment. The risk to the creditor is the credit risk of the bank itself when a cashier's check is accepted.

Certified Check. A certified check is a check in which a bank guarantees that funds are on deposit when the check is certified. The bank earmarks the funds for the creditor. There are certain states where a bank may exercise a right of offset after certifying a check, thereby causing a certified check to bounce. This is a rare occurrence, but it does create risk to a credit grantor.

Cash With Order. In a situation where goods are manufactured for a particular customer, a credit manager may want to receive payment prior to manufacturing. In this case, the check accompanies a customer's order.

Cash on Delivery. The risk to a credit grantor on COD terms is that a trucker may forget to pick up the check on delivery. In addition, a customer could refuse to accept a COD shipment. These risks make other types of cash terms more acceptable to a credit grantor.

Cash in Advance. A credit manager may have a customer order but feel reluctant to ship COD. In this case, cash in advance of shipment may be most appropriate.

Open Account Terms

Most businesses tend to grant customers an industry-wide set of terms. Sophisticated customers will consider their own cost of capital in order to evaluate repayment. Likewise, a credit manager should recognize that customer payment patterns govern the profitability of a sale. Terms are related to the time value of money.

Open account terms are also called ordinary terms or standard terms. Table 8-1 displays examples of commonly used open account terms. The specific terms of 1% 10N30 entitle a customer to a 1% cash discount if the customer pays in 10 days. If the customer forgoes the discount, the full amount is due on day 30.

Many credit managers send new customers a "welcome aboard" letter that includes an explanation of terms. Concise invoices should also reinforce terms. For example, if an invoice is paid by a certain date, the customer can deduct a specified cash discount. If the amount is paid after the specified discount date, the specified net amount should be paid by the net date.

A credit manager may be in a position to convince a customer that taking cash discounts can create profits. The following example may

Table 8-1 **Examples of Open Account Terms**

Terms	Explanation
Net 30	Full amount is due in 30 days.
1% 10N30	A 1% cash discount is earned if paid in 10 days; the net amount is due on day 30.
10th Prox	The full amount is due on the 10th day of the following month.
1% 10th Prox	A 1% cash discount is earned, and the discounted amount is due on the 10th of the following month.
1% 10 MOM	A 1% cash discount is earned if paid in 10 days; the net amount is due the middle of the month.
2% 15 EOM	A 2% cash discount is earned if paid in 15 days; the net amount is due at the end of the month.

prove useful. The formula will provide the approximate percentage cost, on an annual basis, to forego taking discounts.

Equation 8-1. Approximate Cost Formula

$$\text{Approximate \% Cost} = \frac{\text{Discount Percent}}{100 - \text{Discount Percent}} \times \frac{365}{\text{Number of Days Until Paid} - \text{Discount Period}}$$

The formula in Equation 8-1 can be used by a creditor whose terms are 1% 10N30. The results reflect the cost expressed in an annualized percentage.

Equation 8-2. Approximate Cost Example

$$\text{Approximate \% Cost} = \frac{1}{100 - 1} \times \frac{365}{30 - 10} = .01 \times 18.25 = 18\%$$

Recognize that this is a cost to forego a discount. Funds used from day 11 to day 30 cost approximately 18%. If a customer has a source of funds such as a bank, and borrows from the bank at a rate lower than 18%, the customer can create higher profits by discounting. The cash discount becomes an incentive to pay in 10 days.

The results of Equation 8-2 are approximate. The effective annual rate is actually a bit higher. Equation 8-3 shows the calculation for the effective annual rate, which is 20%. This approach is a bit more accurate.

Equation 8-3. Actuarial Example

$$\text{The Effective Rate} = (1.01)^{18.25} - 1.0 = 20\%$$

The results calculated in Equation 8-3 use the terms of 1% 10N30, which were also used in Equation 8-2. However, the annualized rate increased from 18% to 20% due to the magic of compounding. There are 18.25 interest periods in one year (365 ÷ 20); the interest rate per period is .01 ÷ .99 = .01. Therefore, the approximate cost calculated in Equation 8-2 understates the effective rate calculated in Equation 8-3.

There are two assumptions used in these interest rate calculations. First, discounts are taken on the discount date. Second, if discounts are foregone, the full amount is paid on the net date. These parameters can be changed to coincide with actual customer payment habits.

For example, if a customer with terms of 1% 10N30 actually pays on day 60 instead of day 30, the cost is reduced. Equation 8-4 shows the cost to a customer who pays on day 60.

Equation 8-4. Approximate Cost Application

$$\begin{matrix}\text{Approximate} \\ \text{\% Cost}\end{matrix} = \frac{1}{100 - 1} \times \frac{365}{50} = .01 \times 7.3 = 7\%$$

Equation 8-4 shows that a customer can benefit by paying late. The approximate annualized percentage cost to forego a 1% discount and pay on day 60 is 7%. Unless a creditor charges late payment interest, or a customer experiences a supplier holding shipments due to slow payments, the customer may want to lean on a supplier and pay late.

Table 8-2 shows both approximate costs and effective costs for various credit terms. Credit managers should recognize the incentive of offering and carefully enforcing cash discounts. For terms of 3% 15N45, Table 8-2 shows that the real cost of not taking a 3% cash discount and paying the net amount on day 45 is 44%. Any customer foregoing the 3% discount may be in a position where any source of capital simply may not be available to take the discount.

The preceding examples might be useful to a corporation when considering a change in terms. A change in the discount period, the net period, or the discount percentage should change customer payment habits. However, overall corporate profitability also needs to be examined.

Table 8-2 Annual Percentage Costs to Customer to Forego Discounts

Terms	Approximate % Cost	Real Rate
2% 10N30	36%	44%
2% 10N60	15%	16%
3% 15N45	35%	44%

Special Terms

The potential to create profit through the use of special terms mandates an understanding of the alternatives available. For the credit manager, there are unique risks associated with special terms. A clear understanding of any arranged special terms should be communicated among the customer, sales manager, and credit manager in advance. Special terms arrangements can be broken down to consider a special emphasis on electronic payment arrangements.

Consignment Terms. A credit manager may find a marginal credit risk customer who has an ability to sell a product. Goods can be shipped to a consignee without passing title. When the goods are sold by the consignee, a remittance is made to the creditor. If the goods are not sold by the consignee, the consignee may return the goods to the creditor.

High-margin goods such as baseball cards or jewelry are sometimes sold on a consignment basis. In an insolvency, banks with blanket liens on inventory often claim consigned goods as collateral. Creditors who ship consigned goods should receive regular inventory reports, require insurance coverage designating the creditor as loss payee, and consider perfecting a lien under the Uniform Commercial Code.

Contra Account Arrangements. When a customer is also a supplier of goods, a contra account arrangement can be useful. In the event that the customer is not a good credit risk, the credit manager should maintain a balance owed to the customer in excess to the balance due from the customer. Both shipping controls and record keeping need to be carefully maintained in a contra account arrangement.

Letters of Credit. A letter of credit allows a credit manager to substitute the credit risk of a bank for the credit risk of a customer. Standby letters of credit can be an effective tool to use when selling to a marginal account. Export letters of credit facilitate international trade. The risks associated with using letters of credit will be discussed thoroughly in Chapter 11. Payments are made under the terms that are specified in the letter of credit.

Barter Arrangements. Bartering is an exchange of goods in return for goods. Usually bartering involves the use of a clearinghouse system or a reciprocal trade agreement system. A clearinghouse accepts a creditor's merchandise in exchange for trade credits while assessing a transaction fee. The trade credits are then used to acquire goods. Creditors should be concerned about the availability of goods and the limited life of the credits when using a clearinghouse.

Reciprocal trade companies (RTCs) operate as a broker. When RTCs are used, clients exchange goods for credits. However, the company then places a bid for goods at a specified price with the RTC, who in turn acquires the goods for the specified price. Usually RTCs only deal with large transactions, such as General Motors' exchange of 500 Buicks for 250,000 rolls of film and processing from Fuji Films.

Seasonal Datings. Certain industries generate cash flows only once a year. For example, the agriculture industry generates cash flow when crops are harvested. Terms are often established that call for payments to coincide with the timing of the cash flow generated when crops are harvested and then sold. Anticipation discounts are sometimes used as an incentive to customers with seasonal datings.

The seasonal datings pose a problem because accounts receivable balances build up. The credit exposure is increased because of ongoing shipments only being paid for once per year. Anticipation incentives encourage early payment that can be viewed as a vehicle to reduce the dollar exposure in the account.

Electronic Payment Arrangements

Electronic payment arrangements are predominant in certain industries. Prearranged systems for electronic payments can improve the predictability of cash flow. Electronic funds transfers refer to the transfer of dollars; electronic data interchange includes the transfer of the remittance advice.

There are several types of electronic payment arrangements: credit cards, debit cards, stored value cards, online payment systems, wire transfers, and automated clearing house (ACH) arrangements. Standardized forms and procedures are now available. Each of the electronic payment arrangements will be discussed individually. In order to effectively implement electronic systems, managers across functional areas need company-wide policy that fosters cooperation among credit, sales, customer service, purchasing, and transportation departments.

Credit Cards. Credit cards are the most common type of an electronic payment. Consumer credit has been the historical bailiwick for credit card usage. Internet transactions are often paid for through credit cards. According to a study performed by the Credit Research Foundation, credit cards are now used by almost half of the population studied in a business-to-business environment. The purchaser, seller, and credit card company are linked through an electronic network. Credit cards afford convenience but at a cost to the seller.

Debit Cards. Debit cards can be used in a manner very similar to the ways in which credit cards are used. However, unlike the creation of a revolving open account when a credit card is used, the debit cardholder has funds immediately debited from an account. There is no credit created.

Stored Value Cards. A customer can purchase the right to store value in a card by prepaying. The card is used by the holder, and the monetary value is transferred to the seller. Examples include prepaid telephone cards and photocopy cards. A smart card is a stored value card that allows for the electronic transfer of value from a bank to a merchant.

Online Payment Systems. The Internet has provided a unique opportunity to market products. In addition to credit cards and debit cards, online payment systems developed by companies such as PayPal, PayDirect, and Billpoint allow buyers to establish credit electronically. Various tools are used to support the online purchase. Authorization by the online payment service is often based upon savings accounts, checking accounts, money orders, or credit cards.

Wire Transfers. The Federal Reserve allows for the quick transfer of large balances made between financial institutions through the Fedwire. Sometimes a customer with past-due balances may want an order released quickly. In such situations, a credit manager can insist upon a wire transfer to clean up the past-due balance prior to releasing a new shipment. The credit manager should be sure to alert the bank to the incoming transfer and the need to contact the creditor when funds are available so that the order can be released. Foreign exchange wire transfers are made over the Clearing House Interbank Payment System (CHIPS).

ACH Arrangements. Automated clearing house (ACH) arrangements are one of the fastest growing electronic payment mechanisms. Transactions such as utility bill payments or property taxes can be made because a payment was authorized by an individual, a business, or the government, and then a bank is authorized to process the remittance electronically. Many consumers have their paychecks deposited automatically into their bank account via a type of an ACH arrangement. ACH arrangements are sometimes called direct debit programs. They offer an alternative to using checks.

CREDIT AVAILABILITY

The terms credit limit, credit line, and credit availability have historically been used interchangeably. This may no longer hold true. Due to potential lender liability lawsuits against banks, all credit managers should be concerned with the good faith provisions contained in Section 1-203 of the Uniform Commercial Code.

Creditors can potentially be held liable by customers who claim that they have been led to believe that an open-ended availability of credit exists. Creditors should consider avoiding use of "credit lines," which may imply credit will be granted up to a specified amount. Instead, creditors should use language on a credit application that clearly points out that the decision for credit availability is solely at the discretion of the vendor.

Credit managers have a number of concerns regarding credit availability. To whom is the availability of credit communicated? There are some companies that only communicate dollar limits internally. Yet at other companies, customers know that a specified amount of credit can be used.

At some companies, credit availability is only used as a threshold amount to draw attention to an account. The credit manager then can exercise judgment in terms of holding shipments or increasing the dollar exposure. Yet at other companies, the credit availability amount is an absolute threshold for exposure to a customer.

Credit authority is often established through a hierarchy. Table 8-3 presents an example of a hierarchy approach that can be used to assign levels of authority.

Table 8-3 shows that the Division Credit Manager has authority to approve credit to a customer for any amount over $50,000 up to a maximum of $200,000. In some ways, the concept of a hierarchy of credit authority is similar to a loan committee at a bank. As accounts grow larger, the potential risk should be reviewed by higher-level personnel.

Table 8-3 Sample Hierarchy for Credit Authorization

Title	Dollar Authority
Assistant Credit Manager	Up to $50,000
Division Credit Manager	$50,001 to $200,000
Corporate Credit Manager	$200,001 to $500,000
Treasurer	$500,001 to 1,000,000
Vice President of Finance	Over $1,000,000

At many companies, credit is automatically made available to customers up to a certain amount. For example, orders below $200 may be approved by implementing a policy for blanket approval to any customer. The costs of a credit investigation and actual payment experience with small-balance accounts are important factors when considering the blanket threshold amount.

Internal controls are useful in making credit available. Systems that allow for an automatic approval of orders to large, strong companies can reduce the burden of credit personnel reviewing every purchase order. For products with a limited customer market, controls can be used to prevent all orders from entering the manufacturing process until credit is approved.

The use of internal controls is central to the effectiveness of any credit department. Table 8-4 shows a set of codes that can be used to classify customers. The classifications are useful to expedite orders from existing customers. The codes can be distributed internally to sales, manufacturing, and transportation departments.

Table 8-4 shows that customer code “R” is called a refer account. All orders for customers with an “R” code need to be referred to the credit department for credit approval. The “R” code would be useful to control risk for a marginal account.

Table 8-4 Credit Controls for Existing Customers

Code	Classification	Explanation
A	Automatic	Accepted to process all orders.
L	Limited	Credit authorized up to a limited specified amount.
R	Refer	All orders should be referred to credit department for approval.
C	Cash	Customer payments required in advance.
H	Hold	Credit hold on orders. Do not ship.

COLLECTION ACTIVITY

Sound collection actively entails the development of effective policy and procedures. The effectiveness is based upon knowledge of customer habits and use of alternative collection procedures. Failure to communicate clear ground rules can undermine the effectiveness of any collection activity. Records for collection activity should be maintained.

Computer technology is now available that can facilitate collection activity. Certain types of tasks that are routine in nature will lend themselves nicely to the evolving automated applications. The specific decision rules can be developed to trigger the type of mode that is most useful for collecting; then collectors can be automatically alerted to use the appropriate follow up. Management reports can be available online or distributed to keep all interested parties aware of the current situation.

For example, accounts can be classified by size or by risk; then a particular mode of collection is deemed to be most useful. Large amounts might entail a phone call after five days past due; smaller accounts might trigger a letter after 10 days past due. The timing of an appropriate follow up can be automated. Based upon the internally generated decision rules, an account could be placed on hold if a commitment is not honored. Sales personnel and production personnel can be alerted to any developing problems. Distinctive modes for collecting accounts include:

Concise Invoices. The accuracy and design of an invoice, and the promptness in billing are important starting points for collection activity. The name and telephone number of a vendor contact should appear on the invoice. The payment destination should be clear. If a lockbox is used, its location should allow an optimal clearing time for funds.

If a customer complains about a delay in receiving invoices, the creditor needs to investigate the problem. Sometimes a simultaneous mailing of invoices to the customer and credit manager from the billing department can pin down the problem. Technology makes it possible for a credit manager to use a local area network to transmit a copy of an invoice to a customer almost instantaneously.

Collection Letters. The internal policy for the initial letter should be soon after the due date. The sooner the initial contact, the higher the likelihood of collection. There are actually some companies that send out the initial collection letter on the due date.

Some companies use a series of collection letters. Other companies may use one letter and then change modes to telephone collection activity. The size of the account will shape the tactics. The intervals should be systematic. Knowledge of customer habits is crucial to follow-up practices.

Monthly Statements. Monthly statements can be a useful collection device. Some companies pay bills strictly from monthly statements; other companies discard monthly statements. A prudent credit manager might ask customers whether or not they use monthly statements. Sometimes handwritten comments on a monthly statement personalize the statement and result in an effective collection device.

Fax Activity. Faxing is fast and convenient. On the other hand, confidentiality is critical to collection activity. The fax is fraught with several ways for confidentiality to be breached. Credit managers should make it a practice to use a fax cover sheet that clearly identifies the sender, the number of pages, and the intended user. A telephone follow up to the recipient can verify receipt and address any technical problems with the fax transmissions.

Telephone Calls. Pre-call planning is a first step. Learn what time of day and day in the week the person with authority to pay is available. Records of the conversations should be maintained in a computer system or on a call sheet. The goal of the collection call is to get the customer to make a commitment. Any credit hold, accumulation of late charges, necessary updates to credit information, and reasons for the delay should surface during the conversation. Leading questions, a strategic pause, and a professional approach are key ingredients to the conversation. Hold a customer to a commitment by using an effective follow-up system.

Internet. Sending an e-mail can be an effective way to communicate. Some customers are seldom in the office. Most people review their e-mail regularly so that the communication of a problem is less likely to go unnoticed.

Personal Visits. Dollar exposure can justify the costs involved with a personal visit. Visits should be carefully planned by updating credit information, communicating with sales personnel, and bringing along essential documentation. Goodwill visits to large customers can be an effective way to foster improved communications. Visits to collect problem accounts should be conducted professionally. Decisions concerning any questionable topics should be deferred until after the visit. An inspection of the customer's premises can be revealing. The tone of the meeting should be firm but fair. Any commitments from the customer should be confirmed in writing and promptly followed up on.

Collection Agencies. Collection agencies can be effective because of the psychological introduction of a third party. Most collection agencies offer a 10-day period during which the agency does not charge a fee if the account pays within those 10 days of being placed for collection. Collection agency fees can be substantial. There are companies that have actually set up subsidiary collection agencies to act as an in-house collection tool to circumvent agency fees.

Whatever agency is used, creditors should make sure that the agency is bonded. The agency should be willing to furnish financial statements and be licensed in the states where it is collecting. The fees should be competitive. Creditors should also find out the "hit rate," which is the percentage of claims that the agency actually collects. Collection agencies should send reports regularly concerning the status of accounts placed with the agency. Finally, the agency should remit funds and provide reports in a timely manner.

Litigation. Credit managers normally negotiate a fee arrangement and check for any potential conflict of interest when seeking outside legal assistance. If a lawsuit is recommended, the attorney should indicate whether or not there are attachable assets so that the costs of litigation are justifiable. Unsecured creditors may seek a prejudgment writ of attachment and then send in a sheriff to levy on the debtor's assets. A creditor also has the option to docket a judgment to create a lien against the debtor's assets. However, a judgment does not guarantee payment. When a written agreement exists, a creditor can be reimbursed for the costs of litigation. In other cases, the costs of litigating, or the poor likelihood of recovering the debt, suggest that litigation may be fruitless.

Bad Debt Write-Offs. After all collection alternatives are exhausted, an account is written off to bad debts. Policy should require specific authorization to write an account off to bad debts. There should normally be documentation in a credit file that justifies the write-off. Auditors will often pressure credit personnel to write off an account after the account is one year old. A paper trail of collection activity can be useful as a tool to avoid future similar situations.

REVIEWING THE COLLECTION SYSTEM

Both scientific-based approaches and practical approaches can be useful in reviewing a collection system. The scientific-based approach involves the use of collection scoring technology. The technology works in a manner that is similar to a credit scoring system for new accounts. The technology furnishes statistically based scores derived from actual experience. The results can be used to derive scores that predict the likelihood of slow payment or of incurring a bad debt. Predicted payments and bad debts can be compared to actual payments and bad debts to consider adjusting policy and procedures.

In a judgment-based approach, the practical concerns are addressed. Collections often involve practical operating problems. Both policy and procedures should consider the practical concerns. Some of the questions that need to be asked concerning collection activity include:

- How should non-sufficient funds (NSF) checks be handled? Will customers then be placed on a cash-in-advance payment arrangement for future orders?
- Will late payment service charges be used as an incentive for prompt payment? If used, are the charges billed out or are dummy billings used on an aging of receivables? At what rate is interest charged? Who monitors usury concerns?
- How is the sales department kept informed of collection problems? Will the sales department keep the credit department aware of problems?
- Are credit personnel properly trained to use the collections system? Should certain collection tasks be outsourced?
- Will a change of pattern in the collection routine improve the days sales outstanding? How tight can the pattern be made before customers are irritated enough then lost due to being too stringent? Is the company more profitable if marginal accounts are not granted credit?
- Is there an opportunity of collecting in small claims court?
- Who selects the collection agency being used? On what basis is the collection agency selected? Who monitors the effectiveness of the agency?
- Who informs a customer that shipments are being held? When is the sales department notified?
- Who decides when an account should be written off to bad debt?

The best training for credit managers can come from experience. There are usually circumstances that vary from account to account. Technology provides a useful starting point. Then a credit manager needs to ask questions and follow intuition while exercising judgment. A regular periodic evaluation should be made that considers the efficiency of the overall collection system.

DEDUCTIONS

Deductions are sometimes called short payments. A customer might short-pay invoices due to quality problems, transportation claims, returned goods, promotional allowances, billing errors, discount problems, or other miscellaneous reasons. The responsibility for follow up on deductions varies by company. Credit, sales, accounts receivables, customer service, or a combination of departments may be responsible.

Regardless of the responsibility, deductions need quick and systematic follow up. There is a cost to carry deductions in receivables if the deductions are not allowed. There is also a hidden cost of the time involved by employees who are trying to resolve deductions. The task of identifying, verifying, and resolving deductions can become arduous. The follow-up system should include step-by-step procedures and emphasize timing.

Reports can be a useful tool to control deductions. Deductions can be categorized by a number of factors: cause, size, age, and product. Attempts should be made to pinpoint the cause of deductions and correct any internal problems. Ultimately, deductions are resolved in any one of three ways: (1) a credit can be issued for the full amount, (2) the deduction can be denied, or (3) a portion of the deduction can be allowed.

The Credit Research Foundation performed a study of credit and accounts receivable managers concerning the impact of deductions upon receivables. The study showed that on an average, deductions represent 5% of all open accounts receivable. For more details concerning the results of the CRF study, see the CRF web site (www.crfonline.org), where the study can be downloaded.

There are many credit-related issues to consider concerning deductions. Some of the issues that relate to customer deductions include the following:

- Should deductions age out as past-due items on an aging of receivables? (Perhaps only certain types of deductions age out.)
- At what threshold amount should deductions be automatically absorbed? Who decides? (Consider monitoring customers who may test the system that absorbs a specific amount.)

- At what number of days beyond a discount date should unearned discounts be charged back? How is this monitored? (Some credit managers use the postmark on an envelope to monitor discounts.)
- Who monitors cash discounts for the proper amount? (Discounts should be taken on the net invoice amount, not on the gross invoice amount that includes promotional allowances.)
- Who decides whether a quality claim will be allowed? How is that decision made?

Deductions are an important customer relations concern. There are significant costs associated with carrying and resolving deductions. The timely disposition of deductions is also essential to effective collection management. The best strategies for reconciling deductions often originate from questioning the system. What caused the open items? What needs to be done to resolve open items? Can the business practices be improved upon so that the process that caused the deduction to occur be avoided or resolved more expediently in the future?

There has been a recent emphasis placed upon using a team approach to resolve deductions. The team-based process can create an increased level of awareness that can lead to a quicker resolution to problems. Since deductions have many different causes, there is usually someone on a cross-functional team who should be closer to the root cause and better able to move forward than other team members.

In certain industries, outsourcing can offer a fast and cost-efficient approach to resolving deductions. It is effective particularly in retailing, where promotions and pricing changes occur frequently. Outsourcing can provide a viable option to deduction resolution.

CHAPTER 8: FOLLOW UP

Recap of Important Concepts

1. Technology can contribute significantly to the development of an effective collection system. Credit managers are being challenged to harness technology in a cost-efficient manner.
2. Collection activity entails the coordination of a number of factors: clear communication of terms, controls for credit authorization, an effective use of various modes of collecting, and a means to reconcile account balances.
3. Selling terms can be categorized as cash, open account, special, or electronic. Each set of terms should be considered from a risk-reward perspective. Credit managers should be thoroughly aware of the alternative terms and when to establish specific terms.
4. Credit authorization needs to be carefully controlled. A hierarchy can be useful for specific dollar authority levels. Internal codes should be assigned to individual accounts based upon their creditworthiness.
5. Collection activity progresses through various stages. Invoices, monthly statements, letters, fax activities, the Internet, telephone calls, personal visits, collection agencies, lawsuits, and bad debt write-offs should each be evaluated for effectiveness. Credit managers should evaluate the efficiency of the collection system on a periodic basis.
6. Deductions require consistent timely follow up. Deductions should be identified by type. Procedures to verify and resolve open items should emphasize timing and a team approach.
7. The one essential ingredient to a collection system is effective policies and procedures. Collection guidelines should be communicated clearly and applied consistently. The controls should be reviewed regularly. Any changes in corporate goals can be integrated into the overall collection system.

Review/Discussion Questions

1. Why is a systems approach beneficial to credit managers while performing collection activity?
2. What form of cash selling terms is the most restrictive? What form of cash selling terms has the most risk?

3. a. With terms of 2% 15N45, what is the approximate annualized cost expressed as a percent to the customer who pays the net amount on day 45?
   b. If the customer with terms of 2% 15N45 is allowed to pay on day 90, how much is the approximate annualized cost expressed as a percent? (Assume no late payment charge.)
   c. What did you learn from your calculations in 3(a) and 3(b)?
4. How can credit availability become an issue with a customer? To whom is credit availability communicated within an organization?
5. What is an electronic payments system? Furnish two examples of electronic payments.
6. Explain how internal controls can be used to monitor existing customers for credit availability.
7. How can invoices be an important focal point in a collection system?
8. Explain how telephone collection activity should be influenced by the following customer responses during a collection call:
   a. An intentionally provocative response, such as "So what?" from a customer.
   b. An evasive response, such as "I'll look into it."
   c. A customer who is looking for sympathy and saying, "My customers are not paying me, so how can I pay you?"
9. Are late-payment service charges a fair way to control slow-paying accounts?
10. What is a deduction? What are some of the leading reasons that deductions are taken? What can ultimately be done to resolve a deduction?

Test Your Knowledge

1. What is a consignment sale?
2. What is a contra account arrangement?
3. Provide an overview for the use of anticipation discounts.
4. How should unearned cash discounts be monitored?
5. What is the difference between a credit card and a debit card?
6. What is the purpose of using a lockbox system?
7. Discuss the role of monthly statements in collection activity.
8. What should a credit manager try to do before, during, and after a customer visit?
9. What factors should a credit manager consider when selecting a collection agency?

10. A company is considering changing selling terms from 1% 10N30 to 2% 10N30. What factors should a credit manager consider if his or her employer is considering this proposed change? Be thorough.
11. What does ACH represent in terms of a payment arrangement?
12. Why has the use of team building caught on in terms of resolving deductions?

Case Study for Discussion

Technology has changed the approach to collection activity. In what ways has technology enhanced the collection of accounts receivable? Try to pinpoint at least five specific benefits that are made available to credit managers through the enhancements in technology.

Have credit managers properly been able to use the technology that is available? Please consider costs, benefits, and credit department goals when developing your response.

Are there any downsides to the increased reliance upon technology?

Credit Management Online

www.billpoint.com—This is a commercial site that is referenced to provide an example of an online payment system. Billpoint is a unit of eBay Inc. Electronic checks are popular in auction markets. There is considerable potential to develop similar payment systems in other types of markets.

www.chicagofed.org—This site is hosted by the Federal Reserve Bank of Chicago, which is one of the 12 regional Federal Reserve banks. Each of the regional Fed banks has a publication and education link. For example, the Chicago Fed has a publication, *The ABCs of Figuring Interest,* that can be downloaded for free.

www.crfonline.org—The Credit Research Foundation site has numerous research available online. One such study, "Customer Deductions Impact on Receivables," can be purchased. The study provides considerable data concerning business practices that can be useful to reconciling deductions.

www.federalreserve.org—The Federal Reserve Bank site can be used to access any of the 12 regional banks for local research and current economic information. The Fed also provides education-related material concerning the U.S. payment system, check clearing, check truncation, and regulation.

www.getpaid.com—This is a commercial site that can be reviewed to learn more about the potential for collection software. The GetPAID Corporation markets software that can be integrated with SAP or other interfaces. GetPAID can provide the technical support essential to developing an integrated collection system.

www.paypal.com—PayPal Inc. is another commercial site that offers online payment services, which are useful primarily for consumers and small businesses. This site is popular with Internet sellers linked through bank accounts or credit cards. Transaction costs for sellers can be reduced in comparison to using credit card companies.

References Useful for Further Reading

Andreeff, Alexandria, et al. "Electronic Bill Presentment and Payment: Is It Just a Click Away?" *Economic Perspectives* (Fourth Quarter 2001): 2-16.

Banasiak, Michael J., and Gerald L. Kelly. "Predictive Collection Score Technology." *Business Credit* (February 2000): 18-20.

Callahan, Terry. "Customer Deductions: Impact on Receivables." *Business Credit* (February 2002): 56-58.

Corbett, Tom. "The Future of Deductions." *Business Credit* (March 2000): 18-20.

Cronin, Mary J. "Bill Gates, Bill Collector." *Fortune* (October 13, 1997): 157-158.

Fagel, Allen J., and Dennis E. Quaid. "New Life for an Old Remedy: Reclamation from Insolvent Buyers and Bankrupt Debtors." *Business Credit* (January 1998): 46-48.

Fagel, Allen J. "Selling on Consignment: Another Tool in the Credit Arsenal." *Business Credit* (October 1996): 6-8.

Fox, Douglas G. "When Is C.O.D. Not C.O.D.?" *Business Credit* (May 1998): 18-20.

Gallinger, George W. "A Look at Discounts." *P.D. News* (April 1998): 1-3.

Gamble, Richard. "Electronic Invoice Presentment and Payment Can Speed Dispute Resolution and Cut DSO." *Business Credit* (October 2001): 28-29.

Hamilton, Henry K. "The Importance of Shipping Terms." *Business Credit* (February 2002): 68.

Holden, Barbara. "Technology, Teamwork and Trust: Driving Forces in Doing Business with the Government." *Business Credit* (May 2000): 56-57.

Moser, Milton J. "Collecting Foreign Trade Debt." *Business Credit* (March 2000): 28-30.

Nathan, Bruce S. "Selling on Consignment: How to Protect Yourself." *Business Credit* (June 2000): 14-16.

Nathan, Bruce S. "Unpaid Sellers Stoppage of Delivery and Reclamation Rights Against an Insolvent Buyer." *Business Credit* (January 2001): 42-44.

Ochs, Joyce R., and Kenneth L. Parkinson. "Collections Go High Tech." *Business Credit* (May 1998): 27-28.

Ochs, Joyce R. "Managing Collections." *Business Credit* (March 1999): 20-22.

Parkinson, Kenneth L. "Improving Collections with Direct Debit Programs." *Business Credit* (March 1999): 26-28.

Piumelli, Frederick A. "Automating Collections." *Business Credit* (February 2001): 22-25.

Piumelli, Frederick A. "Deduction Resolution as a Change Agent." *Business Credit* (February 2001): 36-39.

Schmidt, Dave. "Technology to the Rescue." *Business Credit* (January 2001): 46-49.

Schmidt, Dave. "Credit and Collections Finds a Home Online." *Business Credit* (October 2001): 47-51.

Weiner, Stuart E. "Electronic Payments in the U.S. Economy: An Overview." *Economic Review* (Fourth Quarter 1999): 53-64.

Wheeland, Rod. "Qualifying Your Collection Agency: Asking the Right Questions." *Business Credit* (February 2002): 57-58.

Chapter 9

FINANCIAL STATEMENT ANALYSIS

"Financial statement analysis is like reading a mystery novel. If you don't start at the beginning, you will be missing a number of clues to help unravel the story."[1]

–George W. Gallinger
Associate Professor
Arizona State University

Generally Accepted Accounting Principles (GAAP) can be defined as the principles of accounting that have substantial authoritative support. Yet there is no universally defined list of specific principles with authoritative support. So credit managers need to become familiar with accounting principles and then focus upon questioning their application to individual financial statements.

Credit managers have different ways of performing financial statement analysis. The analysis is sometimes limited to a quick eyeballing of numbers; at other times analysis entails the use of computers that generate detailed sophisticated spreadsheets. Regardless of the type of analysis, the focus should be placed upon using financial statements to make superior credit decisions.

Financial statement analysis is a subject that can be studied with a number of different focal points. The subject could certainly be a textbook in itself. In order to address the needs of credit managers, there are two chapters of this book that delve into financial statements. This chapter will lay a foundation for the more advanced topics that are contained in Chapter 10.

[1]George W. Gallinger, "Framework for Financial Analysis, Part 2: Financial Leverage and Return on Equity," *Business Credit* (March 2000): 33.

The **Key Learning Objectives** in Chapter 9 are:

1. Identify the role of the independent public accountant in the preparation of financial statements.
2. Examine the usefulness of common-size financial statement analysis.
3. Analyze specific financial ratios that are useful for credit decision making.
4. Delve into contemporary measures generated through the use of financial statements; these measures can be useful for different types of credit analysis.
5. Focus on specific key focal points that are frequently scrutinized by credit managers when analyzing financial statements.

THE SOURCE OF FINANCIAL STATEMENTS

All public companies and many privately held businesses have their financial statements examined by independent public accountants. Independence of the audit provides reasonable assurance that financial statements are free of material departure from GAAP. Credit managers, however, should be able to recognize both the various types of auditors' opinions and the latitude accountants have in using alternative practices that are permitted by GAAP.

Public accountants emphasize that financial statements are prepared by management, not by public auditors. The role of the public auditor is to exercise judgment in determining the fairness of the financial statements according to GAAP. The public auditor then expresses an opinion concerning both fairness and conformity within the parameters of GAAP.

The American Institute of Certified Public Accountants (AICPA) established external auditor opinions in terms of the levels of assurance given by the independent auditor's opinion. The opinion pertains to the fairness of financial statements using the GAAP criteria established by the AICPA guidelines. There are four specific opinions.

1. *An Unqualified Opinion.* An unqualified opinion, also known as a clean opinion, is the highest level of assurance that financial statements comply with GAAP. Auditors, who present an unqualified opinion in the third paragraph of the Auditor's Report,

give their professional opinion that financial statements are presented fairly and are in compliance with GAAP.

2. *Qualified Opinion.* The public auditors will qualify an opinion for any of three specific reasons: a lack of consistency, a major uncertainty, and a question concerning the firm's ability to operate as a going concern. In each of the three, grounds for giving a qualified opinion are spelled out in the Auditor's Report with the use of a fourth paragraph. More complete details for the qualified opinion are then inserted with a note to the financial statements. Prior to 1988, the qualifications for violating consistency were pointed out with the words "except for" in the Auditor's Report. Also prior to 1988, violations for qualifications given because of doubt related to the going concern issue were pointed out through use of the words "subject to" in the Auditor's Report.
3. *Disclaimer.* Sometimes an auditor may not be able to express an opinion concerning financial statements. If limitations are placed upon the scope of the audit, the auditor will issue a disclaimer.
4. *Adverse Opinion.* Financial statements that depart from GAAP to the extent that they do not present fairly the position of the firm will receive an adverse opinion.

Credit managers should exercise considerable judgment when reviewing financial statements and the auditor's report. When more than one accounting procedure is permitted by GAAP, remember that it is the management—not the outside auditor—who decides which practice to use. When a qualified opinion is issued, the credit manager should examine closely the related note to the audit qualification. Moreover, a disclaimer or an adverse opinion should be recognized as posing a serious limitation on possible creditworthiness.

Failure to perform an audit at the requisite level of care has resulted in considerable litigation. When an auditor improperly gives a "clean opinion," a credit manager may be in a position to seek redress. The legal criteria have not always been clear. Under common law, there are three essentials necessary to establish auditor liability: (1) the creditor must have suffered a loss, (2) the cause of the creditor's loss must have been a reasonable reliance on a material omission or on a material misstatement in an audited financial statement, and (3) the auditor must have failed to exercise the proper level of care while performing the audit.

There have been a number of disturbing situations in which the Securities and Exchange Commission (SEC) has required a restatement of the financial statements furnished by large public companies during 2001 and 2002. Several issues that relate to accounting problems need to be addressed by the accounting profession. For example, to what extent are accountants' audit opinions influenced by consulting contracts? Should Arthur Andersen have been prosecuted for failure to comply with document retention in the audit of Enron? These and other questions are at the heart of the confidence in the role that certified public accountants (CPAs) engage in an audit.

In general, public accounting firms function at a very high level of professional competence. Audited financial statements are superior to either a compilation or a review. In a compilation, the internal management team prepares the numbers in the financial statement. In a review, the auditor does not comply with normal auditing standards required by GAAP.

The source for financial statements goes beyond the focus of an audit opinion letter. Credit managers should request personal financial statements when relying upon an individual. Personal statements should be signed and dated. Asset valuation is often inflated on personal statements, so personal statements are often not as reliable as audited statements. Furthermore, some personal statements may include assets held jointly by a spouse. Credit managers should consider the appropriateness of a spousal guarantee or obtain a personal statement that eliminates assets held jointly.

All public corporations must comply with the financial disclosure mandated by the Securities and Exchange Commission. Both 10K annual reports and 10Q quarterly reports provide detailed financial information that is available to the public at www.sec.gov.

Most companies legally maintain two sets of books: one for financial accounting and a second for tax accounting. Since tax laws and financial accounting rules do not coincide, the two sets of books are usually different. Tax returns are not made available to the public; perhaps they should be. Credit managers may encounter customers who claim that financial statements do not exist. In these cases, a copy of a tax return may be of use.

There are occasions when the data presented in financial statements is deliberately misrepresented. Consider saving the envelopes in which financial statements are mailed. False financial statements leave a customer vulnerable to a mail fraud conviction.

COMMON SIZE ANALYSIS

Common Size Analysis is performed on the income statement and the balance sheet. To common size an income statement, simply take each item in the income statement as a percentage of net sales. A common size balance sheet takes each line item in the balance sheet as a percentage of total assets.

Table 9-1 presents income statement data for Blackhawk Retail Company. The income statements pertain to three annual periods; three years is a requirement for public companies in Annual Reports. Common size percentages are in parentheses next to each income statement item.

The three-year common size analysis is helpful to identify trends. Note that Blackhawk Retail Company has been decreasing cost of goods sold as a percentage of sales. At the same time, operating expenses have increased. These trends help to pinpoint the type of questions that should be posed.

For example, is gross profit up due to industry or economic conditions? Has the company changed any marketing policies such as using higher selling prices? Has the company changed suppliers or improved labor cost control? Are these changes temporary? Can selling general or administrative expenses be reduced to improve the operating results?

Common size analysis is not only useful to spot changes or trends internally, but it also is useful in making comparisons to an industry. Table 9-2 shows the common size income statement percentages of Blackhawk Retail Company in comparison to the industry. Industry data

Table 9-1 **Blackhawk Retail Company for the Years Ended December 31**

(000s Omitted)	2001	%	2002	%	2003	%
Net Sales	4500	(100)	4950	(100)	5450	(100)
Cost of Goods Sold	3375	(75)	3564	(72)	3870	(71)
Gross Margin	1125	(25)	1385	(28)	1580	(29)
Operating Expenses	500	(11)	594	(12)	708	(13)
Operating Income	625	(14)	791	(16)	872	(16)
Interest Expense	70	(2)	75	(2)	100	(2)
Pre-Tax Profit	555	(12)	716	(14)	772	(14)
Income Tax	222	(5)	250	(5)	272	(5)
Net Income After Tax	**333**	(7)	**466**	(9)	**500**	(9)

Table 9-2 Blackhawk Retail Co./Industry Comparison
Common Size Income Statement for 12/31/03

	Blackhawk Retail Company	Industry Average
Sales	100 %	100 %
Cost of Goods Sold	71	75
Gross Margin	29	25
Operating Expenses	13	12
Operating Income	16	13
Interest Expense	2	2
Pre-Tax Profit	14	11
Income Tax	5	5
Net Income After Tax	**9**	**6**

is available from the RMA Statement Studies or through agency credit reporting services.

The data in Table 9-2 shows that Blackhawk Retail Company has been able to hold down the cost of goods sold to 71% of sales while the industry average is 75%. The difference could be due to the sales increase and an ability to distribute fixed costs to more units. However, the credit analyst may want to question numbers directly with the Blackhawk Retail Company management.

Common size analysis is also performed on the balance sheet. Table 9-3 includes balance sheet data for Blackhawk Retail Company that includes two year-end dates. The common size percentages are in parentheses. These percentages are derived by dividing balance sheet items by total assets.

The common size data in Table 9-3 can be useful to pinpoint changes. For example, the property plant and equipment percentage increased from 20 to 28% of total assets. A corresponding increase in secured debt from 10% to 18% suggests that long-term secured funds were used to finance the asset acquisition. Since sales have been increasing, these changes appear to be prudent.

As a general rule, a credit analyst should always focus on large common size items in the balance sheet. Somewhat nominal changes in the common size percentage for large line items can be important. For example, Table 9-3 shows that accounts payable increased from 20% to 23% as a common size line item. This increase could be indicative of a slowdown in payments to suppliers.

Table 9-3 Blackhawk Retail Company Common Size Balance Sheets on December 31, 2002 and 2003

(000s Omitted)	2002	%	2003	%
Cash	50	(3)	45	(2)
Marketable Securities	175	(12)	150	(8)
Accounts Receivables	450	(31)	650	(36)
Inventory	600	(41)	580	(32)
Total Current Assets	1,275	(87)	1,425	(78)
Property, Plant & Equipment	300	(20)	500	(28)
Less: Accumulated Depreciation	(100)	(7)	(115)	(6)
Total Assets	**1,475**	(100)	**1,810**	(100)
Accounts Payable	300	(20)	410	(23)
Accrued Wages & Taxes	100	(7)	95	(5)
Notes Payable	150	(10)	135	(7)
Total Current Liabilities	550	(37)	640	(35)
Debentures	50	(3)	45	(2)
Secured Debt	150	(10)	325	(18)
Total Liabilities	750	(51)	1,010	(56)
Retained Earnings	425	(29)	500	(28)
Common Stock	300	(20)	300	(17)
Total Equity	725	(49)	800	(45)
Total Liabilities & Equity	**1,475**	(100)	**1,810**	(100)

The company common size data should also be compared to industry data when analyzing a balance sheet. The analysis is similar to the income statement analysis. However, the balance sheet analysis provides useful information concerning how funds are invested and where the funds are obtained.

Table 9-4 shows the common size balance sheet for Blackhawk Retail Company and the industry averages. The industry balance sheet percentages can vary by the size of the company. For example, small companies may use more debt, carry more receivables, or have fewer dollars invested in property plant and equipment assets. Credit analysts should exercise caution using industry data. Comparable size companies are essential when undertaking an industry common size analysis.

The data in Table 9-4 show side-by-side, company-to-industry common size balance sheets. This type of analysis can be revealing. For example, the Blackhawk Retail Company invests 36% of assets into accounts receivables while the industry only invests 32% of assets into

Table 9-4 Blackhawk Retail Co./Industry Comparison
Common Size Balance Sheets 12/31/03

(000s Omitted)	Blackhawk Retail Company %	Industry Average %
Cash	2	4
Marketable Securities	8	4
Accounts Receivable	36	32
Inventory	32	40
Total Current Assets	78	80
Property, Plant & Equipment	28	25
Less Accumulated Depreciation	(6)	(5)
Total Assets	**100%**	**100%**
Accounts Payable	23	25
Accrued Wages & Taxes	5	6
Notes Payable	7	10
Total Current Liabilities	35	41
Debentures	2	0
Secured Debt	18	20
Total Liabilities	56	61
Retained Earnings	28	19
Common Stock	17	20
Total Equity	45	39
Total Liabilities & Equity	**100%**	**100%**

receivables. Is this difference reflective of extended selling terms, lax enforcement of collection activity, or the extension of credit to marginal accounts?

Common size analysis is particularly effective as a means for pinpointing items that should be questioned. The superior credit analyst is capable of making inter-relationships among the numbers. Asking the right questions can often lead to meaningful financial statement interpretation. Common size analysis can lead to superior questions essential to sound credit decisions.

RATIO ANALYSIS

Ratio analysis is used to provide insights concerning the financial position of a business. In accounting, there are rules established by GAAP to prepare financial statements. No such rules exist for the formulas used in ratio analysis or the interpretation of financial ratios.

For a given corporation, the Value Line Directory, Moody's, Standard & Poor's, and RMA each may furnish a different number for earnings per share. The differences are caused by nuances used by analysts when performing the calculations. For credit managers, the key is to be consistent in applying formulas so that they are useful for comparative purposes. Incidentally, several of the web sites at the end of this chapter furnish ratios and industry norms that can be downloaded.

Ratio analysis is straightforward. Credit managers should look for trends over time for a particular company. In addition, the individual ratios should be compared to a benchmark for a specific industry.

Ratio analysis can be easily broken down into the following categories: (1) liquidity ratios, (2) asset management ratios, (3) debt management ratios, and (4) profitability ratios. Three ratios have been carefully selected from each category based upon their broad usage by credit managers. There are over 60 financial ratios that can be used to analyze statements. Credit analysts may employ industry-specific ratios or variations of the ratios presented for company-specific utility.

Liquidity Ratios

The liquidity ratios are particularly important to short-term creditors. Liquidity measures short-term solvency. The liquidity ratios include: (A) Current Ratio, (B) Quick Ratio, and (C) Payables Deferral Period. These ratios will be calculated using the 2003 data for the Blackhawk Retail Company.

A. **Current Ratio** $= \dfrac{\text{Total Current Assets}}{\text{Total Current Liabilities}} = \dfrac{1{,}425}{640} = 2.2$

The numerator in the Current Ratio is usually cash, marketable securities, accounts receivables, and inventory. Some credit managers include prepaid expenses; other credit managers feel that prepaid expenses should not be categorized as a current asset. The denominator of the Current Ratio represents all debt due within a 12-month period.

A Current Ratio of 2.2 suggests that there is $2.20 in current assets for every dollar in current debt, which is usually a good sign. However, a high Current Ratio is not necessarily good. For example, if a business lets receivables age out and does not turn inventory, the Current Ratio will go up while operations are deteriorating. The credit analyst needs to make a few inter-relationships in order to properly interpret the Current Ratio.

B. **Quick Ratio** $= \dfrac{\text{Quick Assets}}{\text{Current Liabilities}} = \dfrac{845}{640} = 1.3$

Sometimes the Quick Ratio is called the Acid Test Ratio. This ratio is a more stringent measure of liquidity than the Current Ratio. The numerator includes current assets less inventory; the inventory is subtracted because it is the least liquid of the current assets.

A Quick Ratio of 1.3 suggests that Blackhawk Retail Company should have the ability to service short-term debt without selling off inventory. As is the case for all ratios, the Quick Ratio should be monitored for trends from year to year and also compared to an industry norm.

C. **Payables Deferral Period** $= \dfrac{\text{Accounts Payable}}{\text{Purchases Per Day}} = \dfrac{410}{3{,}870 \div 365} = 38.7 \text{ Days}$

The accounts payable deferral period provides a basis for judging a company's willingness to pay its short-term creditors. The numerator is the accounts payable at year end. The denominator is the annual purchases divided by 365 days to get Purchases Per Day. Purchases for a manufacturing company can be found in a multi-step income statement where purchases are part of the cost of goods sold.

The Payables Deferral Period of 38.7 days for Blackhawk Retail Company is generally favorable. The results should be compared to general terms in an industry and general payment habits within an industry. When companies encounter liquidity problems, the Payables Deferral Period usually lengthens.

Asset Management Ratios

For most companies, the largest assets in the balance sheet include accounts receivable, inventory, and fixed assets. Three ratios that can be used to measure the effectiveness of asset management are: (D) the DSO Period, (E) the Inventory Carrying Period, and (F) the Fixed Asset Turnover. Each of these three ratios will be calculated using the 2003 data for the Blackhawk Retail Company.

D. **DSO Period** $= \dfrac{\text{Accounts Receivable}}{\text{Sales Per Day}} = \dfrac{650}{5{,}450 \div 365} = 43.5 \text{ Days}$

There are a number of ways to calculate the Days Sales Outstanding (DSO). In this example, the numerator is the ending accounts receivable balance and the denominator is the annual sales divided by 365 days. The results show that accounts receivable are collected in 43.5 days.

The DSO is closely related to terms of sale and credit policy. As terms lengthen, the DSO period will also be longer. If credit policy is lax, the DSO will also stretch out.

E. $$\textbf{Inventory Carrying Period} = \frac{\text{Inventory}}{\text{Cost of Goods Sold Per Day}} = \frac{580}{3{,}870 \div 365} = 54.7 \text{ Days}$$

The Inventory Carrying Period (ICP) provides the average number of days over which goods are held in inventory. The numerator is the ending inventory. The denominator is the cost of goods sold divided by the number of days in a year. Some credit analysts prefer to use an average inventory in the numerator, and sales rather than cost of goods sold in the denominator.

In the Blackhawk Retail Company example, the results show that goods are held for 54.7 days. Some analysts prefer to use turns per year; simply divide 365 days by 54.7 days to get 6.67 turns per year. Seasonal buildup is common in many industries. However, when the ICP lengthens, credit analysts should be aware of a potential problem moving the inventory.

F. $$\textbf{Fixed Asset Turnover} = \frac{\text{Sales}}{\text{Fixed Assets}} = \frac{5{,}450}{385} = 14 \text{ Times}$$

The Fixed Asset Turnover is calculated by dividing net sales by net fixed assets. Net fixed assets include gross fixed assets less any accumulated depreciation. The Fixed Asset Turnover for Blackhawk Retail Company is 14 times. This ratio is often difficult to interpret.

A high Fixed Asset Turnover may suggest that a company is doing a good job generating sales with assets. On the other hand, if the Fixed Asset Turnover is higher because fixed assets are not being replaced, the company could be heading for trouble in the long run. Also, a company that leases fixed assets may have a misleading Fixed Asset Turnover. Several inter-relationships need to be made to properly interpret the Fixed Asset Turnover ratio.

Debt Management Ratios

Debt Management Ratios are of particular importance to long-term creditors. They include: (G) Debt to Equity Ratio, (H) Times Interest Earned Ratio, and (I) Fixed Charge Coverage. Examples that explain the importance of debt management ratios will be used for the Blackhawk Retail Company in 2003.

G. **Debt to Equity Ratio** $= \dfrac{\text{Total Liabilities}}{\text{Shareholders Equity}} = \dfrac{1{,}010}{800} = 1.3$

The Debt to Equity Ratio is a measure of financial leverage. Some credit analysts subtract intangible assets from the shareholders equity in the denominator to obtain a tangible net worth rather than using total shareholders equity.

The results of 1.3 suggest that the creditors of Blackhawk Retail Company have more invested in the business than the owners. This is not unusual. The extent that leverage is used varies by industry.

H. **Times Interest Earned** $= \dfrac{\text{Operating Profit}}{\text{Interest Expense}} = \dfrac{872}{100} = 8.7$

The Times Interest Earned Ratio (TIE) is of particular importance to bondholders. The TIE suggests the likelihood of servicing or defaulting on debt. The numerator is the operating profit, which is sometimes referred to as earnings before interest and taxes (EBIT). The denominator is the interest expense line item from the income statement.

A TIE of 8.7 suggests that the Blackhawk Retail Company is generating enough operating profit to cover interest 8.7 times. The lower the TIE, the greater the risk of insolvency. As the TIE approaches 1.0, the debt should be restructured or a default is looming.

I. **Fixed Charge Coverage** $= \dfrac{\text{Operating Profit}}{\text{Interest Expense} + \text{Lease Obligation} + \dfrac{\text{SFP}}{(1 - \text{TR})}} = \dfrac{872}{100} = 8.7$

The Fixed Charge Coverage (FCC) is particularly important when a business does a lot of lease financing off the balance sheet. The numerator is the operating profit. The denominator is the interest expense, any lease obligation, and the sinking fund provision (SFP) on an after-tax basis. The lease obligation and sinking fund provision are found in footnotes to the financial statements.

For the Blackhawk Retail Company, the FCC is the same as the TIE. This is because the company does not do any leasing, nor is there a sinking fund on the debt. The FCC is important to creditors in certain industries such as photocopying machines, airlines, rails, and heavy equipment where a lot of leasing occurs. As in the case of the TIE ratio, the higher the FCC ratio, the safer the business.

Profitability Ratios

The profitability ratios are important to all creditors and investors in a business. Three of the most widely used profitability ratios include: (J) Profit Margin, (K) Return on Assets, and (L) Return on Equity. Each of these ratios will be described using data from Blackhawk Retail Company in 2003.

J. **Profit Margin** $= \dfrac{\text{Net Income After Tax}}{\text{Net Sales}} = \dfrac{500}{5{,}450} = 9\%$

The Profit Margin is sometimes referred to as the bottom line margin or the net profit margin. The calculation is simply net income after tax divided by net sales. Recognition of revenue and deferring of expenses can have a significant impact on the Profit Margin.

The 9% Profit Margin calculated for Blackhawk Retail Company should be compared to an industry. Jewelry stores tend to have high margins while grocery stores have tight margins. Cyclical industries tend to have margins that vary with the stage in the business cycle.

K. **Return on Assets** $= \dfrac{\text{Net Income After Tax}}{\text{Total Assets}} = \dfrac{500}{1{,}810} = 28\%$

The Return on Assets (ROA) is a reflection of management's ability to deploy assets profitably. This ratio is calculated by dividing net income after tax by total assets. Since accountants do not place a value on human resources as an asset in the balance sheet, small firms or firms that are not capital-intensive may have much higher ROAs than capital-intensive businesses.

The ROA of 28% for Blackhawk Retail Company is a favorable reflection on management's ability to deploy assets profitably.

L. **Return on Equity** $= \dfrac{\text{Net Income After Tax}}{\text{Shareholders Equity}} = \dfrac{500}{800} = 63\%$

The Return on Equity (ROE) reflects the percentage return being generated by a business for the owners of the business. (The actual return to the owners would come in the form of dividends plus profits derived from the sale of stock that has appreciated in value.) ROE is important because it reflects an ability to raise additional capital.

The Blackhawk Retail Company has an unusually high ROE. For a typical business, the ROE is closer to 15%.

Summary of Ratios

The 12 ratios used to analyze the Blackhawk Retail Company are summarized in Table 9-5. In particular, ratios are a useful tool in terms of appreciating the ability of a company to service creditors. The ratios can signal problems. Credit analysts have the responsibility to question the results. In general, the results of the ratio analysis for the Blackhawk Retail Company are favorable when compared to the industry.

Table 9-5 **Summary of Financial Ratios**

	Ratio	Blackhawk Retail Co.	Industry Average
1.	**Liquidity Ratios**		
	A. Current Ratio $= \frac{\text{Current Assets}}{\text{Current Liabilities}}$	2.2X	2.0X
	B. Quick Ratio $= \frac{\text{Quick Assets}}{\text{Current Liabilities}}$	1.3X	1.0X
	C. Payables Deferral Period $= \frac{\text{Accounts Payable}}{\text{Purchases Per Day}}$	37 Days	40 Days
2.	**Asset Management Ratios**		
	D. DSO Period $= \frac{\text{Accounts Receivable}}{\text{Sales Per Day}}$	43 Days	42 Days
	E. Inventory Carrying $= \frac{\text{Inventory}}{\text{Cost of Goods Sold Per Day}}$	54.7 Days	60 Days
	F. Fixed Asset Turnover $= \frac{\text{Sales}}{\text{Fixed Assets}}$	14X	12X
3.	**Debt Management Ratios**		
	G. Debt to Equity $= \frac{\text{Total Liabilities}}{\text{Shareholders Equity}}$	1.3X	1.6X
	H. Times Interest Earned $= \frac{\text{Operating Profit}}{\text{Interest Expense}}$	8.7X	6.5X
	I. Fixed Charge Coverage $= \frac{\text{Operating Profit}}{\text{Int. Exp.} + \text{Lease Oblig.} + \frac{\text{SFP}}{(1 - \text{TR})}}$	8.7X	6.5X
4.	**Profitability Ratios**		
	J. Profit Margin $= \frac{\text{Net Income After Tax}}{\text{Net Sales}}$	9%	6%
	K. Return on Assets $= \frac{\text{Net Income After Tax}}{\text{Total Assets}}$	28%	18%
	L. Return on Equity $= \frac{\text{Net Income After Tax}}{\text{Shareholders Equity}}$	63%	30%

FINANCIAL TOOLS OF ANALYSIS

There are a number of tools that can be used to analyze financial statements other than common size analysis and ratio analysis. In order to gain a better grasp of the potential to use financial statements, four tools will be introduced. The four tools are: (1) concept of Zero Working Capital, (2) DuPont Analysis, (3) Basic Defensive Interval, and (4) Sustainable Growth. These tools illustrate the potential for credit managers to become creative. Knowing both how and when to use a particular tool requires the use of a considerable amount of judgment.

Zero Working Capital

Net working capital is the difference between current assets and current liabilities. An average company invests about 20 cents into net working capital for each dollar in sales. If a treasurer can cut down on the investment into net working capital, the costs to carry the net working capital can be reduced.

The concept of zero working capital is attained when current assets less current liabilities are equal; then the net working capital is zero. A treasurer could strive to cut down on the level of current assets or increase the level of current liabilities to move toward the goal of zero working capital. Attaining zero net working capital may not be feasible; yet it becomes an important focal point because of the cost of capital associated with carrying working capital. It also creates problems for operating managers.

For example, cutting the DSO and moving toward just-in-time inventory then delaying the payments on accounts payable could each contribute to moving a treasurer toward a goal of zero working capital. The side effect is that it is a challenge to cut DSO and inventory carrying periods. Moreover, suppliers could be upset if accounts payable are not being paid in a timely manner.

The primary purpose for introducing zero working capital is to suggest a need to look beyond a number and appreciate the cause for the number being what it is. Zero working capital needs to be analyzed to get at the cause for the situation. If it is deliberate, it can make a business more profitable. On the other hand, zero working capital can also reflect severe liquidity problems and a looming bankruptcy. The challenge is for credit managers to recognize the root cause of the situation.

DuPont Analysis

The internal management at the E.I. DuPont de Nemours and Company is credited with creating an approach to financial statement analysis. DuPont Analysis has a primary purpose of getting the users of financial statements to recognize that one financial ratio can actually be influenced by several possible focal points. There are actually two equations that have been handed down as components of DuPont Analysis.

The first DuPont Equation focuses upon Return on Equity (ROE). The equation is shown below:

$$\text{ROE} = \frac{\text{Net Income After Tax}}{\text{Total Assets}} \times \frac{\text{Total Assets}}{\text{Common Equity}}$$

The owners of a business are usually interested in improving their ROE. The equation suggests that the ROE can be improved upon if the individual components are examined. The next step would be to consider focal points that lead to increasing the ROE such as changing pricing, cutting expenses, cutting asset levels, or using more debt.

The Blackhawk Retail Company will be used to illustrate the DuPont calculation. The 2003 Income Statement from Table 9-1 and the 2003 Balance Sheet found in Table 9-3 will be used. The ROE is calculated by dividing the net income after tax of \$500 by the total equity of \$800 to arrive at an ROE of 63%. The same result is obtained by using the DuPont Equation below:

$$\text{DuPont Equation:} \quad \text{ROE} = \frac{500}{1{,}810} \times \frac{1{,}810}{800} = 63\%$$

The second DuPont Equation is often referred to as the Extended DuPont Equation. This equation also focuses upon ROE; however, the equation includes more potential focal points. The Extended DuPont Equation is shown below:

$$\text{ROE} = \frac{\text{Net Income}}{\text{Sales}} \times \frac{\text{Sales}}{\text{Total Assets}} \times \frac{\text{Total Assets}}{\text{Common Equity}}$$

To illustrate the extended DuPont Equation, the 2003 Income Statement in Table 9-1 and the 2003 Balance Sheet in Table 9-3 for Blackhawk Retail are used below:

$$\text{Extended DuPont Equation:} \quad \text{ROE} = \frac{500}{5{,}450} \times \frac{5{,}450}{1{,}810} \times \frac{1{,}810}{800} = 63\%$$

By examining the components that are used in the extended DuPont Equation, a broad-based focus can be examined in order to improve the ROE. For example, the profit margin could be improved, asset turnover could be improved, or the company could use more financial leverage. This approach allows management to consider various goals to improve the return on equity.

DuPont Analysis is an approach that involves critical thinking. Too often, financial analysis can become mechanical in nature. By providing multiple focal points, the critical thinking skills are demonstrated to be fundamental to the use of financial analysis. This broad-based focus that involves critical thinking is the main purpose for illustrating the DuPont Equations.

Basic Defensive Interval

Various tools can be used to analyze companies. The Basic Defensive Interval (BDI) can be useful as a tool to measure the severity of a liquidity problem in a given situation. For example, the liquidity of e-commerce companies is sometimes marginal; they tend to burn through cash quickly without generating profits. BDI can be useful to gauge the severity of the liquidity problem.

BDI involves a straightforward, two-step calculation. The first step is to calculate the daily operating expenses, which include cost of sales and operating expenses divided by the number of days in an accounting period. The second step is to divide the defensive assets—which include cash, marketable securities, and accounts receivable—by the daily operating expenses derived in step one. Cash, marketable securities, and accounts receivable are also called quick assets; they represent access to cash in a short period of time.

To illustrate the BDI, the 2003 Income Statement in Table 9-1 and the 2003 Balance Sheet in Table 9-3 for Blackhawk Retail will be used.

Step 1.	Cost of Goods Sold	3,870				
	Operating Expenses	708				
	Daily Operating Expenses	4,578	÷	365	=	12.54
Step 2.	Cash	45				
	Marketable Securities	150				
	Accounts Receivable	650				
	Defensive Assets	845	÷	12.54	=	67.38 Days

The Basic Defensive Interval for Blackhawk Retail is 67.38 Days. The BDI suggests that if sales fall off, there is enough liquidity to cover expenses for a little over two months. Markets for products can dry up in a hurry. Creditors would want to know whether or not the Blackhawk Retail management has alternative sources of liquidity.

The main reason for studying BDI is to point out that certain financial tools can take prominence in particular instances. For example, the BDI could be crucial to a credit manager when a business loses a key customer or in a situation where a marketplace dries up overnight. Credit managers need to become proficient in using tools such as the BDI. Proficiency often comes through experience.

Sustainable Growth

The ability to continue to expand a business is often a key focal point when analyzing customers. Businesses that grow rapidly often experience growing pains. By focusing upon sustainable growth credit, managers have another useful tool.

Sustainable growth provides the maximum rate at which sales can expand through the support from internally generated funds. Too often, businesses fail to adequately plan for expansion by lining up the necessary external funds. Trade creditors often suffer as a consequence because the funds are not available to service obligations.

The calculation is relatively straightforward. Sustainable growth is calculated by multiplying the Return on Equity by the Earnings Retention Rate. The Return on Equity is calculated by dividing net income after tax by common shareholders equity from the prior year. Using the prior year is a departure from the ROE calculation that is typically used; the prior year ROE is used because the calculation is future oriented. The earnings retention is calculated by subtracting dividends from the net income after tax for the current year and then dividing by the net income after tax from the current year.

Blackhawk Retail will be used to demonstrate sustainable growth. The data from the 2003 Income Statement in Table 9-1 and the 2002 and 2003 Balance Sheets found in Table 9-3 will be used. The dividends are not in the financial statements; assume that dividends are 75% of the earnings for Blackhawk Retail.

$$\text{Return on Equity} = \frac{\text{2003 Net Income}}{\text{2002 Common Equity}} = \frac{500}{725} = 69\%$$

$$\text{Retention Rate} = \frac{\text{2003 Net Income less 2003 Dividends}}{\text{2003 Net Income}}$$

$$\text{Retention Rate} = \frac{500 - 375}{500} = 25\%$$

$$\text{Sustainable Growth} = \text{ROE} \times \text{Retention Rate} = 69\% \times 25\% = 17\%$$

The sustainable growth rate for Blackhawk Retail is 17%. This suggests that if the expected growth rate is higher than 17%, the company will need external funds or it will have to make changes in certain operating policies.

The main purpose for introducing sustainable growth is to point out the fact that a calculation can be used to pinpoint questions that credit mangers should be asking. For example, are external funds available to support growth? If debt is to be used, how much risk will be created with a higher debt load to service? Does management have flexibility in altering operations if the growth does not materialize? If the managers for your customers have not considered the questions, the management may not be competent.

Financial analysis skills unfold gradually. The four tools used in this section serve as examples of the types of critical thinking that is potentially applied to credit analysis. Other tools will be explored in the next chapter of this book. Not only do these skills require critical thinking, but they also require the need to keep current with changes in the accounting profession. There are numerous potential accounting-related stumbling blocks that credit managers should be prepared to encounter.

PROBLEMS USING FINANCIAL STATEMENTS

The Bankruptcy filings for Enron, Global Crossing, and WorldCom have one common denominator: accounting issues. In order to use financial statements to make credit decisions, several types of accounting issues and problems must be addressed. Problems range from access to timely information, and the way in which accountants report information, to the actual interpretation of the information available. Credit managers need to become adept at posing questions.

Scrutinizing Footnotes. Footnotes should disclose pertinent accounting information such as inventory valuation, depreciation policies, contingent liabilities, off-balance sheet financing, and the disclosure of certain pertinent events. For many smaller businesses, the credit analyst simply does not have footnotes available. When footnotes are available, they should be carefully scrutinized. Yet, the obligations for special purpose entities that were used by Enron Corporation could not be easily detected. Enron's financial statements were so misleading that the company had to restate prior years' financial statements, which wiped out reported profits and led to (at the time filed) the largest bankruptcy filing in U.S. history.

Revenue Recognition. Recognizing revenue that is not earned can mislead the users of financial statements. For example, Global Crossing used a vehicle called a swap to recognize an increase in revenue. In essence, the swap entailed trading rights to the use of cable resources with other firms. Accounting rules allowed the swaps to be categorized as revenue, misleading investors and contributing to a bankruptcy filing. Xerox Corporation is another business that erred in revenue recognition. Xerox booked over $3 billion in revenue prematurely; the company was forced to restate financial statements from the previous four-year period.

Improperly Capitalizing Expenses. Expenses should be matched to the accounting period in which revenue is recognized. WorldCom can be used as an example of the improper capitalization of expenses. WorldCom may have hidden $3.8 billion in expenses that were capitalized as assets that then showed up improperly in their balance sheet. Recognition of the expenses would have wiped out profits. WorldCom filed a Chapter 11 bankruptcy in July 2002. The WorldCom bankruptcy replaced the Enron bankruptcy as the largest business to file a bankruptcy in U.S. history. Sometimes profits are an illusion; credit managers would be hard-pressed to be able to detect the WorldCom type of an accounting irregularity.

Changes in Accounting Rules. The Financial Accounting Standards Board (FASB) issues rules that public accountants must adhere to. For example, FASB 141 and FASB 142 established new standards to account for the valuation of business combinations and the amortization of goodwill.

The new rules require that acquisition goodwill have an annual test for the impairment of goodwill. This means that goodwill being amortized can vary significantly from year to year. The new accounting rule could have a significant impact on the income statement. This type of rule change makes trend analysis difficult.

Book Value vs. Market Value. Land purchased 50 years ago that is carried at book value may be undervalued. Credit analysts should cultivate a habit of questioning the valuations used by accountants. Liquidation value is usually substantially lower than book value. Moreover, market value could be higher than either book value or liquidation value. Market value is often based upon appraisals, which can vary widely based upon the aggressiveness of the appraisal.

Extraordinary Items. Significant write-offs of losses or recognition of gains can make comparisons difficult. One issue that relates to this topic is the American Institute of Certified Public Accountants (AICPA) decision to exclude losses and costs from the September 11, 2001 disasters from extraordinary items. The logic of categorizing costs as extraordinary is not always clear.

Timing Issues. The accounting period in which revenue is recognized and expenses are reported should be questioned. Moreover, the balance sheet does not always indicate the true timing of all future cash flow. For example, deferred taxes may be recognized if an asset is sold or they may be perpetuated if the asset is retained.

Industry Comparisons. A number of problems can surface when comparing a company to an industry. New economy businesses differ from old economy businesses. For a seasonal industry, if the fiscal year-ends do not coincide, then the comparisons can be very misleading. When accounting practices vary, comparisons can also be misleading. Finally, if a company operates in several industries, the business may need to be broken down into segments to make a valid industry comparison. When a credit manager is extending credit to a subsidiary of a company, the financial statement should be a consolidating statement. A consolidating statement shows the individual subsidiary's position. A consolidated statement combines the subsidiary with the parent.

Technology Issues. Maintenance of records and the use of electronic audit trails are both issues in accounting that carry over to credit managers. Arthur Andersen was found guilty of document shredding in the Enron case; this has led to Andersen's demise. Credit managers need to cooperate with both external and internal auditors when their firm is being audited. A disaster-recovery mechanism should be in place. Technology-related education and training should receive a high priority. Information security should be in place to maintain the privacy for credit department records.

International Financial Accounting. The standards used by FASB are not in place on a worldwide basis. In certain countries, it looks like you are driving on the wrong side of the road; assets are on the right side of a balance sheet while liabilities appear on the left side. There is an International Accounting Standards Board working on common standards. The primary barriers are regulation, such as our Securities and Exchange Commission, and a lack of uniform accounting rules from country to country. Analyzing financial statements from foreign companies can be considered to be a challenge.

Accounting problems and issues require the ongoing attention of credit personnel. Perhaps the best way to keep in touch with the various types of accounting concerns is to attend professional meetings. Both NACM and many of its local affiliates have seminars that deal with accounting issues on a regular basis. Perhaps this topic will receive even more attention with all of the high-visibility bankruptcies that can be related to accounting issues.

CHAPTER 9: FOLLOW UP

Recap of Important Concepts

1. For credit managers, GAAP is sometimes an obstacle to overcome. Since auditors have considerable latitude in reporting financial statements, credit analysts need to become adept at recognizing accounting procedures. Moreover, since accounting rules change, credit analysts need to keep in touch with the new standards used by auditors.
2. The reliability of financial statements varies widely. Audited statements should be scrutinized for the type of auditor's opinion. Personal statements should be signed and dated. The reliability of unaudited statements leaves the credit analyst with much less confidence in relying on financial statements.
3. Common size analysis is an effective approach to financial statement analysis. Common sizing an income statement and a balance sheet over three years can establish operating trends. Industry data is readily available to make comparisons using common size data.
4. Financial ratios can be used to provide detailed insights into the creditworthiness of a business. Ratios can be compared to an industry to reveal strengths and weaknesses for a business.
5. Liquidity ratios are particularly important to short-term creditors. The Current Ratio, Quick Ratio, and Payables Deferral Period each provide insights into the liquidity of a business.
6. Asset Management Ratios are used to measure the effectiveness of management. The Days Sales Outstanding, Inventory Carrying Period, and Fixed Asset Turnover provide a barometer of the management for the largest assets in the balance sheet.
7. Debt Management Ratios are important to long-term creditors. The Debt to Equity Ratio, Times Interest Earned, and Fixed Charge Coverage ratios indicate a firm's ability to manage debt.
8. Profitability Ratios tend to show the effectiveness of the overall management of the business. The Profit Margin, Return on Assets, and Return on Equity each provide an indication of the capability of the managers running the firm.
9. Several financial tools of analysis are couched in the use of financial statements. Zero Working Capital is a way of thinking. A controller may be deliberately slowing down payments to increase profitability at the expense of suppliers.

10. DuPont Analysis broadens the approach to using ratio analysis. DuPont Analysis can be used to shape decisions internally. A credit analyst could use DuPont Analysis to identify the root cause of certain problems.
11. The Basic Defensive Interval can be used to take a close look at liquidity. Creditors are often most concerned with short-term solvency. This calculation is particularly relevant for an e-commerce company that experiences a rapid cash burn rate.
12. The sustainable growth calculation can be used to question companies that are growing rapidly. These are often the types of companies that will experience growing pains in the near future.
13. Financial statement analysis can become quite sophisticated. Interpreting footnotes, recognizing accounting rules, and changes in accounting practices each pose unique reporting problems that need to be recognized and then carefully interpreted.

Review/Discussion Questions

1. In terms of being the most reliable, which auditor's opinion is the best one available?
2. What problems tend to surface when credit managers rely upon personal financial statements?
3. Why should a credit manager consider saving the envelopes in which financial statements are mailed?
4. Data for Ming Research Company and its industry appear below:

	Ming Research in $	Industry Average in %
Cash	10,000	4%
Accounts Receivable	260,000	33%
Inventory	200,000	33%
Net Fixed Assets	150,000	30%
Accounts Payable	250,000	25%
Long-Term Debt	250,000	25%
Common Equity	120,000	50%
Sales	1,200,000	100%
Cost of Goods Sold	850,000	65%
Operating Expenses	200,000	15%
Interest Expense	100,000	10%
Income Tax	20,000	4%
Net Income After Tax	30,000	6%

   a. Calculate the common size balance sheet and income statement for Ming Research.
   b. How does Ming Research common size analysis compare to the industry? Be specific.
   c. Calculate the ratios in Table 9-5 for Ming Research.
   d. Discuss the financial position of Ming Research by identifying any strengths and weaknesses that you perceive.
5. Select an annual report of your choice.
   a. Common-size the balance sheet and the income statement for two years. What changes have occurred in the percentages?
   b. Perform a ratio analysis for the two most recent years. Comment on any changes or trends that you can recognize.
   c. Compare the results from your selected company to an appropriate industry. Comment on any differences that you deem to be important.
   d. Discuss the overall strengths and weaknesses of the company that you have selected.
6. Which of the tools of analysis discussed in the chapter do you believe is most useful to a credit analyst? The tools discussed were Zero Working Capital, DuPont Analysis, the Basic Defensive Interval, and the Sustainable Growth Model. Please support your choice with sound reasoning.

Test Your Knowledge

1. Explain why a Balance Sheet is an important source of financial information for a credit manager.
2. How can an income statement be a useful tool for credit analysis purposes?
3. Give examples of ratios that can be used to analyze a company for each of the following:
   a. Liquidity
   b. Asset Management
   c. Debt Management
   d. Profitability
4. Provide the formula and discuss the usefulness of each of the following ratios:
   a. Quick Ratio
   b. Debt to Equity Ratio
   c. Fixed Asset Turnover

    d. Times Interest Earned
    e. Return on Assets
5. What are some of the problems encountered by a credit analyst when trying to make an industry comparison? Be specific in your response.
6. Carefully summarize each of the four audit opinions used by public accounting firms. Focus your response on the reliability of the opinions.
7. Days Sales Outstanding can generate some misleading interpretation. Discuss the potential limitation of DSO when sales volume is changing.
8. While analyzing the footnotes to a customer's financial statement, you detect a large lease obligation. What impact does the lease have upon your credit analysis? Is there any ratio useful to creditors that take the lease obligation into consideration? If so, explain.
9. A new customer has submitted an unaudited financial statement to you. As a credit analyst, are there any means available to you to verify any of the assets or liabilities that appear in the balance sheet?
10. An existing customer of yours submits a current financial statement. The statement shows a substantial increase in inventory as a common size percentage. What questions would you like to pose to your customer concerning the change in inventory?
11. You receive an audited financial statement from a new customer. After comparing the common size income statement to companies of similar size in the same industry, you notice that the "Cost of Goods Sold" is much lower than the industry norm. What questions would you pose to your new customer concerning this difference?
12. Select an annual report of your choice and perform the following calculations (instructors should consider the use of one particular company if this question is to be reviewed via an in-class discussion):
    a. Determine the Net Working Capital.
    b. Perform a DuPont Analysis.
    c. Calculate the Basic Defensive Interval.
    d. Calculate the Sustainable Growth Rate.

    Based upon your calculations, pose three questions for each calculation (12 total questions) that you would like to ask the treasurer of the company.

Credit Management Online

www.bloomberg.com—This is a commercial site that makes certain information available free of charge. Bloomberg provides quick access to current stock market information and business news.

www.cfo.com—CFO Magazine hosts this site. The site includes articles from the periodical that pertain to issues such as accounting, auditing, GAAP, cash management, risk management, regulation, and education.

www.dnb.com—D&B has several financial statement related products available that are geared toward meeting the needs of credit managers. Financial ratio information together with industry norms can be purchased under D&B subscription arrangements.

www.edgar-online.com—Subscription service to financial information is available at this site. This site is not affiliated with the U.S. Securities and Exchange Commission. Certain information available at this site can be obtained for free at the site hosted by the Securities and Exchange Commission.

www.freeedgar.com—This site requires user registration. Subscription services are available to users including D&B reports. This site is not hosted by the Securities and Exchange Commission.

www.hoovers.com—Hoovers makes current market information, industry information, and company information available. Reports from brokerage firms can be purchased at this site.

www.rmahq.org—The bank trade association RMA provides annual statement studies to subscribers. Common size data together with 16 financial ratios are available. The ratios are broken into quartiles by SIC code.

www.sec.gov—The U.S. Securities and Exchange Commission hosts this site. Public companies are required to furnish financial information that is available for free at this site. There is a quick Edgar tutorial at the site that will accelerate becoming familiar with the information available. Accounting rules and enforcement actions can be reviewed at the site.

www.yahoo.marketguide.com—Yahoo makes comparative data available for the company, industry, sector, and S&P 500. The information is free of charge. Numerous ratios are calculated and made available by typing in the ticker symbol for publicly traded companies.

www.zacks.com—Zacks is a commercial site that makes stock market information and financial ratio information on public companies available for free. A ticker symbol is used to look at the company profile; click on the whole enchilada for detailed financial ratio information.

References Useful for Further Reading

Ainsworth, Pennie, et al. *Introduction to Accounting.* Boston: Irwin McGraw-Hill, 2000.

Emery, Gary W. "Sustainable Growth for Credit Analysis." *Business Credit* (February 2000): 35-39.

Firth, Michael. "Auditor Provided Consultancy Services and Their Associations with Audit Fees and Audit Opinion." *Journal of Business and Finance Accounting* 29 (2002): 661-693.

Foster, Sheila, and Cynthia Bolt-Lee. "New Competencies for Accounting Students." *The CPA Journal* (January 2002): 68-71.

Gallinger, George. "The Defensive Interval: A Better Liquidity Measure." *Business Credit* (September 1997): 26-28.

Gallinger, George. "A Framework for Financial Statement Analysis, Part 1: Return on Asset Performance." *Business Credit* (February 2000): 40-43.

Gallinger, George. "A Framework for Financial Analysis, Part 2: Financial Leverage and Return on Equity." *Business Credit* (March 2000): 33-35.

Gallinger, George. "A Framework for Financial Analysis, Part 3: Tax Effects on Profitability and Sustainable Growth." *Business Credit* (April 2000): 33-36.

Giles, Jill P., and Richard C. Jones. "Accounting and Auditing Issues Surrounding the September 11 Disasters." *The CPA Journal* 71, 11 (November 2001): 10-11.

Heffes, Ellen M. "New Economy Business and Accounting." *Financial Executive* (June 2001): 62-63.

Jacobs, Jay J. "Materiality: It's Not the Same Old Concept Anymore." *Pennsylvania CPA Journal* (Summer 2002): 36-40.

Lewis, Deborah S. "Analyzing Financial Statements." *Internal Auditor* (September/October 2001): 44-48.

Rittenberg, Larry E. "Lessons for Internal Auditors." *The Internal Auditor* (April 2002): 32.

Rosen, Al. "Debt or Equity." *Canadian Business* (October 15, 2002): 25.

Schwartz, Don. "What Price Global Accounting Standards?" *The CPA Journal* (May 2001): 40-48.

Strauss, Norman. "International Financial Accounting Standards: Now the Hard Work Begins." *Financial Executive* (September 2001): 70-71.

Wilson, Arlette C., and Dan Heilger. "Running the Annual Tests for Impairment of Acquisition Goodwill." *Mergers and Acquisitions* (November 2001): 38-40.

Chapter 10:

Cash Flow Analysis and Valuation Essentials

"As long as investors fancy valuations on reported earnings that march steadily upward, you can be sure some managers and promoters will exploit GAAP to produce such numbers, no matter what the truth may be."[1]

–Warren Buffet, Chairman
Berkshire Hathaway Corp.

Cash flow analysis builds upon the concepts introduced in the preceding chapter. Cash flow analysis is an indispensable tool available to assist credit managers. In a climate where accounting rules are being questioned routinely, an understanding of the application of cash flow to credit decision-making is more important than ever.

Through the use of cash flow analysis, a credit analyst can more fully understand the operations of any business. Moreover, one of the most useful applications for cash flow analysis is the application to corporate valuation. Corporate valuation tools have become important focal points. Valuations are often based upon corporate profits that have the potential to drive management into using aggressive accounting techniques.

The **Key Learning Objectives** in Chapter 10 are to:

1. Understand the various definitions and terms commonly referred to as cash flow.
2. Analyze a balance sheet using specific cash flow analysis tools.

---

[1]Warren Buffet, cited in Dana Wechsler Linden, "Lies at the Bottom Line," *Forbes* (November 12, 1990): 106.

3. Examine focal points for the analysis of the Statement of Cash Flows.
4. Focus on the Income Statement by using discounted cash flow as a tool for cash flow analysis by developing a thorough focus upon leveraged buyout (LBO) analysis.
5. Introduce the basics of corporate stock valuation techniques, which are essential to credit managers.
6. Examine cash flow-based tools useful to credit managers in measuring liquidity and bankruptcy prediction.

CASH FLOW

The specific definition used to define cash flow can vary. An economist might define cash flow as the actual cash entering or leaving the firm. An accountant could refer to cash flow as the net income after tax plus the non-cash operating expenses. For most companies, the non-cash operating expenses are depreciation, but sometimes depletion, amortization, and deferred taxes are included as non-cash operating expenses. The study of cash flow analysis draws heavily from the areas of accounting and finance.

For the credit analyst, cash flow represents internally generated funds that can be used to service debt. There are a number of transactions that can make an income statement misleading. For example, expenses could have been reported but not yet paid. Revenue could have been earned but not yet received. Therefore, the income statement often varies significantly from the actual cash inflows and outflows of a firm. The actual cash flows are what is important to the creditor.

Earnings before interest, taxes, depreciation, and amortization is often referred to as EBITDA. The use of EBITDA has become a popular measure to gauge funds available to service debt. However, EBITDA has been discredited to some degree because it does not consider non-cash expenses due to an increase in accounts receivable or inventory. EBITDA also fails to consider debt service, such as the retirement of principal and interest.

One trend in financial marketplaces has been to focus upon free cash flow. Historically, the definition of free cash flow has been the cash flow less dividends. A more contemporary definition of free cash flow is the cash flow that remains after subtracting all dividends and all capital budgeting expenditures that are essential to allow the firm to operate as a going concern; this definition is much more widely embraced by the financial community. The contemporary definition of free cash flow recognizes the fact that fixed assets must be replenished over time in order for operations to continue in the long run.

Cash flow analysis tools are a particularly important focal point for credit analysts. Cash flow analysis of individual financial statements is often quite revealing. The next three sections of this chapter will provide useful tools of analysis for the Balance Sheet, Statement of Cash Flows, and Income Statement.

CASH FLOW ANALYSIS AND THE BALANCE SHEET

Cash flow analysis is often complex. In order to facilitate mastering the essentials of cash flow analysis, specific focal points for analysis will be identified. The most important tools of analysis that pertain to the balance sheet are: (1) the sources and uses of funds concept, and (2) the Cash Conversion Cycle. A detailed discussion of both of these tools will follow.

Sources and Uses of Funds Concept

The sources and uses of funds concept is a focus upon change in balance sheet accounts. All changes in account balances represent either a source or a use of funds. The total "sources" must equal the total "uses" during any given accounting period when analyzing the balance sheet.

Sources and uses can be readily categorized by using the following concepts:

A. Source
- A decrease in any asset account
- An increase in any liability or equity account

B. Use
- An increase in any asset account
- A decrease in any liability or equity account

Table 10-1 provides a balance sheet for Konerko Production Company. The columns represent the January 1 balances, the December 31 balances, and the source or use of funds during the period. Note that the total sources must equal the total uses.

The data in Table 10-1 show a balance sheet analysis for Konerko Production Company that identifies sources and uses of funds. A credit analyst can identify specific account changes and then use analysis skills to determine whether the changes are favorable or unfavorable. For example, long-term bonds were retired using mainly short-term debt. Is the change due to favorable interest rates? Will the short-term debt have to be refunded? If so, what is the likelihood of a bank pulling the plug on a short-term line?

Note that in Table 10-1, the totals for the current assets and the total assets are left off the analysis of sources and uses. This prevents double counting any changes.

An analysis of the balance sheet using a sources and uses of funds approach is usually helpful to identify where a business is heading. All of the sources and uses that are pinpointed in this type of analysis carry through to a firm's Statement of Cash Flows. This statement will be discussed later in this chapter.

One caveat concerning sources and uses may need an explanation. Although "Accumulated Depreciation" is an asset account, when this account increases, a source is generated; when accumulated depreciation decreases, funds are used. This is because accumulated depreciation is a contra-asset. The rules for a source and use are revised for any contra-account. In a very similar way, the rules for debits and credits change when working with contra-accounts in accounting.

Cash Conversion Cycle

For most companies the two largest current assets in a balance sheet are accounts receivable and inventory. The largest current liability is usually accounts payable. The Cash Conversion Cycle considers the time over which receivables, inventory, and payables flow through a business. The survival of many businesses can hinge upon a change in the Cash Conversion Cycle.

The Cash Conversion Cycle is a straightforward calculation. Three of the ratios presented in Chapter 9 are used to calculate a firm's Cash Conversion Cycle. The following equation can be used to calculate the Cash Conversion Cycle:

$$\textbf{Cash Conversion Cycle} = \text{Days Sales Outstanding} + \text{Inventory Carrying Period} - \text{Payables Deferral Period}$$

Table 10-1 **Konerko Production Company**
Balance Sheet Analysis of Sources/Uses

	Jan. 1	Dec. 31	Source	Use
Cash	10	15		5
Short-Term Investment	15	10	5	
Accounts Receivables	205	190	15	
Inventory	230	240		10
Fixed Assets (Gross)	200	220		20
Accumulated Depreciation	60	70	10	
Land	40	40		
Accounts Payable	200	210	10	
Accruals	70	65		5
Short-Term Debt	130	170	40	
Bonds	100	50		50
Common Stock	100	100		
Retained Earnings	40	50	10	—
Total Sources and Uses			**90**	**90**

For example, if a business has a DSO of 35 days, an average inventory of 45 days, and an average accounts payable deferral period of 30 days, the Cash Conversion Cycle would be 50 days. The business would strive to shorten the Cash Conversion Cycle without losing sales. Credit analysts should note that by increasing the payables deferral period to 40 days the Cash Conversion Cycle would be cut to 40 days.

The accounting purist may note that the elements of the Cash Conversion Cycle are not pure offsets. In other words, the size of receivables, inventory, and payables are not equal, so the results are in need of practical interpretation. Yet the Cash Conversion Cycle can often serve as an alarm to creditors by pinpointing a severe problem in working capital management.

CREDIT ANALYSIS OF THE STATEMENT OF CASH FLOWS

In November of 1987, the Financial Accounting Standards Board (FASB) issued statement number 95, which required a specific financial statement known as the Statement of Cash Flows. FASB has been issuing the statements that govern financial accounting since 1972. The

Table 10-2 **Direct Method**
Operating Activities Section SCF

Cash Flow from Operating Activities:		
Cash Receipts:		
Sales Revenue	$10,000	
Interest/Dividend Received	100	
		10,100
Cash Payments:		
Purchases	3,000	
Operating Expenses	3,000	
Interest Payments	100	
Income Tax	1,000	
		7,100
Net Cash Flow from Operations		**$3,000**

Statement of Cash Flows replaced the Statement of Changes in Financial Position.

The purpose of the Statement of Cash Flows is to provide information about a company's cash receipts and payments during an accounting period. The statement is broken down in three types of activities: operating, investing, and financing.

1. *Operating Activities.* These activities affect net income. They include cash inflows such as cash receipts from customers. Cash outflows such as wages, expenses, and taxes are included. In effect, operating activities have the impact of changing the income statement from an accrual basis to a cash basis.
2. *Investing Activities.* The acquisition or divestiture of long-term assets and marketable securities are reported in this section. Loans are also reported in this section.
3. *Financing Activities.* The issuance of stock or bonds is an inflow in this section. Any stock repurchases, debt retirement or dividend payments are outflows in this section. An analysis of financing activities can help to detect a change in the use of financial leverage.

The Statement of Cash Flows can be prepared using either of two formats: the direct method or the indirect method. The direct method adjusts each item in the income statement from an accrual basis to a cash

Table 10-3 **Indirect Method**
Operating Section SCF

Cash Flow from Operating Activities:		
Net Income		$2,000
Adjustments to reconcile net income to net cash provided from operation activities:		
Depreciation	1,000	
Decrease in Account Receivable	4,000	
Increase in Inventory	(1,000)	
Decrease in Accounts Payable	(2,000)	
Decrease in Taxes	(1,000)	
Net Adjustments		1,000
Net Cash Flow from Operations		**$3,000**

basis. Table 10-2 shows the operating section of a Statement of Cash Flows (SCF) using the direct method.

Table 10-2 shows that net cash flow from operations is $3,000 when using the direct method. Credit analysts should note that an income statement format is used when the direct method is used.

Most large companies use the indirect method to prepare the Statement of Cash Flows. The two methods produce the same results. The difference is in the individual line items that are listed in the operating activities section of the statement. The indirect method does not adjust all of the income statement items necessary to convert from accrual to cash accounting. Instead, only activities that impact the adjustment of net income to net cash flow from operations are reported separately.

The indirect method is demonstrated in Table 10-3. The net cash flow from operating activities is $3,000. This amount will always be the same when the results of the direct or indirect methods are compared.

The investing and the financing activities sections are the same under the direct or indirect methods. A complete Statement of Cash Flows is presented in Table 10-4.

The Statement of Cash Flows in Table 10-4 shows a complete statement through the use of the indirect method. Most credit analysts tend to scrutinize the statement to see if funds are being generated internally or externally. In addition, credit analysts may be able to detect a mismatch of funds. For example, if long-term assets are being funded with short-term liabilities, there is an increase in interest rate risk.

Certain ratios can become useful to the analysis of the Statement of Cash Flows. One such ratio is cash flow from operating activities divided by interest expense. The higher the ratio, the better the debtor's ability to service debt. Another important ratio for trade creditors to consider is the ratio of cash flow from operating activities divided by the total current liabilities in the balance sheet. The results provide a measure of a debtor's ability to service short-term credit obligations.

The formatting differences can make the Statement of Cash Flows appear to be complex. However, if credit analysts can keep in mind that the purpose of the statement is simply to identify sources and uses of

Table 10-4 **The Bowman Company Statement of Cash Flows for the Year Ended December 31, 2003**

Cash Flows from Operating Activities:		
Net Income		$2,000
Adjustments to reconcile net income to net cash provided by operating activities:		
Depreciation	1,000	
Decrease in Accounts Receivable	4,000	
Increase in Inventory	(1,000)	
Decrease in Accounts Payable	(2,000)	
Decrease in Taxes	(1,000)	
Net Adjustments		1,000
Net Cash Flow from Operating Activities		3,000
Cash Flows from Investing Activities:		
Purchase of Equipment	(5,000)	
Proceeds from Sale of Land	2,000	
Net Cash Provided by Investing Activities		(3,000)
Cash Flows from Financing Activities:		
Proceeds from Issuing Stock	3,000	
Dividends Paid	(1,000)	
Net Cash Provided from Financing Activities		2,000
Net Increase in Cash		2,000
Cash at Beginning of Year		3,000
Cash at End of Year		$5,000

cash, the analysis is simplified. By breaking the statement into three sections, credit analysts can concentrate on the pertinent changes that have taken place in a business.

PRO FORMA CASH FLOW ANALYSIS OF THE INCOME STATEMENT

In order to provide a clear explanation of valuation techniques, a cash flow model will be introduced. The cash flow model is commonly used to value corporations in a merger, initial public offering (IPO), division spin-off, or leveraged buyout (LBO). This model is widely used in valuing corporate assets. It will be demonstrated through the use of an LBO analysis.

A cash flow model is based upon the development of pro forma income statements. The basis of the model is that the value of any asset is the future cash flows discounted to obtain their net present value. An iterative process can be used by changing key variables. By changing these key variables, the riskiness of the transaction can be more fully understood. This is done by using a computer model that is run over and over to obtain a range of values for a firm.

An understanding of the basic principles of corporate finance is essential to working with concepts related to discounted cash flow models. Students who have not taken a finance course can gain a more thorough appreciation of these concepts by referring to a college-level finance textbook. In particular, the present value concept, cost of capital, and capital budgeting chapters introduce essential skills useful to perform this type of analysis.

A financial analyst might use a model that extends out over a 10-year period so that long-term risk can be scrutinized. For simplicity, a four-year model will be demonstrated. The model will be used to value an LBO candidate by projecting out future income statements. The projected net cash flows will then be discounted back to time zero to obtain their net present value.

Application of a Cash Flow Model to an LBO

Cash flow models have numerous applications. One of the most common applications of a cash flow model is LBO analysis. By focusing upon an LBO, the merit of considering numerous pieces of information will be demonstrated. Once the quantitative model is developed, the next focus will be placed upon the equally important qualitative concerns. An assessment of the overall approach will then be discussed.

The pro forma income statements in Table 10-5 show projected net cash flows in each year under analysis. Note that in 2006 there is an extra line item, called the terminal value, of \$517. This amount is the expected value of the LBO Candidate Co. at the end of 2006. The terminal value is calculated below:

LBO Candidate Co.
Calculation of the Terminal Value in 2006

$$\text{Value of LBO Candidate in 2006} = \frac{\$94(1.10)}{.30 - .10} = \mathbf{\$517}$$

The numerator in the above equation is obtained by multiplying the free cash flow in the terminal year of analysis, which is \$94 in 2006, by the whole number one plus the assumed growth rate after 2006, which is estimated at 10%. The denominator is the cost of equity for the LBO candidate, estimated to be 30%, less the growth rate after the terminal year of 10%. The value of the LBO candidate at the end of the analysis time horizon is \$517.

The final step in the valuation of the LBO Candidate Co. is to discount the net cash flows. Since the cash flows represent flows to equity investors, the appropriate discount rate is the cost of equity. In this example, the cost of capital is 30%. This rate of 30% indicates that equity investors require a 30% return. As market conditions change, this rate changes.

The numerators in the equation used in the final step use the net cash flow, which is the bottom line of the pro forma statements in Table 10-5. The denominators provide the present value of the projected cash flows; this is done to consider the time value of money. The following equation shows the cash flows discounted at the cost of equity in order to obtain the value of the LBO Candidate Co.

LBO Candidate Co.
Discounting the Net Cash Flows (in Thousands)

$$\frac{70}{(1.30)^1} + \frac{77}{(1.30)^2} + \frac{85}{(1.30)^3} + \frac{611}{(1.30)^4} = \mathbf{\$386}$$

Table 10-5 **LBO Candidate Company**
Projected Post LBO Income Statements

(000s Omitted)	2003	2004	2005	2006
Sales[1]	1,000	1,100	1,210	1,330
Cost of Goods Sold[2]	500	550	605	665
Gross Profit	500	550	605	665
Operating Expense[3]	200	220	242	266
Operating Profit	300	330	363	399
Interest Expense[4]	100	110	120	130
Net Income before Tax	200	330	243	269
Income Tax[5]	60	66	73	81
Net Income after Tax	140	154	170	188
Retentions[6]	70	77	85	94
Free Cash Flow	70	77	85	94
Terminal Value[7]				517
Net Cash Flow	**70**	**77**	**85**	**611**

[1]Sales growth is estimated at 10% per year.
[2]The Cost of Goods Sold is estimated at 50% of sales.
[3]Operating Expenses are estimated at 20% of sales.
[4]Interest expenses should include both interest before and after the LBO.
[5]Income tax is estimated at 30% of pre-tax income.
[6]Retentions are used to fund growth and are roughly equal to annual depreciation expense.
[7]The terminal value is the estimated value of the LBO candidate at the end of the final year being analyzed.

The cash flow analysis suggests that the LBO Candidate is worth \$386. The \$386 represents the value to the equity investor, assuming all inputs are accurate. A major error in an estimate used in the analysis or a change in specific variable projections over time could result in serious errors in the valuation.

There are practical concerns when working with pro forma analysis. The best LBO candidates have stable predictable cash flows in each year of analysis. However, this is often not the case. For example, one LBO candidate that ran into problems included a 30% growth rate in net cash flows; however, the actual cash flows that occurred went down 7% after the LBO.

There are two popular risk assessment techniques that credit analysts may consider when using cash flow models. These techniques are sensitivity analysis and scenario analysis. Both techniques entail reconstructing the pro formas.

Sensitivity analysis involves changing one key variable, such as sales growth, to determine the result on the net cash flow for an LBO candidate, a merger target, or a business valuation. Other variables that may be changed include expenses such as interest rates, the operating expenses, and tax rates. The discount rate is also subject to change.

When several variables are changed simultaneously, the process is called scenario analysis. For example, if sales go down, expenses go up and the economy falters, a worst-case scenario would result. For credit analysts, the likelihood of a change in key variables demands use of considerable judgment.

The cash flow model used to evaluate an LBO is the same type of a model that can be used to value common stock, a merger target, an IPO, or a division spin-off. However, there are several other approaches used to perform this type of valuation. The important point to focus upon is that if revenue or expense estimates are off, the valuation will be not be accurate.

Qualitative Concerns in an LBO

There is no one standard definition for an LBO. An LBO could be defined as any situation where a corporation changes its capital structure by substituting debt for equity The important implication to credit managers is recognition of a high-risk situation.

When a company borrows money, retires stock, and pays a substantial dividend to prevent a takeover, the transaction is called a leveraged cash out (LCO). The risk inherent in an LCO can be just as great as the risk inherent in an LBO. A division spin-off could also result in an undercapitalized business. An understanding of the details of high-risk accounts mandates internal policies and controls to monitor total exposure. Knowledge of the qualitative details of LBO funding is essential to dealing effectively with highly leveraged transactions.

The funds provided in the majority of LBO transactions essentially come from three sources and follow a three-tier layering that involves varying degrees of risk for the participants.

1. *Senior Bank Debt.* Commercial banks are the provider of 30% to 60% of funds in typical LBOs. Banks normally obtain up-front fees anywhere from .5% to 4% of loans.

   Banks have the advantage of holding collateral in an LBO. Moreover, banks diversify by industry and geographic area through the use of participation agreements with other banks. Even though banks are collateralized and diversified, the Federal Reserve monitors the overall LBO exposure at banks.

2. *Mezzanine Debt.* Mezzanine debt is more commonly known as the junk bond layer. Generally 20% to 45% of the funds provided in a typical LBO are through use of these types of instruments. Interest rates vary from 2% to 10% above the rate charged on senior funds. Moreover, underwriting fees tend to run from 2% to 3% of the funds raised.

   Mezzanine debt is unsecured and, in almost all cases, is subordinated to the senior bank lender. Historically, investors have been adequately compensated with interest rates that have been high enough to offset the high level of default risk. However, the collapse in the junk bond market in late 1989 and 1990 far exceeded prior default rates.

3. *Equity Investors.* The total equity in an LBO is generally between 10% and 20% of the funding. However, the trend is for new transactions to include a higher proportion of equity. For creditors, the increased equity cushion is a welcome trend.

   There are usually two types of equity in an LBO. First, the management team may contribute to the total funding. The management commitment is important to creditors since it signals confidence in the project. The more management equity, the safer the account for the creditor. Usually the management team will receive additional incentives in the form of stock options.

   The second type of equity investment is usually contributed by either an LBO fund or by venture capitalists. Kohlberg, Kravis, Roberts & Co. and the Blackstone Group are two of the best-known LBO funds. There are several other funds run by smaller companies. The equity fund will generally place significant restrictions on the management team to maximize its control. The equity fund may have an ultimate goal of taking the LBO public, which is sometimes called a reverse LBO.

Assessing LBO Credit Quality

The funding mix that can be used to create an LBO impacts upon the credit quality. Credit analysts need to be aware that a particular funding source will try to protect its own interests first. As business conditions change the overall risk associated with a particular LBO needs to be assessed. Some of the important focal points to monitor the riskiness of an LBO include:

- *The Business Plan.* If profit margins were tight before the LBO, they will probably remain tight after the LBO. Management should be willing to explain where the company is going after the LBO. Another question to be addressed is: Will assets be carved out in order to retire debt?
- *The Growth Rate.* Post-LBO sales growth factored into the pro forma is often not achieved. Companies with a strong market position obviously have an advantage. Also, products that are not susceptible to a rapid technological change provide more predictable cash flows.
- *The Expenses.* Companies with strong unions may not gain anticipated wage concessions after an LBO. Companies that use commodity products, such as oil in the manufacturing process, may have too much volatility in their Cost of Goods Sold to justify extending trade credit after an LBO.
- *Debt Load.* The times interest earned coverage is useful to determine the ability to service the debt load under alternative scenarios. If sales go down and costs go up, will the business have an escape mechanism to survive? The higher the interest expense, the greater the problems if the numbers in the pro forma do not materialize.
- *Over-Estimating the Price of the LBO Candidate.* Major LBO failures have occurred because the price paid for a target was too high. The average American company has a price-earnings ratio of about 25 to 1. Sometimes a simple process such as multiplying earnings by 25 to arrive at a price can be compared to the results used with a sophisticated model. Basic intuition can often help the credit manager recognize that the price paid in an LBO was far too high. When the price is too high, the LBO invariably has a greater likelihood of failure.
- *Industry Factors.* Credit managers should focus industry concerns upon the core business. If the LBO candidate is a low-cost producer, the LBO has a better chance of surviving. On the other hand, if the competition initiates a price war, the business might not survive.
- *Changes in the Economy.* A sound LBO should have limited sensitivity to changes in the business cycle. If a core business is cyclical, such as the housing industry, an LBO is usually not appropriate. If the LBO has debt that is tied to an index, a quick increase in interest rates could take the LBO into bankruptcy.

When these qualitative factors are considered together with the quantitative pro forma cash flow analysis, credit managers can gain meaningful insight. The ultimate decision to extend credit into an LBO is always based upon judgment. Cash flow analysis combined with qualitative analysis is the superior approach to making the most informed business valuation decision.

STOCK VALUATION ESSENTIALS FOR CREDIT MANAGERS

Credit managers should understand how stocks are valued. The growing list of bankruptcies at companies such as Enron, Global Crossing, and WorldCom can be traced to accounting gimmicks. Stock valuation techniques are closely related to the potential for huge accounting frauds.

There are a number of ways in which common stock can be valued. The most common approach is to use good fundamentals. Good fundamentals seemed to go out of vogue during the latter half of the 1990s. Perhaps an examination of fundamental analysis for common stock valuation can be a valuable resource for credit analysts.

Warren Buffet is probably the most widely recognized fundamental analyst. Buffet is the chairman of Berkshire Hathaway Inc. He does not receive any stock options, and his annual salary is only $100,000. Although Buffet's principles seemed out of vogue during the 1990s, Buffet is now once again considered the most highly regarded stock picker in the world.

Buffet subscribes to the principles of his mentor, Benjamin Graham. Graham is the co-author of *Security Analysis*, which is sometimes referred to as the bible of fundamental analysis. Graham is also the author of *The Intelligent Investor*. These books are very highly recommended resources for those readers who are interested in Buffet's approach to stock valuation techniques.

Corporate officers are often under pressure to generate an improvement in earnings. Stockholders simply want to see the value of their investments go up. The pressures can lead to numbers games that can potentially compromise the quality of the financial information reported.

The web site for free EDGAR, the Securities and Exchange Commission site, is www.sec.gov/edgar.shtml. This site has a number of resources available that are potentially useful to both credit managers and to investors. Some of the information available includes:

The *8-K* is a report that includes any material events that are occurring or significant corporate changes.

The *10-K* is a report that is more inclusive than a typical company annual report.

The *10-Q* is the quarterly report that is more abbreviated than an annual 10K report.

A *Proxy Statement* is also called a Schedule 14-A; it reflects all issues for which the stockholders will be voting on.

A *Prospectus* is a thorough disclosure of financial information that is made available prior to issuing any new debt or equity to the public.

Fundamental analysts use public information to employ several stock valuation techniques. They consider the economy, the industry, and the individual stock; this is called a top-down approach. Fundamental analysts often use the following techniques: (1) price-earnings ratio, (2) market-to-book value ratio, (3) market-to-EBITDA ratio, (4) market-to-sales, (5) dividend models, (6) cash flow models, and (7) multiples of unique visitors to web sites.

Price-Earnings Ratio. The market price per share compared to the earnings per share is used. If the market price is $20 and the earnings per share is $1, the price-earnings ratio is $20. Ethics could be compromised by increasing the recognition of revenue or by not recognizing certain expenses; either situation could increase profit and the implied price. If officers are rewarded through stock options, they could purchase the stock at the option price and then turn around and sell the stock. Market participants rely upon timely and accurate information from accountants.

Market-to-Book Value. Book value is the difference between assets and liabilities; it is commonly referred to as owner's equity. The basis for using this approach is a comparison of the market price per share to the book value per share. This is another multiplier approach similar to the price-earnings ratio. If assets are not properly reported, the user can be deceived.

Market-to-EBITDA. Using a multiple of earnings before interest, taxes, depreciation, and amortization is a focus on excluding unusual items found in the income statement from the multiple used in the valuation. This approach is also subject to manipulation.

Market-to-Sales. Using a multiple of sales is often deemed to be crude. Expenses are not part of the process. Yet in industries where there are no profits, a security analyst stretches to find some way to value stock. If revenue is not being properly recognized, the technique is very misleading.

Dividend Models. By projecting future dividends and then discounting them at the investor's required rate of return less the growth rate in future dividends, an implied price can be obtained. There are several dividend models, and each is based upon a different growth rate in future dividends. If management is not honest about reporting profits, the results using the model will be off target.

Cash Flow Models. The model used to illustrate LBO cash flow analysis in the previous section of this chapter can also be used to value common stock. The models rely upon accurate accounting information.

Unique Visitors to Web Sites. As amazing as it may seem, e-commerce companies were being valued based upon the number of unique visitors to web sites. There was reporting of fraudulent information concerning visitors to web sites as management tried to pump up the price of certain stocks. This approach is unusually crude. Needless to say, the blowup in e-commerce stocks has discredited the approach.

Each of the stock valuation models has a focus upon return, timing, and risk. At least in theory, if the inputs were accurate, the models would all lead to the same implied stock valuation. The models suggest what the stock is worth intrinsically—not what the stock is actually selling for in the marketplace. For example, if the implied stock price is $20 and the actual market price is only $15, the stock would be perceived as a good buy.

Stock valuation techniques are subject to considerable manipulation. Keep in mind that the market price is the collective evaluation of the stock price by all market participants. Confidence in management and accounting data are central to each approach using fundamentals. Remember that accounting gimmicks can be used to manipulate the stock price.

Market expectations may tempt managers to manipulate data to mask problems. Credit managers should be aware of the pitfalls and then not be bashful about questioning the numbers. The skills employed in stock valuation can be beneficial because they demonstrate the focal points used in the investment community. These focal points should be examined closely when considering where to look for the accounting gimmicks.

CASH FLOW BASED CREDIT TOOLS

Academia has developed a number of financial tools of analysis that are based upon cash flow analysis. The final section of this chapter will delve into two models that rely upon cash flow analysis. First, Emery's Lambda Index will be used to examine liquidity. Next, Altman's Z-score will be presented as a measure of financial solvency. Both tools have particular relevance to credit management applications.

Emery's Lambda Index

The Lambda Index was developed by Gary Emery, a professor of finance at the University of Oklahoma. The index is useful as a measure of a firm's liquidity. The value of the Lambda Index is that it incorporates cash flow uncertainty into consideration; traditional measures of liquidity, such as the current ratio and the quick ratio, fail to consider the uncertainty of cash flow.

All of the information used to calculate Emery's Lambda can be culled from financial statements. Variations on Emery's formula exist; however, the focus here is limited to Emery's formula. There are three factors that are used in the equation, which is shown below:

$$\text{Lambda} = \frac{\text{Initial liquid reserve} + \begin{array}{c}\text{Total anticipated net cash flow}\\ \text{during the analysis horizon}\end{array}}{\text{Uncertainty about net cash flow during the analysis horizon}}$$

The first term is the *initial liquid reserve*. Cash, marketable securities, and any unused bank lines are included in this term. The unused bank lines can be found in the footnotes to the financial statement. These are funds that can be quickly converted into cash.

The second term in the numerator represents an arithmetic average of the *cash flow from operations* during the prior four years. This number is found in the statement of cash flows; it is the cash flow generated from operating activities. The number is positive if the average during the past four years has been positive; however, if the average has been negative, it is subtracted from the first term.

The third term, which is in the denominator, represents the standard deviation of the cash flow from operations during the past four-year period. The standard deviation is calculated by using the cash flow from operations during the prior four-year period. In finance, the standard deviation is used to measure total risk using the variability of returns. The higher the standard deviation, the greater the risk.

Standard deviation is a bit tricky to calculate, so an example will be used. Many financial calculators are programmed to perform the standard deviation calculation. The data in Table 10-6 show the calculation of the standard deviation for the cash flow from operations for the Prior Co., which is $37,642. This number will be used in the denominator of Emery's Lambda Index.

Emery's Lambda Index for a hypothetical company called Prior Co. will be demonstrated. Assume that the cash plus marketable securities plus bank line availability total $17,000. This is the first term in the index calculation. The second term is the average cash flow from operations which is found in Table 10-6 Step A to be $425,000. The denominator is the standard deviation of the cash flows from operations which is $37,642 also found in Table 10-6 Step F.

$$\text{Lambda Index Prior Co.} = \frac{17{,}000 + 425{,}000}{37{,}642} = 11.7$$

Prior Co. has liquid resources that are equal to 11.7 times its typical operating cash flow needs. The higher the index the more apt a company will have the available liquidity to meet the needs of creditors. The denominator is a key driver in the index. If the uncertainty of cash flow from operations is high, the index drops and a danger signal should be recognized. Also, if a company experiences a severe drain on cash flow from operations due to poor accounts receivable collection and an inability to turn inventory, the index will drop quickly.

Lambda can become a useful gauge for credit managers. The index is useful to measure liquidity for new account analysis and for monitoring existing customers.

Altman's Z-score

Altman's Z-score was developed by Edward I. Altman, a professor of finance at New York University. The model was developed in 1968 to measure financial distress and predict bankruptcy. There are several other bankruptcy prediction models in existence, but the Altman Z-score seems to have stood well over the test of time. The Altman Z-score seems to be the model that most other models are compared to when evaluating bankruptcy prediction models.

The early efforts to predict bankruptcy were based upon univariate models. Such models used one variable, such as a financial ratio, to predict a bankruptcy. The results would be compared against an industry. Needless to say, several variables can have an interactive effect, which

Table 10-6 Illustration of the Standard Deviation Calculation Operating Cash Flows for the Prior Co.

An illustration of the calculation for the standard deviation of cash flow from operations for the Prior Co.:

Year	Cash Flow from Operations
1999	$450,000
2000	370,000
2001	420,000
2002	460,000

Step A. Calculate the average, which is also called the mean:

(450,000 + 370,000 + 420,000 + 460,000) divided by 4 = $425,000

Step B. Calculate the deviation from the mean.

450,000 – 425,000 = 25,000
370,000 – 425,000 = -55,000
420,000 – 425,000 = -5,000
460,000 – 425,000 = 35,000

Step C. Square the deviations from the mean calculated in Step B.

25,000 × 25,000 = 625,000
-55,000 × -55,000 = 3,025,000,000
-5,000 × -5,000 = 25,000
35,000 × 35,000 = 1,225,000,000

Step D. Sum the squares calculated in Step C.

625,000 + 3,025,000,000 + 25,000 + 1,225,000,000 = 4,250,650,000

Step E. Divide by n – 1: there are four years used, so 4 – 1 = 3

4,250,650,000 divided by 3 = 1,416,883,333
(This number is called the variance by statisticians.)

Step F. Calculate the standard deviation. Simply take the square root of the variance in Step E

Square Root of 1,416,883,333 = **$37,642** = **Standard Deviation**

was not taken into consideration with a univariate model. Balance sheet decomposition models then became a focus. These models would focus upon the changing mix of assets such as long term or short term and the corresponding mix of short-term debt, long-term debt, and equity.

Altman designed a multivariate model that was based upon the use of multiple discriminant analysis. Altman's model was designed so that several key variables would be examined simultaneously. The model has its limitations. For example, industry variables are not the same, so the model should be modified to fit a particular industry; many companies are diversified, which makes it difficult to categorize them into any one industry; and the Z-score might be more useful in predicting distress than it is for predicting bankruptcy.

Today, there is considerable experimentation being done with the use of neural network topology models to predict bankruptcy. A neural network integrates computer-based techniques that draw behavior patterns from simulations. Neural network models are potentially useful for credit scoring, the prediction of financial distress, the prediction of slow payments, and the prediction of bankruptcy.

Altman's Z-score is designed to be fit against the data from a particular company. The Altman's Z-score function uses the following equation:

$$Z = .012X1 + .014X2 + .033X3 + .006X4 + .999X5$$

The numbers that appear before each X represent a weight assigned to the variable. Each X is numbered consecutively with the number that appears after the X. The first four variables are expressed as percentages; the final variable is a decimal. The five X variables are explained below:

X1 = Net working capital divided by total assets.

X2 = Retained earnings divided by total assets.

X3 = Earnings before interest and taxes divided by total assets.

X4 = Market value of the common and preferred stock divided by book value of debt.

X5 = Sales divided by total assets.

An application for the Altman Z-score will be made. The data in Table 10-7 are for the Wood Company. The numbers used for the necessary financial data would be culled from the Wood Company financial statements.

Table 10-7 shows the Altman Z-score calculation for the Wood company. A Z-score above 2.99 is favorable. Since the Wood Company has a Z-score of 3.0066, it is not a candidate for bankruptcy. A score below 1.81 is a likely bankruptcy candidate. Altman refers to a Z-score between 1.81 and 2.99 as falling into the zone of ignorance, which means that the bankruptcy prediction is not as definite.

Table 10-7 **Altman's Z-Score Illustration**
The Wood Company

X1 = $500 ÷ $5,000 = 10%	10.0 × .012 =	.12
X2 = $750 ÷ $5,000 = 15%	15.0 × .014 =	.21
X3 = $800 ÷ $5,000 = 16%	16.0 × .033 =	.528
X4 = $2,500 ÷ $2,000 = 125%	125.0 × .006 =	.75
X5 = $7,000 ÷ $5,000 = 1.4%	1.4 × .999 =	1.3986
	Z-Score =	**3.0066**

The Altman Z-score is an example of a financial tool derived through in-depth statistical analysis. The potential to use various tools to analyze financial data can be of significant benefit. Computer software packages often furnish a detailed analysis that includes both a Lambda Index and a Z-score. However, financial data is not a substitute for good judgment. Credit managers should continue to place a high priority on staying in touch with changes as they are occurring.

CHAPTER 10: FOLLOW UP

Recap of Important Concepts

1. Cash flow analysis is an essential skill for credit analysis. The tools useful to complete a thorough cash flow analysis draw heavily from the accounting and finance functional areas of business.
2. Cash flow has several definitions. Moreover there are numerous ways to perform a cash flow analysis. This chapter has provided several definitions of cash flow and numerous tools that can be used to perform a cash flow analysis.
3. When performing a cash flow analysis of a balance sheet the two key focal points should be: (a) the sources and uses of funds concept, and (b) the cash conversion cycle.
4. The Statement of Cash Flows contains three sections that are divided by type of activity: operating, investing and financing. Credit analysis of this statement involves breaking down activities to focus upon the pertinent changes that have occurred.
5. Discounted cash flow models are often used to analyze projected income statements in order to establish a value for a firm. Sensitivity analysis and scenario analysis is performed on key variables in order to identify the risk associated with the valuation. Valuing an LBO, an IPO, a division spinoff or merger is not an exact science. An error in the valuation can lead to serious financial consequences.
6. There are a number of focal points for credit analysts to use to distinguish a sound LBO from a likely LBO disaster. The qualitative analysis needs to be combined with cash flow analysis on an ongoing basis. The financial position of an LBO can change quickly.
7. The valuation of common stock can be a concern because corporate managers may be compromised in attempts to push up stock values so that they can cash in on options. Credit managers should have a foundation in stock valuation to gain insights into potential pitfalls in accounting information.
8. Emery's Lambda Index provides a unique measure of customer liquidity. The index is based upon the riskiness of cash flows.
9. Altman's Z-score is a multivariate model that can be used to forecast financial distress. While there are other bankruptcy prediction models, the Altman Z-score has stood up well to the test of time.

Review/Discussion Questions

1. Distinguish the following terms: "cash flow" and "free cash flow." Which cash flow measure is more important to credit analysis? Why?
2. How are Balance Sheet accounts categorized as a source or use?
3. The Jordan Company has an average accounts payable of 60 days. The company holds inventory for an average of 75 days while the average accounts receivable collection period is 45 days. What is the Cash Conversion Cycle for the Jordan Company?
4. Does the Statement of Cash Flows always follow the same format? If so, explain the format. If not, how can the format vary?
5. Explain how each of the following terms is important to pro forma analysis of an income statement when valuing an LBO:
   a. Projected Post LBO Income Statements
   b. Free Cash Flow
   c. Terminal Value
   d. Discounting the Net Cash Flows
   e. Sensitivity Analysis
6. Provide an overview of the funding layers that are often tiered in an LBO. Try to identify the type of risk taken by each layer that provides funds in an LBO.
7. How does Emery's Lambda Index differ from other traditional measures of liquidity?
8. Examine the five variables that the Altman Z-score uses to predict bankruptcy. Identify an industry where the variables used would not be appropriate.
9. Common stock is valued using several different techniques. How can financial information used to value stock be misused by corporate executives who are paid through incentive based stock options?

Test Your Knowledge

1. What is an LBO?
2. What is the purpose of the Statement of Cash Flows?
3. Identify each of the three sections in the Statement of Cash Flows. What should a credit manager look for when analyzing this statement?

4. The consolidated balance sheet for Thomas Roofing Co. at the beginning and end of 2003 is shown below. Identify the changes as a source or a use in the appropriate column.

	Jan. 1	Dec. 31	Source	Use
Cash	3	4	____	____
Accounts Receivable	40	37	____	____
Inventory	35	39	____	____
Total Current Assets	78	80	____	____
Gross Fixed Assets	46	50	____	____
Accumulated Depreciation	9	11	____	____
Total Assets	115	119	____	____
Accounts Payable	46	41	____	____
Notes Payable	30	29	____	____
Total Current Liabilities	76	70	____	____
Bonds	10	10	____	____
Common Stock	12	15	____	____
Retained Earnings	17	24	____	____
Total Liabilities & Equity	$115	$119	____	____

5. What factors can be used to distinguish a sound LBO from a weak LBO? Be complete and be specific in your response.
6. Calculate the Lambda Index for the Cheli Company based upon the following information:

   Cash flow for operating activities: 1999 = $200,000
   2000 = $210,000
   2001 = $170,000
   2002 = $175,000

   Cash plus marketable securities plus bank line availability are equal to $40,000.

7. The Altman Z-score has been around for several years. What are the strengths and weaknesses of using a bankruptcy prediction model such as the Altman Z-score?
8. Accounting information is particularly important to the investment community. Zero in on at least two valuation techniques used by a fundamental stock analyst that could be influenced by management pressures to keep the stock price at a high level. In other words, if numbers are fudged, which numbers would be likely to benefit top-

level managers who are willing to compromise on accounting rules? How was this accomplished at Enron, Global Crossing, and WorldCom?

Credit Management Online

www.businessweek.com—*Business Week* magazine hosts a web site that provides fresh news concerning hot business topics on a weekly basis. Practical concerns for at least one accounting-related issue appear in almost every issue. There are several links to current business subjects.

www.forbes.com—*Forbes* magazine is the host for this site. *Forbes* seems to do a nice job of stirring up contemporary business issues. There are numerous links to related business topics.

www.fortune.com—*Fortune* magazine hosts this site. The *Fortune* directories can provide a fresh look at the companies that appear in several different *Fortune* directories. There are several useful links to business topics.

www.icpas.org—The Illinois CPA Society hosts this site. The society tackles tough accounting issues. There are links to career services, accounting education, and accounting legislation at the site.

www.nasdaq.com—This is the NASDAQ Stock Market web site. Information concerning NASDAQ stocks can be obtained. There are links to global markets, investor tools, and personal finance at the site.

www.nyse.com—The New York Stock Exchange hosts this site. Information for listed companies can be downloaded for free. There are links to regulation, the trading floor, and the pressroom that can be used to keep in touch with change.

www.valueline.com—Value Line supports an excellent web site for investors. Its company and industry reports include a long-term track record and a short-term forecast. Click on education to gain knowledge that is useful for stock valuation analysis.

References Useful for Further Reading

Altman, Edward I. "A Further Empirical Investigation of the Bankruptcy Cost Question." *Journal of Finance* (September 1984): 1067-1089.

Arnold, Jerry L. "Making Pro Forma Information More Useful." *Financial Executive* (May 2002): 38-41.

Blanchette, Michel, and Garth Livermore. "The Derivative Debate: Criteria to Assess Accounting Practices." *CA Magazine* 134:8 (October 2001): 40-42.

Brigham, Eugene F., and Louis A. Gapenski. *Financial Management.* Ft. Worth, Tx.: Harcourt College Publishers, 2000.

Chlala, Nadi, and Suzanne Landry. "Revenue Recognition: More Stringent Rules on the Horizon." *Ivey Business Journal* 66:2 (November/December 2001): 11-14.

Duncan, James R. "Pressures to Manage Earnings." *CPA Journal* (July 2001): 32-37.

Eaton, Tim V., and James P. Trebby. "Stock Options: Repricing Issues." *National Public Accountant* (December 2001/January 2002): 20-21.

Emory, Gary, and Ronald G. Lyons. "The Lambda Index: Beyond the Current Ratio." *Business Credit* (November/December 1991): 22-23.

Fairfield, Patricia, and J. Scott Whisenant. "Using Fundamental Analysis to Assess Earnings Quality: Evidence from the Center for Financial Research and Analysis." *Journal of Accounting, Auditing and Financial Research and Analysis* (Fall 2001): 273-295.

Gallinger, George. "A Framework for Financial Statement Analysis, Part 4: Statement of Cash Flows." *Business Credit* (May 2000): 32-37.

Gallinger, George. "A Framework for Financial Statement Analysis, Part 5: Prediction of Financial Distress." *Business Credit* (September 2000): 30-33.

Graham, Benjamin, and Warren E. Buffet. *The Intelligent Investor.* New York: Harper Business, Fourth edition, 1973.

Graham, Benjamin, and David L. Dodd. *Security Analysis.* New York: McGraw-Hill, Fourth edition, 1962.

Greider, William. "Crime in the Suites." *The Nation* (Feb. 4, 2002): 11-14.

Howell, Robert. "Fixing Financial Reporting: Financial Statement Overhaul." *Financial Executive* (March/April 2002): 40-42.

Howell, Robert. "Tying Cash Flows to Market Valuations." *Financial Executives* (May 2002): 17-20.

Levinsohn, Alan. "Will Enron's Exploits Bring Reform or Rhetoric?" *Strategic Finance* (March 2002): 63-64.

Marshall, Jeffery. "Lessons from Enron's Debacle." *Financial Executive* (January/February 2002): 10.

Mills, John, Lynn Bible, and Richard Mason. "Defining Free Cash Flow." *CPA Journal* (January 2002): 36-41.

O'Connor, Robert. "Managing High Tech Revenue Streams." *Financial Executive* (May 2002): 44-45.

Reilly, Frank K., and Edgar A. Norton. *Investments.* Ft. Worth, Tx.: Harcourt College Publishers, 2003.

Rosplock, Michael F. "Forensic Financial Tools." *Business Credit* (April 2000): 48-51.

Rosplock, Michael F. "Advanced Analytical Techniques for Performing Forensic Financial Analysis." *Business Credit* (June 2001): 26-31.

Van Arnum, Patricia. "Accounting Reform: Pre and Post Enron." *Chemical Market Reporter* (March 4, 2002): 17-19.

Wood, Dorman L. "SOP 97-2 and Revenue Recognition: Should Credit Executives Know or Care What It Is?" *Business Credit* (September 1998): 12-14.

Zeune, Gary D. "Bloodhounds Not Watchdogs." *Business Credit* (September 1997): 30-32.

Part IV:

Secured Credit and Bankruptcy

Chapter 11

Secured Credit Arrangements and Letters of Credit

"In choosing a bank to handle our export needs we outlined four major requirements: competitive fees, the level of customer service offered, a world-wide presence, and cutting edge technology."[1]

–*Michael M. Zung*
Financial Analyst
Norton Performance Plastics

Identifying the requirements for banking and legal assistance can become complex. A credit manager should be able to establish criteria to select the most appropriate outside support when using secured credit arrangements and letters of credit. This chapter will provide a foundation to use when secured credit arrangements become the appropriate mechanism to control risk.

A secured credit arrangement is one in which a debtor provides collateral to a creditor. There are psychological and financial incentives for credit managers to seek to secure specific accounts. Psychologically, a debtor is more inclined to service an obligation with a secured creditor. Financial incentives are centered upon the ability to generate proceeds from the disposal of assets used as collateral.

The role of the credit manager in utilizing technical skills is contributing to an improved status for the profession. A credit manager can contribute to corporate profitability by recognizing an opportunity to increase sales at an acceptable risk level. The technical skills used to properly secure an account demonstrate the potential for a credit manager to enhance profitability.

[1]Michael M. Zung, "Choosing a Bank for Export Collection Services," *Business Credit* (November/December 1998): 43-44, 47-48.

The **Key Learning Objectives** contained in Chapter 11 are:

1. Identify situations in which credit managers should consider taking a security interest position.
2. Focus on the usefulness of several modes of reducing risk through the use of various credit arrangements.
3. Provide an overview of the Uniform Commercial Code (UCC), the law that governs business transactions in the United States.
4. Analyze the pitfalls in perfecting liens under Article 9 of the UCC.
5. Examine ways in which credit managers can use letters of credit effectively.

In this chapter, the focus is being placed on providing the technical skills essential to work with various sophisticated types of credit arrangements. When secured credit arrangements are properly utilized, creditors reduce risk and contribute to profitability. These arrangements can become complicated by a bankruptcy; the specific concerns of creditors during a bankruptcy will become a focal point in Chapter 12 of this book.

SITUATIONS TO CONSIDER IN THE USE OF SECURED FINANCING

A typical business creditor who sells on open account terms is relying specifically upon the full faith and credit of a purchaser. In the event of nonpayment per terms, the creditor then follows legal procedures to obtain payment. There are not any specific assets that support the unsecured creditor's claim.

Trade creditors are often asked to extend credit into high-risk situations. By obtaining some form of security, a creditor can reduce repayment risk. In the event of nonpayment, a creditor can exercise certain legal rights available to repossess property in order to satisfy a debt.

Examples of situations where secured credit may become useful include:

- *Conversion of an Open Account.* A slow-paying unsecured account can be converted to a secured interest-bearing note.

- *Marginal Accounts.* A start-up business or an undercapitalized business may be too risky to extend credit to without some type of security.
- *A Large One-Shot Deal.* An opportunity to sell an account that cannot justify a high credit exposure can become a situation where security can be used to reduce risk.
- *A Key Account.* A customer who represents a high percentage of total receivables exposure on an ongoing basis may be an ideal candidate to consider for security arrangements.
- *An Export Sale.* International transactions can often entail special types of risk that can be reduced through the use of of a letter of credit.
- *A Long-Term Credit Arrangement.* When a debtor finances a long-term asset, the asset being financed is often secured.

The business credit grantor who obtains security occasionally needs to be able to identify situations when security can be useful. There are certain creditors who will use security for most of their customers. For example, an automobile manufacturer who floor-plans inventory for car dealers may secure all open accounts through a floor-plan inventory financing arrangement. On the other hand, a distributor of metal alloys may only occasionally secure an account. In either case, precise procedures should be established so that the creditor is in a strong legal position in the event of a default by the debtor.

The internal controls that are formulated depend upon the nature of the security. In order to properly use security, a credit analyst should have a complete understanding of the various types of security available. The rest of this chapter will provide a foundation of the pertinent laws and then identify specific opportunities that are available to secure an account.

MODES TO CREATIVELY REDUCE RISK

The one common attribute for any type of security is that it should be of value to the creditor in the event of default. As a general rule, if a business transaction does not make sense without the security, the creditors need to use extreme control when relying upon security. The cardinal rule for securing a transaction is to recognize the probable quick-sale value of collateral and then limit exposure accordingly.

One way of classifying security is to group the collateral by type of agreement. For example, assets could be grouped as real property or personal property. Guarantees could be grouped as personal or corporate. Each classification of security requires specific concerns for the credit analyst to consider.

1. *Real Property.* Real property consists of land, buildings, and anything deemed attached to the land or building. If a creditor accepts real property as security, a public filing is made in the county office. Creditors usually require a title search and can obtain title insurance to protect the creditor against claims not found in a title search.

   Creditors who use real property for collateral should consider obtaining an appraisal to estimate the value of the collateral. Sometimes creditors who believe that they have personal property as collateral can find out that the property is deemed to be real property. If in doubt concerning the status of property, a creditor who relies on personal property should obtain a Landlord Waiver or a Mortgagee Waiver to protect the creditor against claims on assets by a landlord or a mortgage lender.
2. *Personal Property.* Personal property refers to movable assets. All property that is not classified as real property is deemed to be personal property. Personal property can be divided into two categories of goods: (a) those goods kept in the possession of the creditor, and (b) those goods that are in the possession of the debtor.
   A. *A Pledge.* When a debtor places personal property in the possession of a creditor, a pledge occurs. Stocks and bonds can be pledged as collateral. Other assets that are sometimes pledged include the cash surrender value of insurance, a certificate of deposit, or a savings account.

      The creditor should obtain a separate pledge agreement. This agreement authorizes a creditor to sell items pledged in the event of nonpayment. The creditor should take physical possession of items pledged. Finally, creditors should consider notifying an insurance company or bank to block any potential withdrawal of funds by the debtor until the credit commitment is fulfilled.
   B. *Collateral Held by the Debtor.* Typical assets held by the debtor include accounts receivable, inventory, machinery, and equipment. A creditor can perfect a security interest by

following the requirements of Article 9 of the UCC. This type of arrangement is commonly used by suppliers.

Since the topic is somewhat complex, a separate major section of this chapter will be used to develop the subject of perfecting liens under the UCC.

3. *Guarantees.* In general, a business transaction should not hinge solely upon obtaining a guarantee. However, a guarantee does represent a commitment from a third party that can strengthen the position of a creditor. Guarantees may be set up in either of two ways: (1) a Guarantee of Payment, which allows the creditor to present an obligation to the guarantor immediately upon default by the debtor; or (2) a Guarantee of Collection, which requires the creditor to first attempt to collect from a debtor, and if unsuccessful, the creditor may seek payment from the guarantor.
   A. *A personal guarantee* should be signed by the obligor as an individual, not as someone acting in the capacity of an officer of a company. By using a personal guarantee, a creditor can pierce a corporate shield to hold the guarantor responsible for the debt. The guarantor should provide a signed personal financial statement. Be careful because personal assets are often inflated on the financial statement. The creditor can gain a psychological advantage from a guarantor by using a personal guarantee.
   B. *Corporate guarantees* can be difficult to enforce. When a guarantee is obtained from a corporate entity, creditors should consider obtaining a board of directors' resolution that authorizes the corporation to guarantee an obligation. When intercompany transactions are involved, a corporate guarantee can be useful. Also, when a subsidiary is not strong enough to justify open-account terms, a parent company could furnish a corporate guarantee. Selling a joint venture may also provide an opportunity to sell on open-account terms if there are other companies willing to guarantee the obligation of the joint venture.

   Exhibit 11-1 is an example of an Individual Personal Guarantee form. The executed guarantee should be maintained for safekeeping. There are creditors who have collected on guarantees years after writing off indebtedness to bad debts.

4. *Letters of Credit.* A letter of credit is a negotiable instrument that is backed by a bank, in which the bank agrees to pay a vendor upon

presentation and compliance with the terms and conditions specified in the letter of credit. The letter of credit essentially allows a creditor to substitute a debtor's creditworthiness for a bank's creditworthiness. When the documents specified in the letter of credit are accepted by the bank, a *banker's acceptance* is created. Due to the potential complications of working with letters of credit, the final major section of this chapter will sharpen the focus upon using letters of credit.

5. *Mechanics' Liens*. Mechanics' liens are commonly used in the construction industry. This type of lien is placed upon a building, improvements in realty, and in most jurisdictions, on land on which the building is situated. The purpose of a mechanics' lien is to ensure compensation for labor or material furnished for construction purposes. The lien is filed by a contractor, subcontractor, or party supplying labor or materials in the county where the property is located. State laws govern the details that pertain to mechanics' liens.
6. *Trade Acceptances*. A trade acceptance is a form of a time draft. When a creditor ships goods to a customer, the creditor draws a draft on the customer's bank that orders the customer to pay for the goods at a specified time. The creditor can endorse and then discount the

Exhibit 11-1 **Personal Guarantee Form**

Date ____________ 20__

I, ____________________, residing at ________________________________, for and in consideration of your extending credit at my request to (Name of Company) (hereinafter referred to as the "Company"), of which I am ___________, hereby personally guarantee to you the payment at _________________ in the State of _____________ of any obligation of the Company. I hereby agree to bind myself to pay you on demand any sum which may become due to you by the Company whenever the Company shall fail to pay the same. It is understood that this guarantee shall be a continuing and irrevocable guarantee and indemnity for such indebtedness of the Company. I do hereby waive notice of default, nonpayment, and notice thereof and consent to any modification or renewal of the credit agreement hereby guaranteed.

Signature: _________________________

Witness: _________________________
Address: ____

draft or collect from the customer on the date that the draft matures. There are no liens filed. The customer accepts the responsibility to pay, and the draft is not subject to a customer stop payment or a customer claim of nonperformance. Trade acceptances have been popular in Europe for many years; they tend to be used only occasionally in the United States. Trade acceptances are not usually secured by any assets. They provide an alternative way in which to set up a payment arrangement.

Six commonly used modes of protection for creditors have been introduced: real property, personal property, guarantees, letters of credit, mechanics' liens, and trade acceptances. Each of the six modes has its usefulness by reducing certain types of risk. Two of the most complex yet widely used ways to protect trade creditors will be developed more fully: perfecting liens under Article 9 of the UCC and utilizing letters of credit.

THE UNIFORM COMMERCIAL CODE

The legal system that governs business transactions in the United States has been built around state laws. Business laws had been patterned after the English common law legal system, but the state laws varied. The Uniform Commercial Code (UCC) was developed around 1950 and has been adopted by all 50 states in order to make the state laws uniform in nature.

The UCC consists of the following nine articles:

- Article 1: General Provisions
- Article 2: Sales and Article 2A Leases
- Article 3: Commercial Paper
- Article 4: Bank Deposits and Collections and Article 4A Funds Transfers
- Article 5: Letters of Credit
- Article 6: Bulk Transfers
- Article 7: Warehouse Receipts, Bills of Lading, and other Documents of Title
- Article 8: Investment Securities
- Article 9: Secured Transactions, Sales of Accounts, and Chattel Paper

The UCC is now more than 50 years old. There have been a number of revolutionary changes in business practices that could not have been envisioned when the UCC was first adopted. Computer technology and enhancements in communication mandated change. The legal system has a mechanism to keep up with the changes.

There are two main legal groups that are involved in developing business law: the American Law Institute (ALI) and the National Conference of Commissioners on Uniform State Laws (NCCUSL). Both ALI and NCCUSL have been involved in jointly sponsoring laws to unify business laws.

ALI was formed in 1923. It consists of a voluntary group of judges, lawyers, and academics. ALI strives to address uncertainty in the legal system by updating laws so that the laws keep in touch with the changes in business practices.

NCCUSL was formed in 1892. It consists of commissioners from each state who are appointed by their state legislature or governor. NCCUSL examines the laws in a state to determine if certain business practices might be worthwhile to develop uniformly across all states.

ALI and NCCUSL have collaborated in updating the UCC. Each state then has the ultimate decision concerning whether or not to adopt the recommended changes. In 1995, both ALI and NCCUSL recommended changes to the Letters of Credit provisions in Article 5 of the UCC. The changes to Article 5 bring the UCC into conformity with the Uniform Customs and Practices for Documentary Credits, commonly referred to as UPC 500. The revisions to Article 5 of the UCC are generally consistent with UPC 500.

In 1998, both ALI and NCCUSL completed revisions to Article 9 of the UCC. By July 31, 2001, all 50 states had approved the revisions. These revisions are now in effect. Some of the key changes will be discussed in the next section.

Article 9 of the UCC

The purpose of the UCC is to allow the laws that govern business transactions to exist in a uniform manner in all states. The prior section showed how the UCC is divided into nine articles. Article 9 of the UCC pertains to secured transactions involving personal property. In general, personal property includes all property except real estate.

The changes effective under Article 9 of the Code are the first wholesale revisions in almost 30 years. The basic framework remains intact. However, Article 9 now has broader applications. For example, consignment sales now fall under this article. Article 9 now contains specific rules for consumer transactions. Deposit accounts are also included in Article 9.

Documentation deficiencies make Article 9 one of the most frequently litigated sections of the UCC. For the most part, credit managers have become adept at handling the intricacies of the UCC. An attorney could, however, be quite helpful in examining documentation and formalizing procedural concerns.

The two basic documents used to secure personal property are (1) the Security Agreement, and (2) the UCC Financing Statement. There are also a number of other documents that can be useful to a credit manager in connection with the basic documents such as a lien search, a subordination agreement, a board of directors' resolution, or a landlord or mortgagee waiver agreement. The following is an overview of each of the two basic documents and a discussion of other aspects:

The Security Agreement. The customer and debtor agree to certain specific points that govern the lien in the security. Factors such as the specific collateral and the nature of the debt obligation that the collateral secures are included in the security agreement.

The UCC Financing Statement. By properly perfecting a lien on property (properly filing required documents), the Financing Statement becomes a public record acknowledging that a lien exists.

Under the changes in the UCC, the debtor no longer must sign the financing statement. The form has been standardized. A creditor may file a lien but needs the authorization of the debtor to be legally eligible to file the lien. The exact legal name of the debtor must be used. Trade names are not acceptable. To be effective, a lien search that is conducted using the proper name of the debtor should turn up the lien. If a search fails to show up the filing, the filing is not valid.

Another key change under the revised UCC is the location of the filing. For personal property, only one filing is necessary. Liens should be filed with the Secretary of State of the debtor's place of filing registration statements. For example, if a company has filed its corporate charter in the state of Delaware, the lien should be filed with the Secretary of State in Delaware. For a non-registered business, the filing should be made at the executive office if the business has more than one location. For individuals, the filing should be made in the state of the individual's principal residence.

The description of the collateral should be specific in the security agreement; however, the financing statement can include generic descriptions such as blanket liens. Banks sometimes file blanket liens that include all assets now owned or hereafter acquired. It is always preferable to include model numbers and serial numbers of equipment or other complete descriptions of collateral.

If there is any doubt concerning the potential of the security to become a fixture, most attorneys recommend another filing. The second filing should be made in the debtor's county office, or at the place where real estate liens are filed in the jurisdiction.

Exhibit 11-2 contains the standard UCC Financing Statement. The financing statement can be filed electronically in all jurisdictions. Since state laws for filing can vary, some creditors like to use a private company such as Lexis-Nexis Document Services to record liens. Lexis-Nexis performs nationwide filing and search services. Its web site is www.lexisnexis.com.

Documentation Concerns. Creditors should perform a lien search when dealing with secured transactions. The search is used to determine whether any other conflicting liens exist against the debtor. It is always a good idea to search through your own filing to make sure that the lien has been properly recorded.

In general, the first lien filed has a first claim on the collateral. A subordination must be obtained from any creditor that has a prior lien on an asset in order to assure first claim on any collateral. For example, a bank may have a blanket lien on all assets of a company. A creditor can move into a first lien position only after obtaining a subordination from the bank on specific assets. Any leverage to obtain the subordination should be used prior to shipping goods. The bank has a vested interest in making certain the company receives new goods and continues operations so it will be able to subordinate. One exception to the first filing being in a first lien position is the case of a purchase money security interest, which will be discussed later.

A board of directors' resolution should be obtained when there is a question concerning the authority of the person signing the security agreement for the debtor. The board of directors specifically authorizes a particular individual to expressly enter into a secured financing arrangement. Otherwise, a debtor can to try to void a security arrangement because the signor was acting *ultra vires* (beyond the scope of authority).

A waiver from a landlord (if the debtor rents the premises) or a waiver from a mortgagee (if the debtor owns the premises through a mortgage) could be useful. This type of waiver protects the creditor in the event that the debtor fails to pay rent to the landlord or mortgage payments to the

Exhibit 11-2 UCC Financing Statement Form

UCC FINANCING STATEMENT

FOLLOW INSTRUCTIONS (front and back) CAREFULLY

A. NAME & PHONE OF CONTACT AT FILER [optional]

B. SEND ACKNOWLEDGMENT TO: (Name and Address)

THE ABOVE SPACE IS FOR FILING OFFICE USE ONLY

1. DEBTOR'S EXACT FULL LEGAL NAME - insert only one debtor name (1a or 1b) - do not abbreviate or combine names

1a. ORGANIZATION'S NAME				
OR 1b. INDIVIDUAL'S LAST NAME	FIRST NAME	MIDDLE NAME		SUFFIX
1c. MAILING ADDRESS	CITY	STATE	POSTAL CODE	COUNTRY
1d. TAX ID #: SSN OR EIN / ADD'L INFO RE ORGANIZATION DEBTOR / 1e. TYPE OF ORGANIZATION	1f. JURISDICTION OF ORGANIZATION	1g. ORGANIZATIONAL ID #, if any		☐ NONE

2. ADDITIONAL DEBTOR'S EXACT FULL LEGAL NAME - insert only one debtor name (2a or 2b) - do not abbreviate or combine names

2a. ORGANIZATION'S NAME				
OR 2b. INDIVIDUAL'S LAST NAME	FIRST NAME	MIDDLE NAME		SUFFIX
2c. MAILING ADDRESS	CITY	STATE	POSTAL CODE	COUNTRY
2d. TAX ID #: SSN OR EIN / ADD'L INFO RE ORGANIZATION DEBTOR / 2e. TYPE OF ORGANIZATION	2f. JURISDICTION OF ORGANIZATION	2g. ORGANIZATIONAL ID #, if any		☐ NONE

3. SECURED PARTY'S NAME (or NAME of TOTAL ASSIGNEE of ASSIGNOR S/P) - insert only one secured party name (3a or 3b)

3a. ORGANIZATION'S NAME				
OR 3b. INDIVIDUAL'S LAST NAME	FIRST NAME	MIDDLE NAME		SUFFIX
3c. MAILING ADDRESS	CITY	STATE	POSTAL CODE	COUNTRY

4. This FINANCING STATEMENT covers the following collateral:

5. ALTERNATIVE DESIGNATION [if applicable]: ☐ LESSEE/LESSOR ☐ CONSIGNEE/CONSIGNOR ☐ BAILEE/BAILOR ☐ SELLER/BUYER ☐ AG. LIEN ☐ NON-UCC FILING

6. ☐ This FINANCING STATEMENT is to be filed [for record] (or recorded) in the REAL ESTATE RECORDS. Attach Addendum [if applicable]

7. Check to REQUEST SEARCH REPORT(S) on Debtor(s) [ADDITIONAL FEE] [optional] ☐ All Debtors ☐ Debtor 1 ☐ Debtor 2

8. OPTIONAL FILER REFERENCE DATA

FILING OFFICE COPY — NATIONAL UCC FINANCING STATEMENT (FORM UCC1) (REV. 07/29/98)

mortgagee. The waiver by the landlord or mortgagee prevents the landlord or mortgagee from holding a possible prior claim on the creditor's collateral.

When a debtor's name changes, an amended financing statement should be filed to ensure that the lien is properly filed. It is possible to lose a secured status in a bankruptcy proceeding if the filing is seriously misleading. Others parties could be seriously misled. Filing the amended UCC Financing Statement reflecting the name change protects the creditor's interest.

The documentation requirements can be summarized as technical and cumbersome. However, the payoff from a properly perfected lien readily demonstrates the credit manager's utilization of technical skills that can make a significant contribution to an employer.

Remedies for Creditors. In the event of a default, a secured creditor has a right to collateral. If a debtor voluntarily surrenders collateral, the secured creditor may use the proceeds of the collateral to offset debt. When a debtor does not peacefully surrender collateral, the creditor files a lawsuit, obtains a judgment, and then gets a court order to obtain collateral.

The quick-sale value of collateral often does not coincide with the book value of the debt. Any excess received from the sale of collateral belongs to the debtor. In the event of a deficiency, creditors become unsecured creditors for the amount of the deficiency.

As a general rule, the creditors who use Article 9 of the UCC rely upon collateral based upon the estimated quick-sale value. The following guidelines may prove useful for a rough estimate of quick-sale value.

- *Accounts Receivable*. A credit manager should rely upon only 70% to 80% of accounts receivable that are now aged as current.
- *Inventory*. Work in process is often not of any value as collateral. Raw materials and finished goods may justify relying upon 50% of book value, depending upon the secondary market.
- *Equipment*. Delivery and installation of equipment are not of any value. About 80% of the book value may be a justifiable base for equipment. However, the secondary market for the specific type of equipment should be considered.
- *Land and Building*. As a general rule, 80% to 90% of appraised value is used. Location is critically important to the collateral value for real estate.

A few of the common problems that credit managers often associate with perfecting liens under Article 9 of the UCC include:

- Customers are often reluctant to agree to give collateral to a supplier. Negotiation skills are the key to overcoming customer reluctance. Knowing when the creditor has leverage to gain the customer's cooperation is crucial to such negotiations. The credit manager needs to know the customer and be ready to demonstrate a willingness to achieve a mutually agreeable position regarding supply and security.
- Time requirements for filing the UCC form often preclude establishing a properly secured credit arrangement. In a liquidation, it must be remembered that the proceeds from a properly perfected lien are distributed in order of priority claimants. A lien should be perfected over a 90-day period or the lien may be construed to be a voidable preference by a trustee in the case of a bankruptcy liquidation.
- Reliance upon the proceeds generated by the collateral can leave the credit manager with a deficiency. Collateral is not a substitute for sound credit principles and decisions. Caution concerning possible quick-sale market value of collateral after a repossession should be emphasized. A field audit of collateral can help to determine the presence of worthy collateral.

The Case of the Purchase Money Security Interest (PMSI)

There is one particularly troublesome subject that relates to Article 9 and perfecting liens: the Purchase Money Security Interest (PMSI). A PMSI is unique because of the "purchase money" aspect of the specific transaction. Two situations provide opportunities whereby a security interest becomes a purchase money security interest. In both situations, a creditor obtains a priority lien in newly acquired assets.

The first situation occurs when the seller of goods takes a security interest to secure all or part of the sale, using the goods being sold as collateral. For example, a manufacturer or wholesaler selling a product could reduce the credit risk for the vendor by taking a PMSI in the assets sold.

The second situation in which a PMSI can be created is when a third party provides funds to enable a debtor to acquire assets. For example, a bank or finance company could provide the funds for a debtor to purchase assets; these assets are used as collateral by the lending bank or finance company.

Both types of PMSI transactions entail the need for the lien holder to take precautions. Normally, the conflicting security interests rank in priority according to the time the filing is recorded. However, a properly perfected PMSI can have priority over a previously recorded lien. The essential aspect of PMSI transactions is the proper perfection of the security interest.

The credit manager should be concerned with classifying collateral into different categories of goods. For PMSI purposes, goods may be categorized as consumer goods, equipment, or inventory. As remarkable as it may seem, the same item could fall into any of the three categories of goods depending upon the situation. For example, if a doctor bought a microwave oven for use at home, the oven would be classified as a consumer good. If used by the doctor in the office, the oven would be classified as equipment. Finally, if held in inventory by an appliance dealer, the oven would be classified as inventory.

In general, the revisions to Article 9 make it more difficult to attack a PMSI for competing claims. PMSI transactions require the filing of liens with the Secretary of State. Specific filing requirements are influenced by the classification of goods as consumer goods, equipment, or inventory. In order to eliminate uncertainty, the security agreement should specify the manner in which the goods will be used.

Consumer Goods. A credit manager entering into a PMSI transaction in consumer goods is not required to file a financing statement. However, the credit manager's interest in the collateral would not be weakened if a lien is filed.

Equipment. A credit manager taking a PMSI in equipment must perfect a lien on the equipment before or within 10 days after the debtor receives possession of the equipment. By filing before or within 20 days of delivery, the PMSI creditor moves into a first lien position ahead of a previously filed blanket lien that may have covered all equipment. The PMSI lien holder must give new value that enables the debtor to acquire the equipment. Banks or finance companies may want to use a paid proceeds letter when disbursing the funds to an equipment vendor in order to clarify their PMSI position.

Inventory. A PMSI in inventory can be very complex. However, if a credit manager follows the requirements of the UCC and appropriate state laws, a PMSI creditor will receive priority over other blanket security interests in the same collateral.

A PMSI in inventory should be perfected before or at the time the debtor receives possession of the inventory. The PMSI creditor should give written notice via a certified letter to all other creditors who claim a security interest in the inventory of the debtor. The written notice given to the other creditors should state that the PMSI creditor has, or expects to acquire, a purchase money security interest in inventory of the debtor. The letter also should describe the inventory by items or type of product.

There are a few somewhat complex concerns that credit managers could occasionally encounter with PMSI transactions. These concerns include goods that are further processed, commingled funds, inventory proceeds accounts, and the protection of the PMSI stature. These concerns are not often encountered but can become crucial in certain situations.

Article 9 of the UCC requires the use of considerable legal expertise. The law has been updated to meet the needs of the changing business community. There are Business Law courses available at most colleges to gain additional depth in this topic. Perhaps the best way to update skills is through NACM-sponsored workshops, which can be a useful way to become proficient at properly perfecting liens.

LETTERS OF CREDIT

In a letter of credit transaction, a bank promises to pay the beneficiary (creditor) a specified sum upon presentation of the specific documentation. The letter of credit is simply a mode of payment. What is special about a letter of credit is that the credit risk is transferred from the purchaser of goods to the purchaser's bank.

Circumstances in which letters of credit are used can vary dramatically. Moreover, there are specific laws that govern letters of credit. Since over half of the letters of credit issued have discrepancies, credit analysts need to carefully consider the complexities of working with letters of credit.

Standby Letters of Credit

A Standby Letter of Credit is useful when selling to a marginal domestic customer. This type of arrangement is basically a bank guarantee. In the event that a purchaser fails to honor a credit obligation, the creditor may look to the bank for payment.

Exhibit 11-3 shows an example of a Standby Letter of Credit. In this example, the creditor is the beneficiary for an amount not to exceed $80,000. The invoices must be at least 30 days past due in order to draw on the bank for payment. If the customer pays for goods in a timely manner, the letter of credit is never drawn upon. The term "standby" suggests that the bank is standing by to pay in the event of a default.

Article 5 of the UCC applies to any letter of credit that is issued or confirmed in the United States. Also, note that Exhibit 11-3 contains a paragraph concerning UPC 500. The UPC is written into most letters of credit in order to clarify the settling of payments. When Article 5 of the UCC was revised in 1995, it was designed so that it is largely in compliance with UCP 500.

The International Chamber of Commerce (ICC) has established rules for documentary letters of credit. The Uniform Customs and Practice (UCP) were first published in 1933 and have been revised in 1951, 1962, 1974, 1983, and 1994. The current rules are known as UCP 500, which went into effect on January 1, 1994. UCP 500 provides a set of rules used both for international and for domestic transactions.

Exhibit 11-3 **Standby Letter of Credit**

National Bank of Ohio
Columbus, OH

May 1, 2003

The Ethical Creditor Co.
Chicago, IL

We hereby issue in your favor our Irrevocable Letter of Credit for an amount not to exceed $80,000.00 for the account of ___________ and/or _____________ available by your drafts drawn at sight on us and accompanied by the following documents: (1) commercial invoice, (2) copy of truck bill of lading, and (3) your signed statement that the merchandise covered by the invoice has been shipped and a period of at least 30 days has elapsed since the date of the invoice.

This Irrevocable Letter of Credit will expire on December 1, 2003, at our counters in Columbus, OH.

This credit is subject to the Uniform Customs and Practice for Documentary Credits, International Chamber of Commerce Publication Number 500, known as UPC 500.

We engage with you that drafts drawn under and in compliance with the terms of the credit will be duly honored upon presentation if presented on or before the expiring date of this credit.

BY ______________________________
President & Chief Executive Officer

Export Letters of Credit

When the shipment of goods crosses national boundaries, export letters of credit are the most common method of settling payment. A credit manager can reduce the risk of payment problems by obtaining a letter of credit. If the creditor is not comfortable relying upon the credit risk of a foreign bank, the creditor may ask a domestic bank to confirm the letter of credit. By adding a confirmation to a letter of credit, the creditor may look to the credit risk of the confirming bank for payment.

UCP 500 has updated the rules used for letters of credit. Standardized practices, used in various economies and cultures, provide for improved consistency under UPC 500. The export services departments of large U.S. banks often make available one-day seminars to help familiarize credit managers with the UPC 500.

For example, one change established in UPC 500 is that all letters of credit are now irrevocable unless a letter of credit specifically states that it is a revocable letter of credit. This is because the buyer holds the option to revoke or back out of a revocable letter of credit. The UPC 500 does not eliminate revocable letters of credit; it simply means that creditors must watch for the term "revocable" and get it changed before accepting the letter of credit.

Problems Using Letters of Credit

For the creditor who only occasionally uses an export letter of credit, banks will be willing to facilitate letters of credit for a fee. Those creditors who work with letters of credit regularly face numerous types of problems. A few of the typical problems are briefly summarized:

- *Bogus Letters of Credit*. International fraud is not uncommon. When dealing with certain countries, payment arrangements are often difficult. Creditors who have an intuition concerning the validity of a letter of credit should ask their domestic bank to confirm the letter of credit.
- *Bank Fees*. Banks may charge a fee for opening, advising, confirming, amending, extending, accepting, and discounting letters of credit. The fees are always negotiable between the buyer and seller. A seller in a strong position in terms of demand for product may request that the phrase "all fees for the account of opener" be added to the letter of credit.

- *Drafts*. Drafts represent an order to pay the creditor upon acceptance of the documentation in the letter of credit. A sight draft is payable when the drawee bank accepts the draft. A time draft is payable at a specified date after acceptance. Since funds can be tied up for a period of time, the terms specified in a time draft should be considered prior to entering the letter of credit transaction. When a time draft is accepted by a bank, a banker's acceptance is created. Creditors often discount the banker's acceptance at their bank to gain immediate access to funds.
- *Documentation Deficiencies*. Creditors should carefully inspect the terms and conditions in a letter of credit before accepting the letter of credit. An internal documentation checklist is often helpful in minimizing documentation problems. Yet documentation problems occur often. Creditors can request an amendment if the deficiency is detected early. However, UPC 500 is generally considered the operative set of rules to guide credit managers through a documentation deficiency when the UPC is included on the letter of credit.

There is certainly considerable risk borne through problems associated with the use of letters of credit. Yet letters of credit alleviate credit risk when they are used properly. The skills essential for credit managers to master letters of credit will remain at the pinnacle of importance.

CONCLUSIONS

Secured credit arrangements can become one of the most complex topics in credit management. They afford an opportunity to employ skills that demand considerable legal expertise. They also require considerable time to document properly. Moreover, since laws are updated regularly, credit analysts need to keep in touch with changes on an ongoing basis. The benefits derived from reducing risk and contributing to profit are well worth the effort. The final chapter of this book will address bankruptcy issues. Bankruptcy can be closely related to the secured credit arrangements developed in this chapter.

CHAPTER 11: FOLLOW UP

Recap of Important Concepts

1. A secured credit arrangement is one in which credit managers obtain collateral from a debtor. Several situations create opportunities for credit analysts to reduce risk by obtaining security.
2. Real property consists of land, buildings, and anything deemed attached to the land or building. Real property is not often available as collateral to trade creditors; when it is available, there are unique concerns to be addressed.
3. A pledge is created when personal property is placed in the hands of a creditor. Stocks, bonds, certificates of deposit, savings accounts, and the cash surrender value of life insurance are typical types of assets that are pledged.
4. Both personal and corporate guarantees can be used to protect a creditor's interest. Personal guarantees allow a creditor to pierce a corporate shield; they can also provide a psychological incentive. Corporate guarantees are useful when a number of intercompany transactions exist with a debtor and related companies.
5. Mechanics' liens are placed upon real property to make sure that a contractor or subcontractor is compensated for providing labor or material. These liens are commonly used in the construction industry.
6. Trade creditors can use a trade acceptance to potentially strengthen their position when selling marginal customers. The trade acceptance can be discounted at a bank. It is not subject to a customer claim for nonperformance.
7. Article 9 of the UCC is used to perfect liens on personal property held by a debtor. There have been a number of changes made to Article 9 to bring it up to date with current business practices. Accounts receivable, inventory, machinery, and equipment are assets that are often used as collateral.
8. Normally the first filing of a lien prevails in terms of recording a lien on assets under Article 9 of the UCC. There are two exceptions: (a) when a creditor obtains a subordination from another creditor who has filed a prior lien, and (b) when a creditor properly perfects a purchase money security interest.

9. A letter of credit is a mode of payment where the creditworthiness of a debtor is substituted with the creditworthiness of a bank. A standby letter of credit is particularly useful when selling a marginal domestic account. As long as a debtor pays a creditor per agreed-upon terms, the standby letter of credit need not be drawn upon.
10. Documentary letters of credit are the most common method of settling payment on export sales. Credit managers often seek a confirmation from their domestic bank when a creditor is not comfortable with the bank that issued the letter of credit. Credit analysts should anticipate document deficiencies that occur on over half of the letters of credit used. The UPC 500 is particularly important to a credit manager who uses letters of credit for export sales.

Review/Discussion Questions

1. What types of customers are suitable candidates for a trade creditor to consider in the establishment of a secured credit arrangement?
2. What is the difference between a pledge and a secured credit arrangement under Article 9 of the UCC? What type of assets are typically used in a pledge arrangement?
3. How can personal guarantees be useful to protect the interests of a creditor? What factors should a credit analyst take into consideration when considering a personal guarantee?
4. What is the purpose of filing a mechanics' lien? Who has a right to file a mechanics' lien? Where is the lien filed?
5. The following questions relate to Article 9 of the UCC.
   a. Where is a UCC filing recorded?
   b. Does the debtor have to sign a UCC filing?
   c. Why would a credit manager perform a search of UCC filings?
   d. Who should sign the security agreement? If a creditor is unsure of the validity of authority, what safeguards can be taken?
   e. Does the balance owed to a creditor usually coincide with the quick-sale value of an asset? If not, what general guidelines can be used to recognize the potential quick-sale value for assets?
6. Identify three changes made to Article 9 of the UCC as a result of the revisions that became effective July 31, 2001.
7. For a trade creditor, what attributes should a bank possess to represent the interests of the trade creditor who uses letters of credit?

Test Your Knowledge

1. What is a letter of credit?
2. What is the purpose of UCP 500 as it relates to letters of credit?
3. When would a credit manager use a subordination from a bank?
4. Compare and contrast a standby letter of credit with an export letter of credit.
5. Why would a credit manager obtain a confirmation on an export letter of credit?
6. Under what circumstances is a purchase money security interest created? How should a creditor protect a first lien position when obtaining the purchase money security interest?
7. What is the difference between a guarantee of payment and a guarantee of collection?
8. How can a banker's acceptance be created when using an export letter of credit?
9. Compare and contrast a trade acceptance with a banker's acceptance.

Credit Management Online

www.greatland.com—This is a commercial site at which forms for UCC filings can be obtained.

www.liensearch.com—Public records in the United States and Canada can be accessed at this commercial site.

www.law.cornell.edu/uniform/ucc.html—The Cornell University Law School has a considerable amount of material available online concerning the Uniform Commercial Code. Some of the information is free, and other pieces can be downloaded for a fee.

www.lexisnexis.com/documentsolution/about_us.html—This is a commercial site hosted by Lexis-Nexis Document Solutions. There is a considerable amount of information concerning the revisions to article 9 of the Uniform Commercial Code that can be downloaded for free. The site offers a newsletter as well as online filings and searches.

www.mlqattorneyservices.com/ucc.html—Filings and searches can be performed on a same-day basis at this commercial site.

References Useful for Further Reading

Barski, Katherine A. "An Analysis of the Recent Revisions to Article 5 of the Uniform Commercial Code: Letters of Credit." *Commercial Law Journal* 10:2 (Summer 1996): 177-188.

Blakeley, Scott. "Creditor's Claim Unsecured After Debtor's Name Change." *Business Credit* (September 1998): 8-10.

Brinkman, Darren R. "Letters of Credit: The Magic Wand for Minimizing International Credit Risks?" *Business Credit* (November/December 1997): 46-49.

Byrne, James E. "New Rules for Letters of Credit: The International Standby Practices/ISP 98." *Business Credit* (May 1998): 32-35.

Clements, David. "Paperless LCs." *Business Credit* (November/December 2000): 54-55.

Couzzi, Richard. "Trade Acceptance Drafts: The Third Payment Option." *Business Credit* (March 2000): 46-47.

DuPont, Michael, and William M. Hennessey. "A Synopsis of Revisions to Article 9 of the Uniform Commercial Code." *Business Credit* (July/August 2001): 69-71.

Furman, Roger. "Life Becomes Simpler." *US Banker* (December 2000): 62-68.

Gabriel, Henry D. "The Revisions of the Uniform Commercial Code: Process and Politics." *The Journal of Law and Commerce* (Fall 1999): 125-136.

Meadows, Robyn L., Carl Bjerre, and Stephen L. Sepinuck. "The Uniform Commercial Code Survey: Introduction." *Business Lawyer* (August 2001): 1743-1746.

Meyer, Keith G. "A Primer on Purchase Money Security Interests Under Revised Article 9 of the Uniform Commercial Code." *The University of Kansas Law Review* (November 2001): 143-194.

Nathan, Bruce S. "Selling by Consignment: How to Protect Yourself." *Business Credit* (June 2000): 14-16.

Nathan Bruce S. "The Growing Threat of Floating Inventory Liens to Reclamation Claims." *Business Credit* (May 2001): 12-16.

Shaw, Martin. "UPC 500." *Business Credit* (November/December 2001 through June 2002). (This was a seven-part monthly series of articles.)

Weise, Steven O. "An Introduction to Revised Article 9: Part I." *Business Credit* (September 1999): 16-19.

Zung, Michael M. "Choosing a Bank for Collection Services." *Business Credit* (November/December 1998): 43-48.

Chapter 12

Bankruptcy and Reorganization

"A record number of bankruptcies for businesses are being reported. Enron filed the largest Chapter 11 ever, with billions in assets and liabilities. Kmart followed. The notion that a company is simply too large to file Chapter 11 is gone."[1]

–Scott Blakeley, Esq.
Bankruptcy Attorney

The term bankruptcy is sometimes said to have a "broken bench" tradition known as *banca rotta*. In medieval times, in Venice, Italy, when a merchant would fail to repay suppliers in a timely manner, the suppliers would break the benches that displayed the goods for sale. Not only would the merchants have their benches broken, but the common practice included stripping the clothes from the merchant and then tying the merchant to a stake on display in the town square.

Today, the bankruptcy laws are much more debtor oriented. Using readily available legal assistance, most debtors will develop a workout plan prior to actually filing a bankruptcy petition. For the credit professional, there is a need to understand the bankruptcy process. The tactics to consider, in light of the alternatives available, make bankruptcy one of the most complex topics essential to sound credit practices.

Bankruptcy is an integrative subject. In order to master the learning objectives established for this chapter, several of the topics from prior chapters will be useful. Topics such as extending credit, setting up payment arrangements, utilizing cash flow models, appreciating Altman's Z-score model, and arranging security each become an important focal point for bankruptcy analysis.

---

[1]Scott Blakeley, "Chapter 11s on the Rise: Flags and Steps to Protect Your Credit Sales," *Business Credit* (April 2002): 56.

The **Key Learning Objectives** in Chapter 12 include:

1. Review the current bankruptcy data.
2. Understand the various chapters of the Bankruptcy Code.
3. Analyze the priority of claims in a straight Chapter 7 bankruptcy liquidation.
4. Examine the specific concerns of a creditor during a Chapter 11 reorganization.
5. Identify some of the issues, trends, and problems that are bankruptcy-related from a credit professional's perspective.

THE CURRENT BANKRUPTCY SITUATION

The study of bankruptcy is quite timely. Congress has been reviewing new bankruptcy legislation over the past several years. However, at this point the new legislation has not been finalized. The current law was enacted in 1978 and has been amended several times; the most recent substantive changes were made in 1994.

The purpose of bankruptcy is twofold: (1) to provide creditors with an orderly mechanism to assess the risk-reward tradeoff inherent when extending credit, and (2) to furnish honest debtors with a way in which they can move toward a fresh start. One of the key goals is for the legal system to be operationally efficient; this means holding down the legal expenses of the bankruptcy while expediting the process.

According to the Administrative Office of the U.S. Courts, the number of bankruptcies during 2002 was 1,577,651, representing an all-time high. Of the filings, the most were under Chapter 7 and the least were under Chapter 12. A breakdown follows for 2001 and 2002 shown below:

Chapter 7	1,054,975 in 2001 up 5.2% to 1,109,923 in 2002
Chapter 13	425,292 in 2001 up 7.2% to 455,877 in 2002
Chapter 11	11,424 in 2001 down 1.3% to 11,270 in 2002
Chapter 12	383 in 2001 up 26.6% to 485 in 2002

During the first half of 2002, bankruptcy records continued to be broken with filings up to new historic highs. Business filings were down during 2002, but individuals filed at a record pace.

One of the notable trends in bankruptcy filings is the fact that 257 publicly traded companies filed during 2001. The 2001 data set a record for public companies; the number increased 46% from 176 public companies filing in 2000. The slowdown in the economy both domestically and worldwide contributed to the increase in filings in both 2001 and 2002.

Another trend for filings is that very large businesses are declaring bankruptcy. According to Bankruptcy Data.com, seven of the 10 largest bankruptcies occurred from December 2001 to December 2002. Table 12-1 shows the 10 largest bankruptcies since 1980.

Bankruptcy filings have soared to record levels. This chapter will provide an understanding of the basics of the bankruptcy code, then explore essentials of the two key chapters for business filings, and finally, review of some of the key bankruptcy-related issues in credit management.

Table 12-1 The 10 Largest Bankruptcies in U.S. History As of December 27, 2002

Company	Filing Date	Total Prebankruptcy Assets
WorldCom Inc.	July 21, 2002	$103,914,000,000
Enron Corp.	December 2, 2001	63,392,000,000
Conseco	December 18, 2002	61,392,000,000
Texaco	April 12, 1987	35,892,000,000
Financial Corp of America	September 9, 1988	33,864,000,000
Global Crossing Ltd.	January 28, 2002	25,511,000,000
UAL Corp.	December 9, 2002	25,197,000,000
Adelphia Communications	June 25, 2002	24,409,662,000
Pacific Gas and Electric	April 6, 2002	21,470,000,000
M Corp	March 31, 1989	20,228,000,000

Source: BankruptcyData.com

THE BANKRUPTCY CODE

The Bankruptcy Reform Act of 1978 went into effect on October 1, 1979. This was the first major revision of bankruptcy laws since the Chandler Act of 1938. As amended, the Bankruptcy Act of 1978 sets the standards for our current bankruptcy system. There are additional changes that could affect bankruptcy law being discussed in Congress while this book was being written at the beginning of 2003.

When the Bankruptcy Act of 1978 was first passed, all even-numbered chapters were repealed. Since then, one even-numbered chapter has been added. The purpose of the 1978 Act was to streamline and expedite the bankruptcy process. The bankruptcy code consists of the following nine separate chapters:

Chapters 1, 3, and 5. These chapters pertain to general provisions that outline the administration and duties of the parties involved in the bankruptcy proceeding. Chapter 1 contains definitions of the many legal terms used in the bankruptcy code. Chapter 3 contains specific duties such as commencement of bankruptcy, duties of trustees, and the administration of the case. Chapter 5 sets priorities for unsecured creditors, establishes guidelines for nondischargeable debts, identifies preference and other avoidance powers of the trustee, contains duties of the trustee, and contains provisions for creditors' proof of claims.

Chapter 7. This chapter is sometimes referred to as a straight bankruptcy. Business liquidations occur under Chapter 7. Individuals may also file for bankruptcy under Chapter 7. As a matter of fact, most personal bankruptcies are filed as a straight liquidation. Specific liquidation priorities will be developed more fully in a later section of this text.

Chapter 9. Chapter 9 of the code pertains to municipalities and governmental units. The first legislation that allowed for a municipal filing was enacted during the Great Depression in 1934. Since then, fewer than 500 municipal filings have occurred. A Chapter 9 can only be filed on a voluntary basis. There is no provision for the liquidation of assets in a Chapter 9. The bankruptcy process involves filing, confirmation of the plan, and making sure that the plan is properly implemented. The largest Chapter 9 case occurred in 1994; the case involved Orange County, California.

Chapter 11. Chapter 11 pertains to a business reorganization. Most Chapter 11s involve a debtor-in-possession (DIP) of assets; the DIP is attempting to rehabilitate a business. According to the Administrative Offices of the U.S. Courts, there were 11,270 Chapter 11 filings in 2002. The Chapter 11 process is of considerable importance to creditors. Chapter 11 will be developed more fully in a later section of this text.

Chapter 12. The so-called Family Farmer may file a Chapter 12. This chapter is used only with a voluntary petition by family farmers who have debt up to $1.5 million. The purpose of this chapter, which was enacted in 1986, was to provide small farmers with a chance to reorganize debt and retain their land. There were only 13 filings during the year 2000 and an increase to 17 filings during 2001 under Chapter 12.

Chapter 13. Sometimes Chapter 13 is called the Wage Earner Plan. In 2002 there were 455,877 bankruptcy filings that involved a Chapter 13. Individuals with wages or income are eligible to file under Chapter 13. Small businesses are also eligible to file a Chapter 13. To be eligible for Chapter 13, the debtor must have secured debt of less than $871,550 (subject to increases for inflation) and unsecured debt of less than $290,525 (subject to increases for inflation). For the debtor, the advantages of using Chapter 13 are the "cramdown" and "extension" possibilities. A cramdown implies that a repayment plan can be established by the trustee and debtor; it does not include creditor concurrence. The extension of time for repayment in a Chapter 13 can go out over a three-year period; with a trustee concurrence, it goes out over a five-year period to service the debt.

Chapter 15. Chapter 15 establishes the trustee system that is used to administer the bankruptcy code. There are 21 regions that service all bankruptcy courts. Trustees will review cases for debtor fraud. The most typical types of fraud include hidden assets and furnishing creditors with false financial statements. The review of bust-outs also comes within the purview of the U.S. Trustee System. A bust-out can occur through various types of deliberate schemes, often to purchase large quantities and then declare a bankruptcy. To learn more about the U.S. Trustee Program, visit www.usdoj.gov/ust/about_ustp.htm.

Sometimes creditors may refer to a Chapter 22 bankruptcy filing. There is no Chapter 22; the tongue-in-cheek reference to Chapter 22 is used when a company files a Chapter 11 petition twice. Companies such as Trans World Airlines, Montgomery Ward, Crown Books, Converse Shoes, and LTV Steel all went through so-called Chapter 22s.

For most business credit grantors, Chapter 7 and Chapter 11 are the chapters with the highest degree of importance. The mechanics of liquidations under Chapter 7 are important to more fully appreciate the ultimate risk of business failure. The Chapter 11 process poses several challenging questions that are often encountered by business credit grantors. Both Chapter 7 and Chapter 11 of the Bankruptcy Code will be more fully developed in the next two sections of this text.

CHAPTER 7: A STRAIGHT LIQUIDATION

Historically, business schools have emphasized entrepreneurial drive and the success stories in American business. Yet failure is a fact of life. Certain lessons need to be remembered. In particular, a liquidation can be integrated with legal concerns and the financial payoffs to creditors demonstrated through the use of cash flow models by using various parameters.

A Chapter 7 bankruptcy is intended to provide an equitable distribution of assets to claimants on the assets. Claims priority rules establish the liquidating dividends to claimants in accordance with the priority of their claims. Higher priority claims are paid before any distribution to lower priority claims. Pre-petition unsecured claims are near the bottom. However, it is possible for a trustee to negotiate with secured creditors and improve upon a liquidating dividend.

For example, in the majority of liquidations, unsecured creditors do not receive a dividend; these are referred to as no-asset cases. However, a secured creditor may be in a position to negotiate with the trustee and carve out a portion of the secured creditor's claim. A bank that is secured by assets might receive more for collateral by selling off assets than by forcing liquidation. In this instance, a trustee overseeing the proceeding might allow the sale to stray from the claims priority rules.

Although the claims priority rules are sometimes violated, they do provide essential structure. The process of working through a liquidation can be used as a vehicle to provide a foundation for a complete understanding of bankruptcy. Creditors are better able to negotiate with distressed debtors in a Chapter 11 if they understand this rule.

Claims Priority Rules

A Chapter 7 liquidation is subject to a prioritization of claims upon assets. The priorities are clearly established, yet they are often difficult to work through. Proceeds from assets are distributed in a sequence of priorities in a prescribed order.

1. *Secured Creditors*. The secured creditors are first in order of claims on assets. A secured creditor is entitled to have a first claim on proceeds from collateral assets. Any excess amount received from security is returned to the bankruptcy estate. Any deficiency in funds

resulting from the sale of collateral makes the secured creditor an unsecured creditor for the amount of deficiency.

2. *Administrative Expenses.* These expenses represent the cost of preserving the business during the bankruptcy proceeding. Included here are expenses for professional persons used during the bankruptcy, such as accountants and attorneys.
3. *Unsecured Claims for Sales to a Debtor-in-Possession.* The purpose of this priority is to encourage creditors to extend new credit to a bankrupt company. The theory is that the bankrupt company needs inventory to generate new sales and to continue ongoing operations. Only such credit extended after the bankruptcy receives this priority. Creditors need to ascertain that there is a sufficient asset base to cover this priority claim before extending credit to a bankrupt firm. Some companies have a policy of requiring payments on a cash-in-advance basis because sometimes there is not enough money generated from the proceeds to funds these claims.
4. *Wages and Compensation Claims.* Wages earned within three months plus employee benefits earned within six months prior to a bankruptcy filing receive a priority claim limited to $4,150 per wage earner (subject to increase for inflation).
5. *Customer Deposits.* A maximum of $2,100 per claimant (subject to increases for inflation) is next in the order for priority claims. This priority is available to individuals who place a deposit on property or services for personal, family, or household use.
6. *Taxes.* Federal, state, county, or any other type of government agency receives a priority.
7. *Unsecured Creditors.* These claims are often referred to as general creditors' claims. They include the trade creditors, deficiency claims of secured creditors, and debenture holders. A subordinated debenture also holds this type of claim but must turn over proceeds to the party to whom the debenture is subordinated.
8. *Preferred Stockholders.* Preferred stockholders are paid after all creditors are paid in full. Since there is seldom enough available to fund creditors, the preferred stockholders usually receive nothing from the proceeds in the liquidation.
9. *Common Stockholders.* Last in line is the common shareholder who bears the residual risk. Any remaining funds are paid to common stockholders after all other claimants are paid in full.

A superpriority claim can be authorized by a court during a Chapter 11 proceeding. The superpriority claimant has priority over all administrative expenses and other types of pre-petition unsecured claims. Debtor-in-possession financing is a typical example of a superpriority claim being granted to the Chapter 11 debtor's lender.

The court could authorize a superpriority claim when a debtor in a Chapter 11 is unable to obtain new credit during the Chapter 11. If the Chapter 11 proceeding is converted into a Chapter 7 liquidation, the superpriority claimant has the first claim on all unencumbered assets (sometimes behind a Chapter 7 trustee's fees and expenses).

Liquidation Case Study

In order to provide a more complete explanation of the liquidation process, a hypothetical case study will be used. A balance sheet that lists all obligations (claims) at the time of liquidation is furnished in Table 12-2. This balance sheet is used to determine who is entitled to proceeds in the liquidation.

The numbers used in the KPT Manufacturing Company liquidation can be revealing. Note that the owners and bond holders were completely excluded from liquidating dividend payments. Also note that the First Mortgage holders realized a substantial dividend. Finally, note that unsecured creditors were hurt because of a forced sale of assets and the high cost of administrative expenses.

Computer models are available to help credit managers work through various liquidation scenarios. By understanding the implications of a liquidation, credit managers are better able to evaluate the risk-reward tradeoff in a bankruptcy.

The KPT case study is an example of a liquidation using the claims priority rules. By understanding the sequence of the payout for the proceeds, negotiations in a Chapter 11 proceeding can be conducted with a clear understanding of the potential results. A debtor could offer creditors a stake in the securities of a reorganized firm as an alternative to a straight liquidation. This arrangement in a Chapter 11 could violate the claims priority rules, yet it may be in the best interest of all parties involved in the bankruptcy proceeding.

The "what if" scenarios can make liquidation one of the most complex topics in finance. As a matter of fact, in most liquidations the unsecured creditors can only expect to receive a small fraction (if anything) of total claims.

Table 12-2 **KPT Manufacturing Company**
Balance Sheet – June 30, 2003

Cash	$ 25,000	Accounts Payable	$ 750,000
Accounts Receivable	825,000	Accrued Taxes	100,000
Inventory	750,000	Notes Payable to Bank	250,000
Total Current Assets	1,600,000	Total Current Liabilities	1,100,000
Fixed Assets (Net)	400,000	First Mortgage Bonds	400,000
		Subordinated Debentures	300,000
		Total Debt	1,800,000
		Preferred Stock	50,000
		Common Equity	150,000
Total Assets	**$2,000,000**	Total Liabilities and Equity	**$2,000,000**

Assumptions:

1. First mortgage bonds are secured by fixed assets.
2. Bank holds the subordination from the debentures.
3. Proceeds in the liquidation include:
   a. $700,000 from the current assets.
   b. $300,000 from the fixed assets.
4. Administrative expenses are 20% of the proceeds.
5. No accrued wages, pension obligations, or sales to debtor-in-possession are included.

Task: Determine distribution of the $1,000,000 liquidation proceeds working through priorities.

Step 1. First Mortgage Bonds receive $300,000 from the sales of the fixed assets. The bonds are unsecured for the $100,000 deficiency. (See Assumptions 1 and 3.)

Step 2. Administrative expenses receive $200,000. (See Assumption 4.)

Step 3. Accrued taxes receive $100,000 as a priority creditor. (For simplicity, assume no other priority claimants.)

Step 4. Determine the payout percentage for unsecured creditors. The $600,000 paid out so far indicates that $400,000 remained to be paid. The remaining unsecured debt totaling $1,400,000 consisting of: accounts payable $750,000, bank debt $250,000, first mortgage bonds $100,000, and subordinated debentures $300,000.

Step 5. Remaining proceeds ($400,000) ÷ remaining creditors' claims ($1,400,000) = .285714 on the dollar, as follows:

Accounts Payable	.285714 × $750,000 = $214,286
Bank Debt	.285714 × $250,000 = $ 71,429
First Mortgage	.285714 × $100,000 = $ 28,571
Subordinated Debt	.285714 × $300,000 = $ 85,714

Step 6. Funds that would have accrued to subordinated debentures go to the bank. (See Assumption 2.) The $1,000,000 liquidation proceeds are distributed as follows:

	Payout	Book Claim	% of Book Claim
Accounts Payable	$ 214,286	$ 750,000	29 %
Accrued Taxes	100,000	100,000	100
Notes Payable Bank	157,143	250,000	63
First Mortgage Bonds	328,571	400,000	82
Subordinated Debt	0	300,000	0
Preferred Stock	0	50,000	0
Common Equity	0	150,000	0
Administrative Expenses	200,000	0	NA
Total Paid Out	**$ 1,000,000**	**$ 2,000,000**	**50 %**

CHAPTER 11: REORGANIZATION

In a Chapter 11 proceeding, a business attempts to reorganize. The primary focal points include initiating a case and examining the proceeding to include responsibilities of both the debtor and the creditor. In this section of the text, the focus is placed upon the process of a Chapter 11. The final section of this text will delve into some of the complex legal concerns relevant to creditors during a bankruptcy.

Initiating a Chapter 11 Proceeding

A bankruptcy petition is filed in a U.S. Bankruptcy Court. The petition may be filed by a debtor or creditors. A petition may be filed where the principal assets of a debtor are located, typically in the U.S. Bankruptcy Court closest to the corporate headquarters. Alternatively, the petition may be filed in the state of incorporation or other registrations of the debtor. However, the venue may be transferred to another district court in the interest of justice or for convenience. The jurisdiction can be important to a case. U.S. Bankruptcy Courts do not have the same track records for expediting cases or for successfully rehabilitating debtors.

Most bankruptcy petitions are initiated by the debtor. The filing of a voluntary proceeding creates an order of relief. At this time, there exists a stay on collection activity for debt incurred prior to the filing.

An involuntary petition may be filed by creditors under either Chapter 7 or Chapter 11. There are two circumstances in which creditors may file an involuntary petition: (1) When the debtor has 12 or more total creditors, at least three of the creditors whose claims, not subject to bonadife dispute, aggregate more than $11,625 (subject to increases for inflation) may join together to file a petition. (2) When the debtor has fewer than 12 total creditors, any one creditor with a claim of at least $11,625 can file the involuntary petition.

Normally a debtor has 20 days to contest an involuntary petition. The court could order a trial to determine whether or not the involuntary petition is acceptable to grant relief to the petitioners. Creditors are urged to seek legal counsel prior to filing an involuntary petition. Relief on an involuntary petition is conditional on proving the debtor's inability to pay debts as they mature.

Regardless of the voluntary or involuntary nature of the petition, once a bankruptcy case is initiated, an automatic stay is created. The stay protects the debtor from both collection and judicial activities that originated before the commencement of the bankruptcy proceeding.

Chapter 11 Timeframe

A large Chapter 11 proceeding could easily take two years to complete. However, the LTV Corp. bankruptcy case spanned a seven-year period. The size of the business filing, the complexity of the issues that relate to the case, and the jurisdiction overseeing the case each can play an important role. The costs of administering the case run up when the proceeding drags out.

The duration of a Chapter 11 can be reduced significantly through a prepackaged Chapter 11. The main purpose of a prepackaged Chapter 11 is to speed up the proceeding and cut costs. For example, the related fees during the Revco bankruptcy exceeded $40 million. Moreover, the stigma of being involved in a protracted bankruptcy case is detrimental. USG Corp. was able to file a prepackaged Chapter 11 in March 1993 and then emerge from bankruptcy 38 days later. By soliciting the creditors' votes before a filing, a prepackaged bankruptcy can be significantly reduced.

The DIP During Chapter 11

The debtor in a Chapter 11 is commonly referred to as a debtor-in-possession (DIP). The DIP continues to operate a business as a going concern during the Chapter 11 proceeding. The Bankruptcy Code grants the DIP an exclusive right to file a plan of reorganization for 120 days. The bankruptcy court often uses its authority to extend the debtor's period of exclusivity beyond the 120-day period.

The debtor often experiences a liquidity crisis after filing Chapter 11. A motion is sometimes made by the DIP to the court to allow for the DIP to obtain financing. Banks often obtain a security interest in unencumbered and post-petition assets and a superpriority administrative claim when DIP financing is allowed. The fresh infusion of funds can alleviate the liquidity crisis often faced by companies that enter Chapter 11.

Another motion sometimes made by the DIP is for the authorization to use cash collateral. Cash collateral represents the proceeds obtained from the sale of a creditor's collateral. For example, if a bank is financing a car and the DIP sells the car, the funds derived from the sale of the car are cash collateral. The court will usually authorize a debtor's use of cash collateral conditional on granting the secured creditor adequate protection in the form of replacement liens.

The DIP is required to submit a disclosure statement that includes a schedule of creditors. The bankruptcy court requires the DIP to submit monthly financial statements during the Chapter 11 proceeding. With court approval, the DIP may elect to reject executory contracts. Executory contracts are contracts where each party has material obligations to perform. If the debtor elects to retain and exectory contract, monthly payments obligations that arise after the filing of the petition may be payable to the creditors during the Chapter 11.

Eventually a DIP emerges as a reorganized business or the assets are sold or the business is liquidated. The ultimate resolution of the Chapter 11 is contingent upon approval of a reorganization plan. The success or failure of the plan often depends upon how the business's worth is allocated to classes of creditors and the shareholders.

The Creditors During a Chapter 11

Creditors often face a number of difficult decisions during a Chapter 11 proceeding. Once a petition is filed with the court, the creditor should stop direct collection activity with the debtor. Usually the debtor continues to operate the business as a DIP. However, creditors can make a motion to have the court appoint a trustee to run the business. This might occur if there is gross mismanagement or fraud.

One of the first actions taken by a creditor should be to investigate the potential to exercise reclamation rights. Under Section 2-702 of the UCC, a creditor may reclaim goods shipped to a debtor. There are state-by-state variations concerning the law that governs reclamation.

In general, a creditor who seeks reclamation should send a written notice to the debtor within 10 days of the receipt of goods by the buyer. The notice of reclamation must be sent to the debtor within the 10 days; therefore, use of a letter, sent by expedited delivery with a return receipt is recommended. The period for reclamation is extended to 20 days for a bankruptcy case; the 20 days commence after the receipt of goods by the debtor. The creditor should follow up with an attempt to obtain the goods from the debtor using local counsel due to variations in state laws. Usually the creditor will not be able to reclaim goods where the buyer is in bankruptcy; however, the creditor can often times obtain an administrative priority claim for the goods. Courts have been divided on the issue of floating inventory liens claimed by banks on goods shipped by suppliers that go into inventory. The key point for creditors is to act quickly and seek local legal counsel.

During a Chapter 11 proceeding in large cases, the 20 largest creditors are usually invited to sit on a creditors' committee. Although a creditor may have to invest considerable time, the potential rewards can be substantial. Creditors evaluate the debtor's reorganization plan. The creditors also examine the potential for fraud. Interrelated company transactions or the removal of major assets by the debtor can create a need to monitor the bankruptcy to protect the interest of creditors.

Creditors are urged to file a proof of claim with a bankruptcy court. The proof of claim should be sent with a certified letter. Creditors should follow up to ensure that they are on the schedule of creditors. However, filing a proof of claim is not an absolute requirement. In fact, a proof of claim is not necessary where the debtor is a Chapter 11 and the creditor's claim is listed in the debtor's schedules in the correct amount and not disputed, contingent and unliquidated.

In 1998, Form B10 became the standard proof of claim form to use during a bankruptcy. Exhibit 12-3 shows Form B10, which can be downloaded at www.uscourts.gov/bankruptcycourts.html. When the form is submitted, it should be typewritten or black ink should be used to complete the form. Usually copies of invoices are attached to the form. Forms must be submitted in a timely manner.

A creditor with a pre-petition supply contract may be asked to make post-petition shipments under the contract. It is recommended that the creditor receive a written request from the debtor affirming the supply contract that stipulates agreement to pay post-petition obligations. The creditor may then request a court order that approves the post-petition contract. The creditor should also consider seeking to have the post-petition obligations prioritized as administrative expenses.

A decision to make new shipments to a DIP is difficult. Some creditors insist on cash in advance. However, the DIP is often in a poor working capital position. Any fresh credit extending on an open account basis should reflect that shipments are being made to a DIP on the invoices. In the event of a liquidation, the shipments made to a DIP have a priority claim. However, there is a possibility that funds will not be available to cover this priority claim in the liquidation.

Eventually creditors vote on a reorganization plan. In order to approve a plan, over one-half of the voting creditors in a class holding at least two-thirds of the amount of claims must approve the plan. Creditors may present their own plan after a debtor's period of exclusivity ends.

A plan can be difficult to evaluate. For example, if creditors are offered equity in a swap arrangement, how would it compare to a cash bid? The liquidation value can be estimated through the use of a cash flow model. However, one goal of a Chapter 11 is to avoid a liquidation. Creditors ultimately vote on the plan to preserve their own best interests.

Exhibit 12-3 **Form B10 - Proof of Claim**

FORM B10 (Official Form 10) (4/01)

UNITED STATES BANKRUPTCY COURT ________ DISTRICT OF ________

PROOF OF CLAIM

Name of Debtor

Case Number

NOTE: This form should not be used to make a claim for an administrative expense arising after the commencement of the case. A "request" for payment of an administrative expense may be filed pursuant to 11 U.S.C. § 503.

Name of Creditor (The person or other entity to whom the debtor owes money or property):

Name and address where notices should be sent:

Telephone number:

☐ Check box if you are aware that anyone else has filed a proof of claim relating to your claim. Attach copy of statement giving particulars.

☐ Check box if you have never received any notices from the bankruptcy court in this case.

☐ Check box if the address differs from the address on the envelope sent to you by the court.

THIS SPACE IS FOR COURT USE ONLY

Account or other number by which creditor identifies debtor:

Check here if this claim ☐ replaces ☐ amends a previously filed claim, dated: ________

1. Basis for Claim

- ☐ Goods sold
- ☐ Services performed
- ☐ Money loaned
- ☐ Personal injury/wrongful death
- ☐ Taxes
- ☐ Other ________
- ☐ Retiree benefits as defined in 11 U.S.C. § 1114(a)
- ☐ Wages, salaries, and compensation (fill out below)

Your SS #: ____ ____ ____

Unpaid compensation for services performed

from ________ (date) to ________ (date)

2. Date debt was incurred:

3. If court judgment, date obtained:

4. Total Amount of Claim at Time Case Filed: $ ________

If all or part of your claim is secured or entitled to priority, also complete Item 5 or 6 below.

☐ Check this box if claim includes interest or other charges in addition to the principal amount of the claim. Attach itemized statement of all interest or additional charges.

5. Secured Claim.

☐ Check this box if your claim is secured by collateral (including a right of setoff).

Brief Description of Collateral:

☐ Real Estate ☐ Motor Vehicle

☐ Other________

Value of Collateral: $________

Amount of arrearage and other charges at time case filed included in secured claim, if any: $________

6. Unsecured Priority Claim.

☐ Check this box if you have an unsecured priority claim

Amount entitled to priority $________

Specify the priority of the claim:

- ☐ Wages, salaries, or commissions (up to $4,650),* earned within 90 days before filing of the bankruptcy petition or cessation of the debtor's business, whichever is earlier - 11 U.S.C. § 507(a)(3).
- ☐ Contributions to an employee benefit plan - 11 U.S.C. § 507(a)(4).
- ☐ Up to $2,100* of deposits toward purchase, lease, or rental of property or services for personal, family, or household use - 11 U.S.C. § 507(a)(6).
- ☐ Alimony, maintenance, or support owed to a spouse, former spouse, or child - 11 U.S.C. § 507(a)(7).
- ☐ Taxes or penalties owed to governmental units - 11 U.S.C. § 507(a)(8).
- ☐ Other - Specify applicable paragraph of 11 U.S.C. § 507(a)(____).

**Amounts are subject to adjustment on 4/1/04 and every 3 years thereafter with respect to cases commenced on or after the date of adjustment.*

7. Credits: The amount of all payments on this claim has been credited and deducted for the purpose of making this proof of claim.

8. Supporting Documents: *Attach copies of supporting documents,* such as promissory notes, purchase orders, invoices, itemized statements of running accounts, contracts, court judgments, mortgages, security agreements, and evidence of perfection of lien. DO NOT SEND ORIGINAL DOCUMENTS. If the documents are not available, explain. If the documents are voluminous, attach a summary.

9. Date-Stamped Copy: To receive an acknowledgment of the filing of your claim, enclose a stamped, self-addressed envelope and copy of this proof of claim.

THIS SPACE IS FOR COURT USE ONLY

Date	Sign and print the name and title, if any, of the creditor or other person authorized to file this claim (attach copy of power of attorney, if any):

Penalty for presenting fraudulent claim: Fine of up to $500,000 or imprisonment for up to 5 years, or both. 18 U.S.C. §§ 152 and 3571.

The Expedited Small Business Chapter 11 Proceeding

A small business can elect to be placed on a fast track during a Chapter 11 proceeding. For the purposes of qualifying as a small business, the criterion used requires that the business has aggregate secured and unsecured debt not exceeding $2,000,000. This type of bankruptcy moves along more quickly, which can reduce administrative costs and increase the likelihood of emerging successfully from the bankruptcy proceeding.

The hearing to approve a disclosure statement is not required. The debtor has an exclusivity period of only 100 days to present a plan of arrangement. The disclosure hearing can be combined with the hearing for the confirmation of the plan of arrangement. By shortening the process, the debtor is more likely to survive the Chapter 11.

BANKRUPTCY: PROBLEMS AND ISSUES

The one constant in a capitalistic system is change. As laws are applied and case decisions establish precedents, certain unexpected outcomes occur. A myriad of problems and issues can be attributed to bankruptcy law.

For creditors, some of the most relevant problems, issues, and trends include: (1) voidable preferences, (2) fraudulent conveyances, (3) bankruptcy prediction models, (4) alternatives to bankruptcy, and (5) automation of bankruptcy courts. These topics will each be examined in this section of the chapter.

Voidable Preferences

English common law recognized the need to prevent any injustices or abuses that could result due to collusion between a debtor and a creditor. A "preference" is a payment or business transaction entered into within 90 days of a bankruptcy that allows for a creditor to receive a preferential payment or benefit. In the case of transfers to insiders, the preference period extends to one year before the bankruptcy is filed.

The preference period is extended from 90 days to one year for insiders. The logic of the extended preference period is that someone with insider knowledge has greater control over a debtor. This control can cause a debtor to give preference to certain creditors.

Legal defenses exist for creditors that pertain to preferences. One such defense is called the "ordinary course of business" defense. Normal trade credit transactions are acceptable. So if a debtor typically pays net 30-day terms on the 45th day, the transaction should customarily be allowed to stand. However, if a material change in payment habits is detected, certain payments may be considered preferences. The creditor must also satisfy objective industry criteria that the payment was made according to ordinary business terms.

Another preference-related defense is called the "new value" defense. The new value defense limits the exposure of a preference to the value of goods or services provided to a debtor on credit extended after the receipt of a preference.

There is also a "contemporaneous exchange for new value" defense that may be used by creditors. For example, if a creditor furnishes $5,000 in new product and a debtor pays $5,000 for the product on the same day, a contemporaneous exchange for new value has occurred. The simultaneous nature of the transaction should not be attacked later as a preference. Credit transactions do not qualify for this defense. Moreover, if the customer's check bounces, the contemporaneous exchange for new value defense will not qualify.

Fraudulent Conveyances

The basic premise that underlies a fraudulent conveyance is the practice of conveying the debtor's assets to a third party so that the debtor is left judgment proof. Both state laws and the bankruptcy code contain statutes that pertain to fraudulent conveyances. The fraudulent conveyance laws can be traced back over 400 years to English common law.

Today the laws remain murky yet have a new important application. There have been leveraged buyout transactions where the application of fraudulent conveyances have been used by unsecured creditors. If a bank has provided funds as a secured lender to fund an LBO and the debtor is rendered insolvent or with unreasonably little capital, the bank's lien could be at risk. The payoff to unsecured creditors could be substantial.

In the LBO of *Wieboldt Stores, Inc. v. Schottenstein,* the bankruptcy court found a fraudulent conveyance to exist. Also, in the O'Day Corporation case, a bank lost its security interest in another LBO fraudulent conveyance ruling. However, in *Moody v. Security Pacific Business Credit Inc.,* the court ruled that the secured lenders' rights should not be voided. Sometimes the issue can come down to a test for solvency. Should the Balance Sheet test or Liquidation Value of Assets test be used? Clearly, the issue remains unresolved.

Creditors should seek legal counsel when dealing with a fraudulent conveyance case. Applicable laws may ultimately decide the potential application for fraudulent conveyance laws.

Bankruptcy Prediction Models

The ability to predict bankruptcy prior to the actual filing would furnish a tremendous edge to a creditor. Academics have conducted a number of studies that use financial ratios to predict bankruptcy. Most of these studies isolate specific financial ratios or combinations of financial ratios in an attempt to detect observable trends. Current research suggests that industry-specific ratios may provide more accurate results.

Edward I. Altman, a professor of finance at New York University, is perhaps the most renowned academic to work on bankruptcy prediction models. Altman has used a multivariate model that includes five weighted financial ratios to predict bankruptcy. The results are presented in statistic called a Z-score. Altman's model was illustrated in Chapter 10 of this book.

The crux of the issue concerning bankruptcy prediction models is somewhat similar to the credit scoring models discussed in Chapter 6 of this book. One of the problems often expressed by credit practitioners is that the release of the financial data comes too late to be useful to make effective credit decisions. Yet there have been significant inroads made that allow for technology to contribute to a wider use of models to predict bankruptcy. There are computer programs that furnish credit managers with a Z-score. This information can become useful to credit decisions.

Alternatives to Bankruptcy

The high costs associated with bankruptcy proceedings encourage both the debtor and creditor to seek ways to avoid bankruptcy. Two specific alternatives to bankruptcy include (1) an assignment for the benefit of creditors and (2) an out of court workout. Each of these alternatives will be explored.

Assignment for the Benefit of Creditors

An Assignment for the Benefit of Creditors, often called an assignment, is a way to liquidate a business outside of bankruptcy. The assignment is a voluntary transfer of all of the debtor's property to an assignee. The assignee sells off the debtor's assets and distributes the proceeds to creditors. Any excess proceeds are returned to the debtor. Any deficiencies become a bad debt for creditors.

There are state laws that govern the use of an assignment. The administrative costs can be lower than in a Chapter 7 liquidation. The results of an assignment are the orderly liquidation of assets and a pro rata distribution of cash to creditors based upon their claims. Rarely are there enough funds available to pay creditors in full. An assignment has the advantage of being speedier and less costly than a bankruptcy; however, the assignment simply is not appropriate in many cases due to complexities of debtor-creditor relationships. Situations in which a business is deteriorating quickly can afford an opportunity to use an assignment.

Out of Court Workout

An out of court workout is an informal reorganization of a business. The debtor continues to operate a business as a going concern. The goal of the out of court workout is to gain a moratorium on debt payments and/or to get creditors to agree to a pro rata settlement. Sometimes creditors are offered additional debt or stock in a business in order to gain acceptance for the out of court workout. State laws govern out of court workouts.

An out of court workout is done on a voluntary basis. The agreement does not require the consent of all creditors. However, creditors that do not agree are forced to sue the debtor and collect on any judgment. Creditors face the issue of whether the proposed composition is superior to a formal bankruptcy proceeding. In an out of court workout, there is usually a creditors' committee that will impose a number of covenants upon the debtor.

There are circumstances that make a formal bankruptcy preferable to either an assignment or an out of court workout. A formal bankruptcy provides a mechanism that includes a statement of the affairs of a business that is made under oath. A bankruptcy can bind dissenting creditors to the deal. Moreover, a bankruptcy can allow for the rejection of executory contracts, recapture of preferential payments, and prevention of fraudulent conveyances.

Automation of Bankruptcy Courts

Due to technological improvements, the ability to use the Internet makes electronic modes of working with bankruptcy a reality. The U.S.

Bankruptcy Courts are at varying levels of preparedness. Most bankruptcy courts appear to be utilizing the potential of the Internet nicely through a service known as PACER. Bankruptcy dockets and other official case information can be reviewed through the PACER service for any available online bankruptcy and district court. Direct links to all courts that offer PACER are listed at http://pacer.psc.uscourts.gov/cgi-bin/links.pl.

One web site useful for bankruptcies in Canada is located at www.bankruptcycanada.com. Here information that pertains to specific provinces can be reviewed. Proposals and trustees comments can be listened to through the use of Real Player, an audio device used in conjunction with the Internet.

Enhancements in technology will continue to make improvements in the information available. The feeling of being overwhelmed with paper is being replaced with improvements in sharing meaningful information. For credit managers, an understanding of the important aspects of bankruptcy becomes more important than ever because there is so much valuable information available.

CHAPTER 12: FOLLOW UP

Recap of Important Concepts

1. There have been a record number of bankruptcies filed since January 1, 2000. Not only are more individuals filing but also more publically traded companies are seeking the protection available by filing bankruptcy.
2. Chapter 7 of the Bankruptcy Code is used for straight liquidations by both businesses and by individuals. Credit analysts should be aware of the priority of claims used to distribute the proceeds in a liquidation.
3. A business reorganization is conducted under Chapter 11 of the Bankruptcy Code. The bankruptcy process can be initiated through either a voluntary or an involuntary petition filed in a U.S. District Court.
4. The debtor-in-possession has certain responsibilities during a Chapter 11 case. The DIP must present a disclosure statement and monthly financial statements, affirm or reject executory contracts, and strive to ultimately emerge form the Chapter 11 case by working through a viable reorganization plan.
5. The creditors often face a number of difficult decisions during a Chapter 11 case. Creditors should consider exercising a right of reclamation. The decision to extend fresh credit to a DIP can vary by circumstances. Creditors often can benefit by serving on a creditors' committee. The ultimate vote on a reorganization plan addresses the decision of whether the debtor is more valuable as a going concern or in a liquidation.
6. Chapter 13 of the Bankruptcy Code is used by individuals with regular income and by small businesses. Chapter 12 is used by the Family Farmer to reorganize debt. A municipality would file a bankruptcy petition under Chapter 9 of the Bankruptcy Code.
7. Noteworthy trends in Chapter 11 include the use of prepackaged bankruptcy, the availability of DIP financing through a bank, the use of cash collateral by a debtor, and the use of the small business expedited timeframe by qualifying small businesses.
8. The treatment of a creditor in a preferential manner can create a need to return payments received within a 90-day period of a bankruptcy. The *Deprizio* ruling is an example of a situation where the

preference period can be extended to one year for insiders. There are several legal defenses that exist to protect payments from being classified as preferential.

9. A fraudulent conveyance is a transfer of a debtor's assets to a third party so that the debtor is left judgment proof. There have been LBO transactions where fraudulent conveyance law has benefited unsecured creditors at the expense of secured lenders.
10. Bankruptcy prediction models have examined financial ratios to predict bankruptcy. Credit practitioners often have Z-score information available through software packages that are used to perform financial statement analysis. The ability to forecast bankruptcy is intuitively appealing.
11. An assignment for the benefit of creditors or an out of court workout can be used as an alternative to bankruptcy.
12. U.S. District Courts are gradually moving toward automation. There have been significant enhancements made concerning the flow of relevant information.

Review/Discussion Questions

1. Under which chapter(s) of the Bankruptcy Code would each of the following debtors file a bankruptcy petition?
   a. An individual
   b. A Family Farmer (total debt $500,000)
   c. A small corporation (total debt $100,000)
   d. A municipality
   e. A corporation going out of business
   f. A corporation seeking to rehabilitate
2. What is the purpose of the Absolute Priority Rule used in a Chapter 7 proceeding?
3. What is a supermajority claim in a Chapter 11 proceeding?
4. What is a prepackaged bankruptcy under Chapter 11?
5. Must a creditor file a Proof of Claim in order to receive a liquidating dividend? Explain your response.
6. Why is the *Deprizio* ruling important to creditors?
7. Who is asked to serve on a creditors' committee? What do members of the creditors' committee do?

Test Your Knowledge

1. Under what circumstances can a creditor or creditors file an involuntary bankruptcy petition? Be specific.
2. What is a Chapter 11 bankruptcy? What is a small business Chapter 11 proceeding?
3. What is an assignment for the benefit of creditors?
4. What is the voting requirement needed for creditors to approve a Chapter 11 reorganization?
5. What factors should a credit manager take into consideration when asked to ship to a debtor-in-possession?
6. Under what circumstances may a creditor exercise a right of reclamation? Describe the process to be used by a creditor who is exercising the right of reclamation.
7. What is a voidable preference in a bankruptcy proceeding? Identify two defenses that can be used by a creditor in order to defend against a voidable preference.
8. Compare and contrast an out of court workout and an assignment for the benefit of creditors.
9. Use the absolute priority rule to perform a liquidation. The cash received in the liquidation is $1,500 of which $400 is received from the sale of fixed assets and $1,100 from the sale of current assets. Your task is to allocate the $1,500 in proceeds from the liquidation to the appropriate claimant.
   - Assume administrative expenses are $300.
   - Assume that debentures are subordinated to the bank.
   - Assume that accounts payable are not related to DIP sales.
   - Assume the mortgage bond is secured by fixed assets.

Accounts Receivable	1,000	Accrued Taxes	100
Inventory	1,100	Bank Debt	1,300
Total Current Assets	2,100	Accounts Payable	800
Fixed Assets	2,000	Subordinated Debentures	1,100
Total Assets	**4,100**	1st Mortgage Bond	300
		Common Equity	500
		Total Claims	**4,100**

Web-Based Assignment

Select a recent bankruptcy of your choice. Find out the docket number for the case. What information is contained in the docket? When is the first meeting of creditors? What activities are on the agenda at the first meeting of creditors? What other useful information can you find online about the bankruptcy proceeding? (Note to instuctors: You may want to use one particular bankruptcy to assign to the entire class. This can lead to enriching discussion in class.)

Credit Management Online

www.abiworld.org—The American Bankruptcy Institute hosts this web site. There is data for bankruptcy by chapter, by U.S. District Court and by state. There are articles concerning legislation, international bankruptcy laws, and U.S. court opinions. Much of the data is free; ABI members do have access to additional information.

www.bankruptcycanada.com—This site contains information concerning most aspects of business and personal bankruptcy in Canada.

www.bankruptcydata.com—This is a commercial site. There is a considerable amount of information that is available for free. However, subscribers can access premium services for a fee. There are links to specific cases and courts.

www.uscourts.gov/bankruptcycourts.html—The U.S. bankruptcy courts are hosted by the federal government at this site. Bankruptcy forms and a basic overview of bankruptcy chapters are available through links at the site. There are links to the web sites for U.S. bankruptcy courts. The place to file a proof of claim and the dates for creditor meetings can be reviewed when a specific U.S. court is accessed through the links at the site.

www.usdoj.gov/ust—The U.S. Department of Justice Trustee Program web site contains information pertaining to the US Trustee Program. There are 21 regions that cover all of the district courts. Fraud prevention is one of the key goals of the program.

www4.law.cornell.edu/uscode/11/—The Legal Information Institute at Cornell Law School hosts this site. The entire Bankruptcy Code Law can be reviewed at the site.

References Useful for Further Reading

Avery, Wesley H. "The Top 10 Things You Should Do If Your Client Is a Creditor in a Bankruptcy Case." *Business Credit* (February 2002): 24-25.

Blakeley, Scott. "Chapter 11s on the Rise: Flags and Steps to Protect Your Credit Sales." *Business Credit* (April 2002): 56-57.

Blakeley, Scott. "Dealing With a Major Customer's Second Chapter 11 Filing." *Business Credit* (May 2001): 8-10.

Blakeley, Scott. "Debtor-in-Possession Financing in the Spotlight." *Business Credit* (January 2003): 30.

Blakeley, Scott. "A Proper Purpose for Commencing an Involuntary Bankruptcy Petition: Preserving a Preference Action." *Business Credit* (May 1998): 8-16.

Fagel, Allen J. "New Life for an Old Remedy: Reclamation from Insolvent Buyers and Bankruptcy Debtors." *Business Credit* (January 1998): 46-48.

Frieswick, Kris. "Worldwide Workouts." *CFO* (July 2002): 73-75.

Kaiser, Kevin M.J. "European Bankruptcy Laws: Implications for Corporations Facing Financial Distress." *Financial Management* (Autumn 1996): 67-85.

Kupetz, David. "Assignment for the Benefit of Creditors: Salvaging Value from a Sinking Ship." *Business Credit* (April 2003): 70.

Lee, Scott W. "Bulk Sales Transfers: Protection for Creditors." *Business Credit* (July/August 1997): 9-19.

Musika, Terry L., and Charles R. Goldstein. "How Can Creditors Use Regional Bankruptcy Data?" *Business Credit* (October 1997): 26-27.

Nathan, Bruce S. "Beware of the 91- or 92-Day Preference Period: The Preference Zone Expands." *Business Credit* (January 1999): 8-10.

Nathan, Bruce S. "Extending Credit to a Chapter 11 Debtor. Let the Creditor Beware: The Risk of a Failed Chapter 11." *Business Credit* (May 1999): 14-16.

Nathan, Bruce S. "Out of Court Settlements." *Business Credit* (March 1998): 8-12.

Nathan Bruce S. "The Right to Reimbursement of a Committee Member's Professional Fees: Yes and No." *Business Credit* (February 2001): 11-12.

Nathan, Bruce S. "Section 546(g) Return of Goods: A Leg Up for Unsecured Creditors." *Business Credit* (October 1998): 32-34.

Nathan, Bruce S. "A Trade Creditor's Ability to Assert an Administrative Claim from a Debtor's Post-Petition Rejection of Pre-Petition Purchase Orders: Not So Fast!." *Business Credit* (April 2003), 19-21.

Nathan, Bruce S. "Unpaid Sellers Stoppage of Delivery and Reclamation Rights Against an Insolvent Buyer." *Business Credit* (January 2001): 42-44.

Pearson, John K. " The New Bankruptcy Claim Form." *Business Credit* (April 1998): 20.

Rasnak, Sandra Taliani, and Joe Brown. "The U.S. Trustees." *Business Credit* (April 1998): 30-33.

Tatelbaum, Charles M. "The Automatic Stay in Bankruptcy: How Long Is It Effective?" *Business Credit* (February 2000): 58.

Tatelbaum, Charles M. "A Look at Bankruptcy from Behind the Bench, Part II. *Business Credit* (May 1999): 26-29.

Tatelbaum, Charles M. "National Bankruptcy Review Commission Further Studies Preference Issues." *Business Credit* (June 1997): 4.

Wise, Jim. "Chapter 13, UCC and Work Groups on the Horizon." *Business Credit* (July/August 1996): 7-8.